OF SEVERAL BRANCHES

Essays from the *Humanities Association Bulletin*

OF SEVERAL BRANCHES

ESSAYS FROM THE
Humanities Association Bulletin

Edited by
GERALD McCAUGHEY
and
MAURICE LEGRIS

Published in association with the
University of Alberta by University of Toronto Press

Printed in Canada
Reprinted in 2018
ISBN 978-1-4875-8734-5 (paper)

Preface

> There is not one of us who may not qualify himself so to improve the average amount of opportunities, as to leave his fellow creatures some little the better for the use he has known how to make of his intellect. To make this little greater, let us strive to keep ourselves acquainted with the best thoughts that are brought forth by the original minds of the age. . . .
>
> —John Stuart Mill, *On Education*

In offering this collection of essays, it is our intention that we may all keep ourselves acquainted with what may not presumptuously be called "the best thoughts," but what we might legitimately say is representative of the best material that has appeared in the *Humanities Association Bulletin* over the past decade. In our four years of editorship of that journal we have been consistently motivated by the desire to make the "official voice" of this heterogeneous organization one that will be heard and judged by scholars throughout the "wide world" of the humanities. That such judgment of Canadian scholarship constitutes an important part of the evolution from "Colony to Nation" is an obvious truism; that such judgment already takes place is equally true. That the *Humanities Bulletin* should become a bona-fide "academic" journal is, we believe, one further contribution, however small, to that evolution. That the *Bulletin*, under a succession of hard-working editors, has always contained material of lasting value will be amply illustrated in this attempt to place on permanent record essays gathered from a wide variety of issues on very diverse subject matter.

We wish to thank all those sincere and dedicated people who have shared our view of the need for such a volume, especially the Managing Editor of the University of Toronto Press, Miss Francess G. Halpenny; and Dr. Walter Johns and the Publications Committee of the University of Alberta, whose generous grant has made publication possible. We wish to thank, also, those Executive Members of the Humanities Association who have supported our views of the necessary evolution of the *Bulletin*, particularly Dr. F. E. L. Priestley, who has been unusually generous of such support and has graciously agreed to write the introduction which follows. Naturally, to those scholars without whom neither the journal nor this book would have been possible, our debt remains foreover unpaid. Their faith remains our pride. We hope you, as readers, will share in that pride.

GERALD MCCAUGHEY

Notre but pour le *Bulletin de l'association des humanités* durant nos quatre années à la rédaction a été constamment d'en faire une publication bilingue ayant trait à tous les aspects des études humanitaires; c'est-à-dire que nous n'avons que souligné l'œuvre de nos prédécesseurs. Mais ils étaient, eux, peu fortunés : le *Bulletin* débuta, en 1954, de façon assez modeste, et ce n'est que depuis ces quelques dernières années que le tirage atteint un chiffre impressionant et que s'y abonnèrent les bibliothèques des principales universités au Canada et aux Etats-Unis.

Malgré ce début sans éclat, le *Bulletin* publia dans ses premières années des articles importants; ce volume tient alors à conserver ce qui serait autrement tout à fait perdu. Il tient aussi à attirer l'attention à des écrits plus récents qui sont de valeur durable.

Ce livre est témoin de l'activité savante et intellectuelle au Canada dans le domaine des humanités. Il est pour nous une source de fierté. Il est aussi, nous semble-t'il, une indication que l'humanisme dans ce pays bilingue promet des richesses exceptionnelles.

MAURICE LEGRIS

Contents

Introduction

When in 1950–51 the Humanities Research Council of Canada undertook the formation and organization of a Humanities Association of Canada, the general terms in which the intentions and purposes of the new body were defined allowed for a good deal of variety in interpretation. The Association was to be a national body with local branches across Canada, "designed to appeal to everyone, amateur or professional, who had an interest in one or more of the different humane studies." As soon as this general statement began to be translated into terms of practical action in the setting up of local branches and a national executive, and the planning of their activities, it became clear that one could include in the general purpose several very specific and imperative needs, not all obviously compatible in actual practice. In planning the programmes for a local branch, for example, one could interpret "having an interest" with rigour or with a tolerant hope; one could aim at preaching to the converted or at proselytizing the Gentiles; one could interpret "amateur" as dabbler, novice, or semi-professional. If the aim were interpreted as a spreading into the unenlightened and apathetic community outside the academic walls of some understanding and appreciation of the humanities, a very necessary task for the survival of our disciplines, this clearly called for special sorts of programmes, and for special approaches by the professionals. If, in other words, any sense of a radical difference between amateur and professional were retained, the task of appealing to both at the same time became very difficult.

It was very evident, furthermore, that the task of engaging public understanding and appreciation of our disciplines is not, for most academic professionals, one for which they have been trained or to which they have given much thought. Like all professionals, including professional scientists, the basic assumptions of their own discipline, the fundamental principles, the techniques of research and of interpretation, have so long been a virtually unconscious part of their mental habits that it is only by a very deliberate and painstaking effort that they can recapture imaginatively the naïve and unsophisticated state of the layman. The relative rarity of scientists able to convey to the general public any real conception of what science is, what the scientist does, and how he does it, is well recognized. There is little reason to believe that the task of conveying to the general public what the humanities are, what the scholar in the humanities does, and how he does it, is any easier, or capable of being done successfully by any greater number.

It is quite natural, therefore, that the Humanities Association has had only what might be called qualified success in this sort of endeavour. In some branches, where the relation of university to the larger community was propitious, and where the local executive made special and careful efforts, a good deal has been achieved. Elsewhere, other aims and intentions have become more dominant.

For at the national level, the Association almost inevitably becomes a purely professional body. One can conceive that it need not have become so. One can imagine that if it had been given generous support by subsidy in its formative years, and if it had achieved the large and varied membership its founders presumably hoped for, a dominantly non-academic national executive might have developed, and non-academic delegates might have attended the annual meetings in large numbers. But as it has turned out, this is not so, and at the national level it has become almost solely an academic body. And this means that its aims have tended to be the aims of professionals. This in turn has tended to encourage professional aims at the local level. To some extent, these tendencies are the result of circumstances, as I have suggested; to some extent they were inevitable.

From the outset, it was clear that there were highly important professional needs which a national association could go some way towards satisfying, and these needs were undoubtedly in the minds of the founders of the Humanities Association. Most scholars in the humanities in Canada felt urgently the necessity of a national organization, an association of professional scholars teaching and doing research in the humanities. Such a body could do much to weld together the relatively scattered groups of scholars, to give them a medium of mutual intercourse, and to provide periodic meetings at which they could exchange ideas and stimulate each other. It was never perhaps very clear how the national organization could function in relation to the wider community beyond the world of scholarship, but it was always perfectly evident how it could function as a national body of scholars. In many ways, this could be said to be the one highly important purpose of the Association which presented the fewest problems in its execution. This is consequently the purpose in which it has probably come nearest to success.

But paradoxically, the successful establishment of the Association as a national body of scholars in the humanities at once opposed a threat to this purpose. Each discipline within the humanities began to form its own national body, and to press for a professional fragmentation of the humanities into separate disciplines. If to some this seemed subversive, a betrayal of the whole interdisciplinary principle of the Association, to others it served to emphasize even more strongly the need for the Association. This has in fact been well demonstrated by many of the programmes at the anuual meetings, which have been designed to bring together scholars from all the disciplines of the humanities, both those with their own professional body and those without one, and to choose themes whose illustration in several literatures will throw light on each, or themes relating the other arts to literature, or literatures to philosophy, and so on. Careful preparation of programmes has repeatedly asserted the function of the Association, the demonstration of the relatedness of the humanities, and of a professionalism beyond the narrow professionalism of the single discipline.

And for the larger audience, beyond those in attendance at the annual meetings, this function has been carried on by the *Bulletin* of the Association. From its humble beginnings as a mimeographed newsletter, keeping branches and members informed of the activities of the branches across Canada, the *Bulletin* has become, under its more recent editors, a journal competently designed and printed, publishing essays contributed by members. It has received the full support of the Association of Canadian University Teachers of English, who accept it as their own organ of publication. With similar support from the other professional groups it could indeed become fully the journal of the Humanities Association. If it is in part a journal of particular scholarship in the humanities, as the selections Professor McCaughey has included in Part III of this volume indicate, by its inclusion of such essays from various disciplines it reaffirms a primary aim of the Association in asserting the unity of the humanities. But it also allows, as the essays in Part I show, more general considerations of problems affecting the humanities as a whole, and it attracts a wide range of articles like those in Part II, less specialized than those in the third section, less generalized than those in the first, and perhaps best described by the editor's term, "approaches." The general quality represented in the present volume indicates why, in a very short time as a full-fledged journal, the *Bulletin* has already established itself in libraries and bibliographies. I fervently hope that it will be given in future the full support of the members and of the executive of the Association. In the meantime, I congratulate the editors, and particularly Professor McCaughey, on this testimony of the Association's real achievement.

F. E. L. Priestley

PART I

Humanities in the Twentieth Century

MARSHALL McLUHAN

The Humanities in the Electronic Age

It was Peter Drucker, former professor of philosophy and now Dean of the School of Management of New York University, who said in effect at the outset of his *Landmarks of Tomorrow*:

For the first time in human history higher education is not a privilege, a frill or a luxury. It is a necessity of production. This is not to say that higher education is being supplanted by commerce, but rather that the age-old gap between them is harder to find. In a recent book, *Classrooms in the Factories*, Clark and Sloan report that the annual budget for classroom teaching in industry is more than four times the annual budget for primary, secondary, and higher education. And that estimate takes no account of the extensive training programmes for military personnel. The G.E. management centre for executive training at Crotonville on the Hudson has four classes of forty executives each year. The budget is $46 million. Never did he know the true meaning of liberal education, says Peter Drucker in the book already mentioned, until he entered the field of management consulting. He refers to the immediate relevance of encyclopedic liberal knowledge in the conduct of current corporation design and action. Indeed, the corporations are much more aware of their need for high-level liberal education than are the universities. The Ciceronian ideal of the *doctus orator* is current again. In *The Liberal Hour*, Kenneth Galbraith has a chapter on "Economics and Art," in which he both ridicules the old commercial notion of arts as frivolity and urges the relevance of art as navigational guide in all business today. The supremacy of design in creating and markets is one factor. The

HAB vol. xxxiv (xii), no. 1, fall 1961. From an address to the annual meeting of the Humanities Association of Canada, 1961.

other factor is that the artist's designs provide the advance models of future development. Careful study of new artistic models gives any firm ten or twenty years breathing spell in planning and development. The old-fashioned business man who played it off the cuff and read only the current signs is now doomed by the speed of the new technology. So the artist moves from the ivory tower to the control tower in modern industry.

With regard to the new needs of industry in the electronic age a recent spokesman insisted that one out of every ten elementary school children must proceed to a Ph.D. if the American situation is to be maintained. No matter what the area of study be, so it be done in depth, that is the vision of American business in education today, for good or ill.

On all hands today it is plain that actualities are much in advance of our thought and theory. When everything changes at once because everything has become inter-dependent, we can expect from the very heart of change a plangent cry for permanence and stability. A second-grade teacher, just after Sputnik, asked her class to write poems about the event. She was quite amazed at the results and showed them to me. One of them I wrote down. It went:

> The stars are so big
> The moon is so small
> Stay as you are.

That, whether verbalized or not, is the message and the logic, not of the mechanical age just past, but of the electronic age in which we stand as the primitives of an undeveloped and unknown culture. Those of us who have had special regard for the ancient disciplines that passed out of our schools years ago will see them return and flourish as never before. The generations immediately ahead of us will scorn the recent decades and even centuries as periods of triviality, frivolity, and of planned obsolescence. We shall see all communities, as well as all commodities and dwellings, assume a stubborn, depth character of organic persistence, as if built by Frank Lloyd Wright. Survey programmes will disappear from the curricula of studies as the panic for permanence drives us into ever greater depth understanding of all kinds of knowledge and action.

I say this without enthusiasm. It is not exhilarating to foresee the inexorable discovery of one's own childish ways of thought. Many a teenager today in his passionate pursuit of a crash programme in adulthood looks on parent and teacher alike as superficial and banal in their modes of routinized living. The situation is the same on the non-personal level. We are all familiar with the computation based on a survey of present-day scientific development: that of all the greatest scientists who ever lived, 95 per cent are living right now. Does this mean that there is more human intelligence now than before? Not at all. But it does mean that we have hit upon some means of activating intelligence that is new. A. N. Whitehead pointed to the discovery of the nineteenth century as the discovery of the technique of invention. Bertrand Russell pointed to the great achievement of the twentieth century as the technique of suspended judgement. That is, the discovery of the process of insight itself, the technique of avoiding the automatic closure of involuntary fixing of attitudes that so easily results from any given cultural situation. The technique of open field perception. Both the discovery of the method of invention and the discovery of the technique of insight not only concern scientists but humanists, and have been freely used by both of what C. P. Snow calls the two cultures. So much so, indeed, that the resonant statistic of about 95 per cent of the greatest scientists of human history now being alive may apply equally to poets, painters, and philosophers. Perhaps we in this group ought really to ask ourselves why we tend instinctively to reject the idea that we might be living in the greatest of all intellectual and artistic periods, even though we may endorse the ebullient scientific estimate of our time. At any period of the past, humanists have been distinguished by a love of ruins and by a gloomy sense that change and decay invest the scene. Perhaps Lord Macaulay hit upon a new strategy. Convinced that he did live in the greatest of all human centuries, he compensated for his non-humanist buoyancy by giving us the memorable image of the New Zealander who would one day arrive to sit upon a fragment of London Bridge in order to sketch the ruins of St. Paul's. Petrarch in a famous passage which has often been misread as a glorious prophecy of the great Renaissance so near to him, actually stood amidst the ruins of Rome and stated that just as surely as there had been uninterrupted decline from Augustan days to his own time, so in the years that lay ahead there would be continuous decay of such classical treasures and skills as still remained. Gibbon was faithful to the same perspective when he tells in his *Autobiography*:

> It was at Rome, on the fifteenth of October, 1764, as I sat musing amidst the ruins of the Capitol, while the barefooted friars were singing Vespers in the temple of Jupiter, that the idea of writing the decline and fall of the city first started to my mind.

May I suggest a face-saving device in this humanist obsession with ruins and decay? The humanist is a Luddite, as C. P. Snow calls him, because he gets a thrill of imagined potential from the fragmentary, and tends to feel that the complete structure offers no mode of creative empathy or participation. Thus the humanist is more fascinated by the incomplete *Hyperion* of Keats than by the complete *Prelude* of Wordsworth.

It has been said that had Milton broken off his *Paradise Lost* at the end of the fourth book, his reputation would stand above any poet of antiquity. The fragment we possess of the *Faerie Queene*, perhaps, spurs more speculation than would a completed twenty-four-book structure. Let me return a moment to the observation of A. N. Whitehead's, that the great discovery of the nineteenth century was the discovery of the technique of discovery. At least in *Science and the Modern World*, where he makes this statement, Whitehead does not explain his point. Edgar Allan Poe, whom Baudelaire and Valéry regarded as the nineteenth-century Leonardo da Vinci, did explain the point in his "Philosophy of Composition." The technique of invention is to begin with the *effect* one wishes to achieve and then to go *backward* to the point from which to begin to produce that effect, and only that effect. In a sense this technique of starting with the effect, before seeking the causes and means for the effect, is the perfection of assembly-line method. It is a method of organized ignorance. Because, whether one wishes to make a car or a poem, a guided missile or a detective story, it is necessary to begin with the solution or effect. Dickens found that writing for serial publication compelled him to plan ahead. And assembly-line methods imply complete analysis and total reconstruction *backwards* from the end-product. This power of advance segmental analysis of each phase of a complex operation was bequeathed to us by Gutenberg and his movable types. It is a technique made obsolete by electrically recorded tapes. The assembly line yields now to galaxy clusters of simultaneous operations which are made possible by the exact synchronization of the information on tapes. The humanist will observe, however, that no matter what period or technology is in question, the artist has always solved the new problem both for the engineer and for the human community, by his new advance models for sensibility and awareness. The exact models of coming forms provided by artistic intuition are like "the providence that's in a watchful state," which, as Ulysses says to Achilles in Shakespeare's *Troilus and Cressida,*

> Knows almost every grain of Plutus' gold,
> Finds bottom in the uncomprehensive deeps,
> Keeps place with thought, and almost like the gods
> Does thoughts unveil in their dumb cradles.

The ever new models of the artist are for the correction of the perceptual bias inflicted upon any human community by ever new technology. In the past century, indeed, we have come to rely almost wholly on art for the nutrition of fresh impulse and the alerting of hypnotized senses. No previous society ever regarded art this way. But no previous society ever underwent the successive brain-washings and hypnotic trances that ours has done from a succession of new technologies.

Now to come to the Bertrand Russell point—that the great discovery of the twentieth century concerns the technique of the suspended judgement. The technique of insight itself is a natural phase to succeed the nineteenth-century discovery of the technique of invention, because it is the means of abstracting oneself from the bias and consequences of one's own culture. If a merely negative criterion were needed it would be easy to infer from the dismay and incomprehension which the later work of Harold Innis has caused in the minds of his admirers that he had finally hit upon a discovery of a very considerable and a very exacting nature.

Innis' concern in the *Bias of Communication,* and later, is with the technique of the suspended judgement. That means, not the willingness to admit other points of view, but the technique of how not to have a point of view. This is identical with the problem facing physicists in correcting the bias of the instruments of research, and it draws attention to the fact that the historian, the poet, the critic, and the philosopher, now as always, face exactly the same situation as the scientist. This is easy to see in larger historical retrospect. Failure to see it in the present may be the result of what Gallbraith calls "vested interests in acquired knowledge" of involvement or anxiety or stupefaction or fatigue. But there are now some quite new factors in the over-all situation which need to be specified. Whatever may prove to be the weaknesses of Teilard De Chardin's work, he will always have the credit of having correctly defined the major change of our age. In the *Phenomenon of Man* he observes:

> It has been stated over and over again. Through the discovery yesterday of the railway, the motor car and the aeroplane, the physical influence of each man, formerly restricted to a few miles, now extends to hundreds of leagues or more. Better still, thanks to the prodigious biological event represented by the discovery of electro-magnetic waves, each individual finds himself henceforth (actively and passively) simultaneously present, over land and sea, in every corner of the earth.

The end of mechanism, the extension of organic interdependence to every phase of experience and human association is what has happened to us. Behind us are twenty-five or more centuries during which the Western world perfected the means of moving the *products* of human discourse and human ingenuity to every corner of the earth. This was done mainly by the alphabet and print and their derivatives in transport and industry. By abstracting sight and sound, by arresting the movements of speech and thought in a visual code, we extended the techniques of mechanical analysis and packaging to the whole of human discourse and learning.

But what has happened with the electronic advent is not that we move the products of human knowledge or labour to all corners of the earth more quickly. Rather we dilate the very means and *processes* of discourse to make a global envelope of sense and sensibility for the earth. From the moment of the telegraph, extra-sensory perception became a daily factor in shaping the human community and private perception alike. It is not the products of perception and judgement which now reach us by electric media, but involvement in the entire communal process of interfused co-existence. Each one of us, actively or passively, includes every other person on earth. The world no longer offers the possibility of the separatist, centre-margin structure which is featured in all our institutions, legal, educational, political. Centres-without-margins, inclusive consciousness, inclusive organization, these alone are viable or relevant to the new electric age. One can readily sympathize with a ferocious intellectual Luddite like Jacques Barzun, who in an inclusive negation of our new age, says: "Away with Art, Science, and Philanthropy." He finds all three so monstrously demanding and possessive that he is probably right in concluding that the free-wheeling days of solitary *laissez-faire* are finished, and the House of Intellect must be builded anew and by other means.

The sheer dilation of sight and sound and touch and movement to encompass the earth is entirely consistent with Bertrand Russell's point that the great discovery of the twentieth century is the technique of suspended judgement. For as our private senses now go beyond us to the ends of the earth, as our wits go out of us, it becomes necessary for us to develop a consensus among our outer senses or media. And the pressure towards this consensus has given us a clairvoyance about the *process* of human awareness which we call insight. Even now we continue to act a good deal as if our outer senses, the electronic media, were still private. Madison Avenue is the collective Archimedes of our time. Archimedes had rightly observed: "Give me a place to stand and I will move the world." Today, looking at our globally dilated senses, he would comment: "Well, I'll be fulcrummed. Why, I can stand on your ear, on your eye, on your skin and move your world as I wish."

Up until the advent of electromagnetism the Western world had merely externalized and exchanged the products of thought and experience. We are quite unprepared for the much higher educational demands of the present situation in which we must share the actual processes of thought and experience of all mankind. But this new necessity not only compels us to inspect our own processes of thought and perception more carefully than in any previous age, but it urges us to the most earnest inquiry into all past art, literature, and culture in order to benefit from all past discoveries about the processes of insight. The humanities are moving out of their centuries-old consumer and appreciation phase into a depth phase of rigorous producer-orientation. Instead of merely establishing a perspective for past cultures, our tendency today is to reconstruct entire past cultures from within. A whole galaxy of procedures is available to this end. But the result is very different from the perspectives and views of the past that became possible at the Renaissance. Instead of a fine background and foreground, with central and peripheral organization, the to' al reconstruction procedure is less visual than empathic. It is a structure of simultaneous and organic inter-relationships.

This change of structure resulting from new means of information is of the greatest relevance in understanding the changed situation of the humanities today. We have in the past century moved out of a mechanical into an electric, organic culture. That is, we have increasingly moved out of a segmental, specialist phase of knowledge into a period of interplay and, as it were, dialogue among all kinds of knowledge. And whereas the mechanical age had been one of centre-margin structures, the electronic age is inevitably one of multiple centres-without-margins. Under conditions of simultaneity of access to information, Cuba is not a margin politically, nor is Laos. They are centres as much as London or Moscow or Washington, yet our assumptions are still otherwise. Hence our confusion.

In the world of Top Management, the same confusion reigns. More development has occurred in the past decade of management, say the leading consultants, than in the previous fifty years. And the change is all decentralist. Delegated authority simply won't work under conditions of electric information movement. Instead, only the "authority of knowledge" will work. And this means that a manager today has to know the over-all operation. Let me cite from a recent article by a Toronto University doctor of philosophy, who is now one of the leading management consultants on this continent. In explaining the sudden reversal of specialization in all areas of industry by the phenomenon of "job enlargement," Bernard Muller-Thym says:

> The first thing to be discovered was that pyramidal organizational structures, with many layers of supervision, and with functional division by specialty, simply did not work. The communication chain between top scientific or engineering leadership and work centres was too long for either the scientific or managerial message to be communicated. But in these research organizations where work actually got done, when one studied them he found that whatever the organization chart prescribed, groups of researchers with different competences as required by the problem in hand were working together, cutting across organizational lines; that they were establishing most of their own design criteria for the work as well as their intended patterns of association; that individually or from a working centre they arranged to tap directly into more senior sources of competence; and

that the patterns of their group association at work followed the organization of their competences as human knowledges.

So much for "the forty-year-old assumption of specialization as a means of attaining organizational efficiency—an assumption which expressed itself in functional forms of organization at the managerial level and in minimization of task at the worker level."

Today one of the most interesting developments in American education concerns the new honours programmes for the top students. This programme is steering away from the old centre-margin pattern of lectures towards the inclusive centre-without-margin pattern of the tutorial.

Another major upset in centre-margin patterns of education concerns the idea of university extension. Just as business is discovering that higher and higher education is needed for the ever enlarging jobs of management, so the adult community in general has become aware of the life of learning as natural and delightful and as necessarily extended throughout adult life.

Another way of getting at this in terms of the humanities in the Electronic Age is to reflect on the fact that A.T. & T., by far the largest business in the world, with a gross annual product equal to that of the entire Canadian economy, does nothing but move information. No wheels, no shafts, no belts, just the movement of information. The coding and moving and use of information will soon be the main business of all mankind. And as the work force withdraws from its present industrial occupations, with the aid of automation, learning will be the paid occupation of all mankind from infancy onward. The entire globe will be a single campus, for such in large measure it is at the present hour.

Our existing ideas of educational organization are still of the centre-margin pattern of institutionalized structure that is taken for granted by the baffled administrator as he meditates on the explosion in student population and the explosion in learning. How is this centre-margin pattern to be maintained *and* TV fitted into it? How is the entire community to receive a higher education *and* present standards of instruction to be maintained? The answer is simple, and it has been rendered many times by other new structures in the electronic age: decentralize. Create multiple new centres. Abandon centre-margin patterns of the old hierarchy of specialties and functions. Enthrone the living dialogue in centres and between centres, since the entire new technology of our age demands this greatest of all humanist forms of instruction, not as an ideal, but as a daily necessity of action in every area of our communities.

The humanities, then, are about to enter their greatest period of cultivation and expression in the electronic age. But they will assume different relations to each other than we have latterly known them to have. In the ancient world and in the medieval period the trivial and quadrivial studies were, in the main, centres without margins. They are returning as such, but where there were seven before, there may soon be seventy. And there will be no more incompatibility of the *Two Cultures* that C. P. Snow has reminded us of. The real trouble has been that the literary and verbal culture has followed the nineteenth-century logic of mechanism and specialism just as far as the scientists have followed the merely statistical logic of numbers. With the computer we all move out of the age of number and statistics into the age of the curve and the simultaneous awareness of structures. With satellite broadcasting a few months off we move, scientist and humanist alike, into a world of instant and inexpensive access to anything and anybody on the globe. The divorce in our world is not now, nor will it be, between the scientist and the humanist but between the mechanist and the electrician. Our scientists as much as our humanists are caught in the old forms of the departing mechanical culture which all have contributed to for centuries. We now live electrically, but we continue to think in the older modes of mechanism. Even the wheel itself, which we abstracted from animal form, is being reabsorbed into the organic in the jet age. In the Polaris missile the fuel and the engine are one. Both cease to exist at the same moment. Yet the mark of obsolescence is now, as always, hypertrophy. Witness the motor car.

When he set out to give us his *ABC of Relativity*, Bertrand Russell explained:

> Many of the new ideas can be expressed in non-mathematical language, but they are none the less difficult on that account. What is demanded is a change in our imaginative picture of the world. . . . The same sort of change was demanded by Copernicus when he taught that the earth is not stationary and the heavens do not revolve about it once a day. To us now there is no difficulty in this idea, because we learned it before our mental

habits had become fixed. Einstein's ideas, similarly, will seem easier to generations which grow up with them; but for us a certain effort of imaginative reconstruction is unavoidable.

One major difference between the age of Copernicus and that of Einstein is the fact that there was nobody who could apply the ideas of Copernicus to anything but poetry and painting. Today the most abstruse theories go into action even before they have had their day in science fiction.

Yet today, as never before, the task of the humanities is to keep clear and lively the modes of discourse and the forms of mental life. More than ever before humanists are called on to understand many new languages born of the new forms of new knowledge. Nor will these new languages obviate the older ones. Jet travel and satellite broadcasting will foster the grasp of languages, ancient and modern, in a simultaneous cultural transparency. The concept of history of the philosopher Heidegger recommends itself as a natural model for the humanities in the electric age. It is the idea of the poetic of history, of history as a kind of unified language, the inner key to the creation of which can be grasped by a deepening sense of the spiritual energy encompassed in the ceaselessly growing life of words. The ideal Marriage of Mercury and Philology, of spiritual values and perfected method, will be consummated, if ever, in the electronic age.

CAMILLE DOZOIS

The Catholic Church in the Mid-twentieth Century

Because of their personal convictions, men tend often to overlook certain beliefs or opinions held by others, or simply choose to ignore them as unimportant. For the humanist scholar, such an attitude would be unpardonable. For his task is to make accessible to man all that is human, all that affects man's life and thought. Religion is one of these factors of human existence, whether one considers it as a general social phenomenon or concretely as a system of thought and life expressing itself in history. As such, it must be assessed and evaluated by the humanist scholar, made relevant and meaningful for the present generation and that of tomorrow.[1]

No attempt, obviously, will be made here to establish the significance of either religion or Christianity or Catholicism for mid-twentieth century man. The task is too vast and, within the confines of this essay, certainly quite impossible. Rather, our purpose will be to sketch briefly that reality which is present-day Catholicism, to present the elements of what has been called its "mounting vitality,"[2] and to outline what seem to be the principal causes of this renewed vigour.

In recent years, even columnists of secular newspapers and magazines have noted the changing mien of the Church. Indeed, the Church is at present actively engaged in a critical re-appraisal of her place and role in the world. Since 1959 especially, when the late Pope John XXIII summoned an ecumenical council embracing the entire Catholic world, this public examination of collective conscience has made history. This event, as well as others of recent years, shows that, in describing present-day Catholicism, contemporary changing trends and attitudes must be taken into careful consideration.

HAB vol. XVI, no. 1, spring 1965.

The Church has lost much of the negative and defensive attitude formerly developed as a reaction against the Protestant Reformation and, more recently, against the attacks of rationalists and modernists. Pope John XXIII, speaking at the opening of Vatican Council II, on October 11, 1962, expressed the Church's growing positive attitude in this way:

> The Church has always opposed . . . errors, and often condemned them with the utmost severity. Today, however, Christ's Bride prefers the balm of mercy to the arm of severity. She believes that present needs are best served by explaining more fully the purport of her doctrines, rather than by publishing condemnations.[3]

Growing increasingly conscious of the influence she possesses, the Church is, as a result, in a position to stress new dimensions in her relationship to the world at large. The present council, Vatican II, was not convoked to combat error or to establish defences against outside influences considered pernicious; rather, it was meant as a positive reflection concerning the Church's role toward mankind. This is well noted in the opening paragraph of the very first document to be approved and published by Vatican II:

> This sacred Council has several aims in view; it desires to impart an ever increasing vigour to the Christian life of the faithful; to adapt more suitably to the needs of our own times those institutions which are subject to change; to foster whatever can promote union among all who believe in Christ; to strengthen whatever can help to call the whole of mankind into the household of the Church.[4]

Together with the consciousness of her influence, there has grown within the Church a deeper awareness of the responsibilities connected with this influential role. These responsibilities entail, for the Church, a growing faithfulness to God and His message on the one hand, a greater fidelity also, on the other hand, to man to whom this message is to be given so that he may grasp it and respond to it. There is no area of human knowledge and activity which has not become a concern of the Church. This has not always been so, historically. But today the Church realizes more than ever that she would be unfaithful both to God and to man if she were not to encompass in her solicitude every aspect of human thought and life: Bible studies, theology, philosophy, history, archaeology, medicine, biology, physics, psychology, sociology, education, economics, social and racial problems, government, politics, art, communications; these and many more are contemporary concerns of the Church.

This new attitude of the Church towards the modern world is "an attitude of solicitude, understanding, admiration and friendship."[5] It is a revolutionary attitude, one which, even within the Church, is sometimes very difficult to accept. There are bound to be strong opinions voiced both for and against it. One need but consider for example the present-day discussions concerning family planning, the population explosion, the question of religious liberty, etc., to see what difficulties lie in a sound and objective seeking of truth. The quest for truth is always revolutionary. It is often a source of embarrassment: it forces one to think, to re-assess one's position, even to change what falls short of the ideal. Yet, the Church today is committed to this line of action and to the spirit of renewal which is its logical consequence. And, although to some observers she treads most cautiously, she has no fear of what this may mean for her. For today, more than at any time in her history, does she seem convinced of those words spoken by her founder: "the truth will make you free men."[6]

Despite the obvious fact that this spirit of renewal has not yet pervaded with equal depth and efficacy all areas of Catholic life and thought, it seems similarly obvious that a new trend has firmly established itself within the Church. She has become, in fact as well as in spirit, revolutionary "in a revolutionary age." This attitude could and indeed should be explored at greater length. A leisurely evaluation of this trend and of its implications for present and future generations would prove most interesting. However, only the origins of the new attitude will here retain our attention.

Many would attribute today's trend within the Church to the straight-forward sincerity and zeal of the endearing Pope John XXIII. Yet, he was merely the occasion for this trend to express itself; he was the catalyst, as it were, enabling the Church to show its renewed vitality. The cause of the new current in Catholic life and thought must be sought further afield. Such changes are not wrought overnight; they have to be prepared, based, launched. Although the influences are manifold, three of them stand out as major factors in the current trends within the Church.

The first of these is the intellectual renewal in the Church, which must be traced back mainly to the impulse given by Pope Leo XIII.

Leo XIII was not himself a radical. As R. H. Schmandt puts it: "He was neither a reactionary nor by any means a doctrinaire liberal. Perhaps the more neutral term 'progressive' best characterizes him."[7] Yet, Leo was the man who, in his very first encyclical, *Inscrutabili Dei Consilio* (April 21, 1878), outlined a programme of reconciling the Church with the modern world, the man who could say: "I want to see the Church so far forward that my successor will not be able to turn back." Although not a revolutionary, Leo XIII was a man of vision. He saw the necessity for the Church of making her message meaningful to the world. To realize this, Leo also clearly grasped the necessity of approaching scientifically both poles of the relationship—God and man. And he set out to make his vision a reality.

A profound knowledge of God's message would involve a scientific approach to the Scriptures, to tradition, to theology itself and to its allied disciplines, especially philosophy. Leo XIII encouraged and stimulated the work of objective appraisal of the Scriptures, particularly by his encyclical *Providentissimus Deus* of November 18, 1893, and by the foundation of the Pontifical Biblical Commission on October 30, 1902. Tradition, on the other hand, that reflection—carried on throughout the ages of the Church's history—on the message received from God through the Bible, was lifeless and meaningless, unless vivified by objective historical research. And so Leo opened other closed doors: the Vatican archives were made accessible to scholars for research in 1881. Moreover, it was most important that this message, reflected upon in the Church's life, be expressed in an ordered, intelligent synthesis if all of its implications for modern man were to be discovered and applied. What was needed was a suitable framework, a skeleton upon which to build this body of living truth. It was in scholastic philosophy and theology, particularly in the system of St. Thomas Aquinas, that Leo saw the scientific approach he was seeking. Scholasticism, with its qualities of precision and clarity, would form an adequate synthesis of revelation and tradition on an adaptable yet coherent system of thought. It would be all the more so if the contributions of biblical and historical studies and those of the secular sciences were not set aside in favour of purely rational and notional constructs. And so, with the encyclical *Aeterni Patris* of August 4, 1879, the revival of theological studies in the Church was given its major contemporary forward thrust.

Together with this impetus for renewal in the ecclesiastical sciences are to be considered the great strides taken, also by Leo XIII, in the considerations of man's situation in his world. Leo's keen pastoral sense made him aware that the man to whom God's message is addressed was involved in a vast technological, political, and social upheaval. It is here that the second major factor influencing contemporary Catholic life and thought shows itself. It might be called the integration of secular values into the religious framework of Catholicism. Through his teachings, Leo XIII urged the development of the present-day interest and competence, within the Church, in such diverse fields as those of sociology, politics, economics, and the sciences. He gave the lead on the burning social and political crises of his time, especially through his epoch-making statement on the conditions of workers, *Rerum Novarum*, on May 15, 1891. Such official concern with the human realities both within and outside the Church was also to spark the growth of an increased lay involvement in Church affairs and open new avenues for ecumenical dialogue, as had the new attitudes towards the ecclesiastical sciences.

The impulse given by Leo XIII was not immediately felt. Concerning the other fields of Catholic life and thought, one must keep in mind what J. Macquarrie says about Leo and the revival of neo-scholasticism: "It must be remembered, however, that it took time before the effects of Leo's recommendation began fully to show themselves."[8] It was not until after both World Wars, which themselves had a deepening influence in man's understanding of God and of his fellow man, that the full impact of the renewal, launched by Leo XIII and vigorously fostered by Pius XII, became strikingly apparent. And this is precisely the hour of Pope John XXIII and of Vatican II.

It would however be a sorry mistake to claim that the present trend within the Church is due only to the renewal and integration of both ecclesiastical and secular intellectualism. This intellectualism would have been mainly arid if it had not been directed concretely to present pastoral problems but solely to questions of speculative or historical interest. This is why the influence of existential and personalist philosophies on the Church's pastoral and theological outlook must be deemed a third major factor in changing present-day Church attitudes. The emphasis of these philosophies on life-situations, on the reality of human encounter and of interpersonal relationships have undoubtedly affected the Church's understanding, both theoretical and practical, of such realities as faith, prayer, ethics, and social problems. Even when their excesses had to be curbed, as was the case for situation ethics in the 1950s,[9] these philosophies have, in their reaction to a too-rigid notional theology, complemented Catholic intellectualism and have contributed to a better-balanced Church attitude in the mid-twentieth century. Particularly have they been most useful in such areas as biblical studies, moral and pastoral theology, social and political thought. And most often they have formed an integral part of the theological renewal within the Church, an intimate and inseparable element of the Church's assimilation of secular scholarship for her own speculative or pastoral work.

It would be very difficult to explain, without such a background, such documents as Pope John's *Pacem in Terris* and the published or forthcoming statements of Vatican Council II[10] and the world-renowned scholarship of men like K. Adam, J. Daniélou, H. de Lubac, R. de Vaux, B. Haring, B. Lonergan, R. A. F. MacKenzie, J. Maritain, K. Rahner, E. Schillebeeckx, P. Teilhard de Chardin, V. White, and so many others. Indeed, if one does not consider the above-mentioned factors, the current attitude and trends within the Catholic Church are well-nigh impossible to fathom.

NOTES

1. For the relation of religion to the humanities, see the excellent work by C. A. Holbrook, *Religion, A Humanistic Field,* Humanistic Scholarship in America: the Princeton Studies, edited by R. Schlatter (Englewood Cliffs, N.J.: Prentice-Hall, 1963).
2. K. S. Latourette, *Christianity in a Revolutionary Age* (London: Eyre and Spottiswoode, 1961), IV, 19. In chapter II (pp. 15–21) the author gives an adequate overall picture of the Catholic Church in the nineteenth and twentieth centuries.
3. English text from *The Pope Speaks,* VIII (1963), 213.
4. *Constitution on the Sacred Liturgy,* December 4, 1963. NCWC translation.
5. Address of Pope Paul VI on the Christian concept of economics, given to a congress of employers and managers at Naples, June 8, 1964. The full text is given in *Herder Correspondence* (special issue, 1964), pp. 20–21.
6. John 8:32.
7. In *Leo XIII and the Modern World,* edited by E. T. Gargan (New York: Sheed and Ward, 1961), p. 35.
8. *Twentieth-Century Religious Thought: The Frontiers of Philosophy and Theology,* 1900–1960 (New York: Harper and Row, 1963), p. 278.
9. Instruction of the Holy Office, February 2, 1956. English text in J. C. Ford and G. Kelly, *Contemporary Moral Theology* (Westminster, Maryland: Newman, 1958), I, 121–123.
10. Such as those on the Church, on the Jews, on religious liberty.

MICHEL BRUNET

Towards the Discovery of a New Quebec

Within any society, it can be said that a true revolution occurs when people see themselves in a new perspective, get a more precise consciousness of themselves, and choose new goals for their collective action. Such a revolution has actually been in the making for the last twenty years among Quebec's French Canadians. Its effects constitute nowadays a real challenge for every English-speaking Canadian citizen.

The fact is that English-speaking Canadians are poorly prepared to understand what is going on in French Canada. For many generations they lived with the conviction that they alone had the right answers to the country's problems. Indeed, they had many good reasons to believe that Canada's prosperity and future were exclusively entrusted to their care.

Many facts long encouraged English Canadians to keep this good opinion of themselves. The English-speaking peoples of the world—Great Britain, the United States, British North America, Australia, New Zealand and British South Africa—formed a privileged group of nations. They enjoyed a high standard of living. Their political institutions represented a great achievement of human history. All the civilized nations of the world had adopted the representative system of government which first reached its full development in the English-speaking States. Great Britain had been the leader in the industrial revolution. The United States had become the most power-

HAB vol. XVI, no. 1, spring 1965. Text of an address delivered during French Canada Week at the University of Alberta campus in Edmonton, January 1965. A part of this article previously appeared in *Queen's Quarterly*, autumn 1956.

ful and prosperous country of the world. Canada itself had made a genuine contribution to the evolution of the representative system of government and to the economic development of the English-speaking world.

In the field of international politics, the might of Anglo-Saxondom was felt and respected on every continent and sea of the world. His or Her Majesty's navy ruled the waves from the beginning of the eighteenth century until the First World War when the American navy came to her rescue. The British Empire had been larger than that of the Romans and of the Spaniards. When Germany twice attempted, during the first half of this century, to dominate Europe, her back was broken by the Great Alliance concluded between the British peoples and the United States. In both World Wars, British Canada could be rightly proud of her contribution to the Great Alliance's victory.

From the Treaty of Utrecht in 1713 to Germany's and Japan's unconditional surrender of 1945, the history of the English-speaking peoples has almost been a fairy-tale. One can easily understand why and how they gradually convinced themselves that their institutions, their language, their culture were superior to those of all the other nations. Were not their deeds and their success the demonstration of this superiority? Their neighbours' and rivals' admiration or envy encouraged them in that way of thinking. They sincerely came to the conclusion that God Himself had given them the leadership of the contemporary world. Is it necessary to quote Rudyard Kipling, Joseph Chamberlain, Senator Beveridge, and John Foster Dulles?

This infatuation has long prevented the leaders of the English-speaking nations from realizing that, during the last twenty years, a new equilibrium in international politics and economics has brought an end to this former privileged position. The English-speaking peoples of the world are just beginning to discover that the glory of the Great Alliance and of Anglo-Saxondom belongs to the past. It is now urgent to proceed to an "agonizing reappraisal." The process, which has already begun, is a painful one.

In Canada, the English-speaking and British-minded citizens had additional reasons to nurse their feeling of superiority. They only had to compare their fate to that of their French-speaking fellow-citizens to conclude that they were right in their approach to the political and economic problems of the country. Had not Canada's historical evolution from the Treaty of Paris to the Second World War eloquently demonstrated that the English-speaking population had exerted with success and for the good of all Canadian citizens its leadership in all the fields of collective action? Indeed, French Canadians had not always agreed with their English-speaking fellow-citizens' viewpoints and decisions. But, finally, they had been compelled, after some protest, to bow down. Was that not proof that they had first been ill-informed and that they had realized, after a while, that the policies adopted by English Canada's leaders did serve the best interests of all the Canadian population?

One must not then be surprised to learn that English Canadians have built themselves a set of rationalizations to legitimize their dominant position in the economic and political life of the country and to explain the French Canadians' way of life and attitude in their dealings with English Canada. The fact is that the survival of the *Canadiens,* as a distinctive group having the means to act collectively in some fields, constitutes one of the major problems of Canadian political, economic, and social life. The problem has existed since the British Conquest and occupation of Canada two hundred years ago; there is every indication that it will endure for many more generations.

The French-Canadian problem may be approached and has been approached in a variety of ways. First, there is what might be called the optimistic approach. It has been displayed at many after-dinner speeches and at those meetings of *bonne entente* where Canadians and *Canadiens* have indulged in the bad habit of not telling one another what they really think. The exponents of the optimistic approach like to believe that there are only small—very small—differences between the English-speaking majority and the French-speaking minority. Eloquently, they invite both groups to forget what divides them and to emphasize all the factors which are supposed to unite them. In the name of national unity, they expect the French Canadians to accept all the decisions made by the majority and they want the minority to let itself be persuaded that these decisions are for the common good. They pretend that Canadians and *Canadiens* form one Nation-State under the leadership of the federal government, which they consider as a national government. To placate the *Canadiens,* they pay lip-service to French-Canadian culture and to the so-called unique French-Canadian contribution to the building of Canada. They even go so far as to pretend, in spite of all the facts to the contrary, that this nation is bilingual and biethnic. These nice, sugar-coated words used to please tradition-minded French Canadians of former generations who accepted the old nationalistic-messianic interpretation of the past and present history of their nationality. The trouble is that the new generations have rejected that interpretation.

The optimistic approach has long been adopted by federal politicians—both Canadians and *Canadiens,* by well-wishers and, in general, by all those who through habit, ignorance, or inertia cannot face the facts as they are. This approach explains and settles nothing. It has only soporific effects and deceives both the Canadians and the *Canadiens.* It muddles the fundamental issues of the Canadian union, and has been and is still the cause of many misunderstandings and maladjustments. Most of the time when a serious clash breaks out between *Canadiens* and Canadians, it is because the leaders of both groups have been blinded to the differences which actually exist between them. Faced with a decision taken by the English-speaking majority which they are not prepared to accept, the *Canadiens* resist and protest, feeling strongly that they have been pushed around. On the other hand, the English population, having been told and therefore sincerely believing that the *Canadiens* of Quebec are like all the other Canadians, tries in vain to understand their behaviour and is prone to denounce their ill-will and their separatist leanings.

A second approach may be designated "the big-brother attitude." Among the Canadians there are many who have always considered the *Canadiens* as a backward population that has unfortunately been unable, since 1760, to take full advantage of the political liberty and of the material prosperity brought to them by the British Conquest and the colonization of the St. Lawrence Valley. This paternalistic approach is that of all colonizers and majorities towards colonial peoples and minority groups placed under their rule or, if one prefers, under their leadership. They sincerely believe that they really bring happiness and well-being to the population upon whom they impose their language, their laws, their political institutions, their economic domination, their foreign and internal policy, their ways of thinking and living.

This big-brother approach, which was general among the first generations of British settlers who came to Canada after the Conquest, still exists today. When the English-speaking majority sees that the *Canadiens* apparently do not fully appreciate the blessings of being associated with British Canada and that they show no special gratitude towards the Canadians, it concludes that it is because they are ill-bred, ignorant, biased, and "priest-ridden." Fortunately these old accusations are not thrown out as often as they used to be. But many contemporary Canadians, as their fathers and forefathers did, still eagerly hope for the day when the *Canadiens*, receiving a better education and having got rid of their so-called prejudices and of clerical rule, will suddenly discover—at last!—that it is in their best interest to amalgamate completely with the English-speaking majority. Then, it is said, they will be free from the old fetters which are supposed to have prevented them from gaining access to a more modern and dynamic way of living.

It is important to note that many French-Canadian intellectuals, rejecting the traditional and time-worn assumptions of French-Canadian thought and realizing the shortcomings of the old leaders of their people, were formerly tempted to adopt this big-brother approach. They liked to consider themselves more enlightened than the majority of their compatriots. Most of today's French-Canadian intellectuals have changed their minds in this respect. They have realized that their own future is linked to that of French Canada. They have also discovered that the French Canadian population is eager to adopt all the reforms which will enable it to enter into and master the twentieth century. These days one can still find the big-brother approach among French-Canadian businessmen, employees, engineers, and politicians who make their living with British Canada or need for their own promotion to make friends among English-speaking people. One can easily understand why they speak and act as they do. But one must not pay much attention to their statements. They speak first for themselves, they represent a very small minority, and it pays them to say things which people who listen to them like to hear.

There is a more recent approach to the French-Canadian problem. It is the "social-leftist" interpretation of the relations between Canadians and *Canadiens.* It has been developed by a few sociologists and intellectuals who have, wittingly or unwittingly, been influenced by Marxist theories about the class structure or capitalistic society. According to the social-leftist approach the population of Canada should be no longer divided between French-speaking and English-speaking citizens, but between the haves and have-nots, between the employers and the employees. The exponents of this theory pretend that French-Canadian and English-Canadian workers and underdogs throughout Canada will forget their divisions as members of different cultural groups and unite together to get a bigger part of the economic loaf. They seem convinced that the class struggle will completely modify the two-century-old pattern of ethnic relations in Canada. One cannot deny that the French Canadians want to improve their standard of living and get all the advantages of progressive social security legislation. To achieve this legitimate aim, they are not opposed to working in collaboration with all Canadian citizens and groups that seek the same ends. But, as it has been clearly proven during the last few years, they also realize that the betterment of their individual standard of living requires an extension of the Quebec government's power and cannot be dissociated from the collective progress and influence of their nationality in the Canadian union. The social and school legislation of the Lesage government, its policy aimed at protecting and enlarging provincial autonomy, and the later evolution of the labour movement in Quebec whereby the French-Canadian Federation of Labour's membership increases every week, have compelled the most clever partisans of the social-leftist approach to change their frame of reference.

The optimistic approach, the big-brother approach, and the social-leftist approach all give one-sided and false interpretations of the French-Canadian problem. To understand the peculiar position of the French-Canadian nationality in the Canadian union, one has to put aside all preconceptions and to face the facts as they are. At the same time one must take the risk of hurting the feelings of many people.

Throughout the English-speaking provinces, the *Canadiens,* who number less than one million, have a status which is almost that of immigrants. They are involved in an accelerated process of complete assimilation into the majority. However, they desperately try to survive as a cultural group. In their struggle for *la survivance française* they occasionally receive some support from their Quebec compatriots. They have a few French radio stations and newspapers. Sometimes they can look at French TV programmes. In some districts they send their children to French schools and colleges. In this respect, federal grants to university education have been a real boon for them. They have organized and still control some French parishes and dioceses. They use bilingual bank-notes printed by the Bank of Canada, and the Post Office Department sells them bilingual stamps—most of the time through the agency of English-speaking and unilingual federal functionaries. They receive bilingual cheques when the Ottawa government owes them money. They are free to use the French language when they write to the federal government, and they are entitled to get, sometimes with much delay, French publications from its various departments. And that's all! This situation cannot last for many more generations before the assimilation of these scattered and small French-speaking groups is complete. The case is somewhat different for the French Canadians living in Ottawa.

In New Brunswick, where they number about 40 per cent of the population, there is perhaps a future for French-speaking citizens as a distinctive cultural group. But one must not forget that if the Atlantic provinces (Newfoundland, New Brunswick, Prince Edward Island and Nova Scotia) are one day united—and there are many factors working in that direction, the *Acadiens* will still remain an uninfluential minority. One can suppose that the *Acadiens* would then prefer to be annexed to Quebec.

The population of the English-speaking provinces is now tranquillized. Since the census of 1951, it knows that the "French and Popish domination" so long feared has always been a myth. The censuses of 1956 and 1961 have given additional proofs that there will be no "revenge of the cradle" for the *Canadiens*. The chill given to the English-speaking majority when the figures of the 1941 census were published looks today like a good joke.

The situation is quite different in Quebec. There the *Canadiens* have always been and will always remain the majority of the population. It is about time for the English-speaking inhabitants of all the provinces to abandon the illusion that the *Canadiens* living in Quebec will in the long run be themselves assimilated by the English-speaking majority of North America as if they were mere immigrants in the St. Lawrence Valley. Quebec is the land where their forefathers established the *nation canadienne* in the seventeenth and eighteenth centuries when France, their mother country, was at the summit of her power. They remember that they have a past of their own on this continent. For one century and a half the *Canadiens* lived alone in the St. Lawrence Valley and dominated the hinterland of North America. They have their traditions; their cultural, economic, and political institutions; their professors, scientists, writers, artists; their collective ways of thinking and living; their common sorrows; their common aspirations. They actually form a nationality whose members are bound together by specific ties of cultural homogeneity. They are animated by consciousness of themselves as a group and, what is more important, they have means of expressing this consciousness. They feel a bond of sympathy toward one another which is different from that which they experience towards the members of another nationality. For generations they have shared a common life, and they are giving the proof that they want to continue this life in the future.

This nationality exists in a provincial state, part of a federal union. And the *Canadiens,* even if they are the majority, are not alone in the province of Quebec. Because of the British Conquest and colonization of the St. Lawrence Valley, they were deprived in the nineteenth century of their right to full self-determination. They were annexed to the Kingdom of Canada. However, on account of historical and geographical circumstances, they have survived as a distinctive collectivity, and they had no choice but to survive. The English-speaking population that settled in Quebec was never strong enough to assimilate them. They are now more than four million. By the end of the century they will be six or seven million. They alone can and will determine the nature of their survival as a community. This is the fundamental reason why the provincial rights issue has been and is still, in Quebec, a struggle for self-government.

The political events of the last twenty years have emphasized more clearly every year the fact that the *Canadiens* make some essential distinctions between the Ottawa government and the Quebec government. For them, the central government represents the rule of the English-speaking majority. Especially since the Second World War, when they realized how small was their actual influence on the general policy of the country, they have come to see it as a political instrument to enforce the decisions of the Canadians. On the other hand, even when Mr. Duplessis was the *chef*, they have gradually learned to consider the Quebec government as the most powerful means at their disposal for supporting their collective action and assuring their progress as a nationality. This evolution in their political and social thinking was inevitable because their provincial government is the only one in Canada which they control as a majority. It would be unrealistic to deny these facts. What would be the English-speaking Canadians' attitude toward the federal government if the latter were under the control of a French-speaking majority and if they were the majority of the population only in one province? Would they accept to sacrifice the autonomy of "their" provincial government in the name of the "national unity" preached by the French-Canadian majority?

The words of Lord Durham, who still remains the best historian of Canada, still ring true: "I found two nations warring in the bosom of a single state." Since Durham's Report, the British-American nation, which built the second Kingdom of Canada with the help of her mother country, secured and now exercises her right to full self-determination. This collective freedom could not be given to both nations. Self-determination has naturally been the privilege of the stronger.

However, some leaders of British Canada, more clear-sighted than Lord Durham, had realized as early as the 1820s that the complete assimilation of the *Canadiens* was already impossible. Hinks, Baldwin, and their successors made a deal with the French-Canadian spokesmen in the legislature of United Canada and used them as junior partners to win responsible government. This victory, however, was placed in the hands of the British majority who utilized it mostly for their own benefit. But the *Canadiens* could say that they participated in the government of the country, and they were satisfied. Since the British Conquest and occupation of their country they had learned to be satisfied with little.

A better compromise was reached in 1867 with the creation of the Province of Quebec. The *Canadiens* had been lucky enough to keep a limited freedom of collective action as a nationality within the new federal framework. They at least had control over a provincial government. Indeed, it was, for three generations, a very limited control. The English-speaking minority in Quebec was very powerful. Its status was that of a dominant group in a colonial territory. In fact, the Bank of Montreal and the Montreal Anglo-American plutocrats dominated without any challenge Quebec's politics till the 1950s. Even Mr. Lesage and Mr. Levesque have recently been reminded that bankers and insurance company managers, who administer money which does not belong to them, still believe in the second half of the twentieth century that they are more powerful than the voters and their democratically elected representatives.

Moreover, during the first eighty years after Confederation, the French Canadians hardly knew how to use the provincial government given them in 1867. Pressure groups, among which the Quebec English-speaking capitalists and the Catholic clergy were the most active and the most powerful, were completely free to organize, protect, and increase their vested interests. For too many years, the French-Canadian politicians were mere errand-boys at the service of the English-Canadian and American entrepreneurs and of the Catholic bishops. One should not be surprised or scandalized by this fact. To understand it, it must not be forgotten that from 1760 to 1867 the political leaders of French Canada had always been an uninfluential small minority in the executive branch of the government—before and after the establishment of responsible government. They had no political tradition, and their experience in managing public affairs was very limited when they took charge of a provincial government in 1867. In fact, the *Canadiens* did not know what self-government meant and had developed a narrow conception of the role of the State and of the importance of political power. Here lies the main reason why pressure groups have been so long able to dominate Quebec politicians and politics at the expense of the common good. Both the Church leaders and the *Montreal Gazette*, which was the mouthpiece of St. James Street, agreed to preach that the best provincial government was the one which governed the least.

A totally new political and social thinking now inspires French Canada's most dynamic leaders in all fields of collective action. This new approach to politics and public affairs manifested itself during Duplessis' years. It is about time to take a less emotive look at this recent period of our history. The Union Nationale leader's defence of provincial autonomy and his strong opposition to federal centralization were the signs that the French Canadians of the 1940s and 1950s, contrary to their forefathers, had begun to realize that good government by the English-speaking majority in Ottawa is no substitute for self-government by a French-Canadian majority in Quebec. Now receiving a better schooling, enjoying a higher standard of living, and under the impact of an accelerated industrialization, the *Canadiens* have made many important discoveries since Mr. Duplessis came to power in 1944.

The Union Nationale victory was first a protest vote against the policy imposed by the English-speaking majority on the Quebec voters during the Second World War. The federal Liberal party's broken promises, the plebiscite of 1942, Mr. Cardin's resignation, and the adoption of military conscription had left deep wounds in Quebec. People had no more confidence in the Ottawa government. They had concluded that their representatives in the federal capital had very little influence. Even Mr. Saint-Laurent could not change his fellow Quebeckers' minds in this respect.

When, in 1953, Mr. Duplessis appointed a provincial commission of inquiry into constitutional problems, he received enthusiastic support throughout the province. This investigation was in fact a plebiscite on provincial autonomy and on the role of the state as an instrument to serve the common good of the population. The institution, in 1954, of a provincial tax on personal incomes gave more authority and a new prestige to the provincial government. Taxing has always been the best means for a state to get respected. The rich people of Quebec, and among them there were many members of the English-speaking minority, understood that the provincial government was less under their influence than it used to be. In fact, Duplessis was so afraid of the money-lenders—he had not forgotten his lost struggle of 1939 against them—that he refrained from borrowing money and tried to pay with the provincial yearly revenues all the expenses of its government from 1944 to his death in 1959. One must not then be surprised to learn that Quebec suffers today from a delay in its public investments and needs increased revenues.

The Catholic Church herself was told that the Quebec government had full jurisdiction over education and that her action in that field was under its authority. It happened when Université Laval and Université de Montréal, with the support of some bishops, let it be known in the fall of 1956 that they were not opposed to accepting the federal grants to universities. Three years before, Mr. Duplessis had refused these grants. Threatened with the projected creation of a state university, the Church bowed down before Duplessis' decision. McGill University had no choice but to do the same. Its principal, Dr. Cyril James, who was the main architect of the federal plan to help the universities, had himself discovered that the provincial government was stronger than he had thought.

Duplessis greatly contributed to the firm establishment of the authority of the provincial state. His critics say that he had only in mind the aggrandizement of his own personal power. They are wrong because they refuse to see that at the same time he worked, in the long run, to the benefit of the provincial government. His policy was a response to new challenges. His successors had no choice but to pursue the same policy with some new accents and with more definite goals. They have taken profit of Duplessis' pioneer work.

When Duplessis died in September 1959, Paul Sauvé was acclaimed by the whole province. He declared that he would continue to extend the powers of the provincial state in order to give to the population the reform legislation it was asking for. The French Canadians demonstrated by their reaction to Sauvé's programme that they were strongly in favor of a positive state. They had discovered that they could now influence through their votes the action of the only government where their representatives constituted a majority. Sauvé's sudden death in January 1960 was seen as a catastrophe.

At the general election of 1960, the voters gave their support to a completely renovated provincial Liberal party. The latter had presented a very progressive programme. Moreover, the French-Canadian electorate was convinced that Mr. Lesage, Mr. Lapalme, Mr. Gérin-Lajoie and Mr. Lévesque were the right men to satisfy their demand for a positive state. They were not deceived.

When the Lesage government called a general election, in the fall of 1962, on the issue of nationalizing the private electricity companies, it adopted as its electoral slogan: "Masters in our own house." Nobody knows if the leaders of the Liberal party have thoroughly analysed the implications of this slogan but there is no doubt that for the young generations of French Canada it means a breaking from the past and a leap into the future.

A new French-Canadian man is born. He lives at a new rhythm, in a new mood, and in a new climate. He is against power abused and injustice encrusted. He already has a sense of resistance overcome and triumph achieved. He has the will for winning. He wants to settle as soon as possible many problems which past generations ignored or did not dare to cope with.

A problem almost solved during the last few years is that of the exact role of the Roman Catholic Church in the new French-Canadian society. The Church leaders, most of them at least, have demonstrated that they are willing to abandon powers and responsibilities which had been formerly entrusted to them by the population itself. They are no longer opposed to the state's taking its full jurisdiction in the fields of health and education. At the time of the Vatican Council, the Quebec Church is one of the most progressive, and one cannot expect a major power struggle between the Church and the state in the near future.

The most ticklish problem in Quebec now is how to gradually modify the former pattern of the relations between the English-speaking privileged minority and the French-Canadian majority. Very few people have the courage to discuss this major issue publicly. However, the most clear-sighted leaders of both groups privately admit that the situation which has prevailed since the British conquest can no longer be maintained. The young French-Canadian generations are in no mood to tolerate for many more years a state of affairs which their fathers and forefathers were compelled to accept. Already some gestures have been made. In a few industries and companies, French-Canadian labourers and employees are no longer obliged to use the English language at their work. Thousands of English-speaking Quebeckers are learning French. Many young English-speaking parents want bilingual schools for their children. But these first steps, even if they are in the right direction, are not sufficient. A special commission on inter-ethnic relations in Quebec should be established to prepare a programme in order to help the English-speaking minority to adapt itself to a new Quebec and, at the same time, to educate the French Canadians to accept as their fellow countrymen, no matter what their ethnic origin, all those who want to make their living in

Quebec. A system of public non-denominational schools has become an urgent necessity.

Strong and quick action is required for economic expansion. Quebec has many of the weaknesses of an under-developed region. Its economy suffers from severe unemployment, a slow rate of growth, and bad habits acquired by the Anglo-American and the few French-Canadian entrepreneurs and businessmen who have operated in Quebec. Economists who have seriously studied the problem conclude that Quebec cannot rely only on private investments to create the jobs it needs to absorb the thousands of young men and women who are looking for work every year. The new political leaders, having no special admiration for the *laissez-faire* economy of the so-called "good old days," are conversant with the serious situation they face. Some among them realize perfectly that only a far-sighted policy of advanced and systematic socialization could help to cure the basic economic ills of the province. However, they have to be very prudent, not so much in fear of scandalizing the Church or the voters but because they do not want to frighten the capitalists whose investments are much needed. Nevertheless, they know that these investments will not be sufficient to prevent a major crisis of unemployment. They place their hope in the establishment of a provincial pension fund which will constitute a reserve of capital.

Finally comes the question of the relations of Quebec with the federal government and with the other provinces. French Canadians of past generations were ready—some among them were even eager—to consider the Ottawa government as a "national" one. They sincerely wanted it to be truly representative of the two cultural groups whose close association was necessary to build a continental union of Canadians and *Canadiens*. Unfortunately, the English-speaking and British-minded majority had decided that Ottawa was and would remain its "national" government and used it as an instrument to enforce its conception of "national unity." Consequently, the Quebec French-Canadian voters gradually came to the conclusion that their representatives in the Ottawa government were mere "yes men." And "yes men" they were!

Since the Second World War, the French Canadians of Quebec have shown less interest every year in federal politics. Having been refused participation as equals in the decision-making in Ottawa they have totally reconsidered the nature of their association with the Canadian federation. The majority among them now see the Ottawa government as that of English Canada and as a link between the Quebec government and the rest of the country. They are almost completely indifferent to what is happening on Parliament Hill.

From 1945 to 1957, they voted for the federal Liberal party, not because they had faith in a party which had deceived them for more than thirty years with false promises but because they had no choice and felt some admiration for Mr. Saint-Laurent. Nevertheless, they stubbornly refused to listen to him when he tried to influence their votes in provincial politics. This intervention was even looked at with indignation. In 1958, Mr. Saint-Laurent having been ousted from the party leadership by its English-speaking members who did not want it to become a racial or regional group, they voted for the Conservatives. They had no more confidence in Mr. Diefenbaker's party than they had in Mr. Pearson's but they had not forgotten the war years and wanted the Quebec federal Liberal politicians to know it. The two federal elections of 1957 and 1958 also reminded the French Canadians that English Canada does not need their vote to form a government in Ottawa. Once more, they could see the actual size of their influence on Parliament Hill. Even the most optimistic among them opened their eyes.

In 1962 and 1963, the Quebec voters divided their votes between the Liberals, the Creditists, and the Conservatives. Their attitude clearly shows that they do not take federal politics seriously. Is it not revealing to learn that the House Committee on the Flag received no project from Quebec French-Canadian associations? Every one knows that the response would have been much different a generation ago. In fact, the recent flag debate gave more grounds for the French Canadians of Quebec to disengage themselves from federal politics. The public reaction to the decision of inviting the Queen to commemorate the building of Confederation illustrates the same feeling. On the other hand, French Canadians now believe for the first time in provincial politics. They are engaged, as we have seen, in the process of nationalizing their provincial political institutions with the help of a new generation and a new kind of leaders.

Actually, French Canadians have discovered that they have the collective means to organize their national life by themselves and for themselves. They now have the knowledge and the will to shape their own future in the St. Lawrence Valley. In doing so they have to change the two-century-old pattern under which they have lived since the British Conquest and their subsequent annexation to English Canada. It is a great and difficult undertaking which begins first inside Quebec. But it also puts into question the nature of the new Quebec's relations with the Ottawa government and the rest of Canada. This problem must be solved because Canada's future is here at stake.

Quebec's revolution—there is no use hiding the fact that there is a revolutionary mood in French Canada—requires a rebuilding of the Canadian union. A new political equilibrium exists in today's Canada. Quebec can no longer be considered as a mere province among ten provinces. This myth long served the interests of English Canada in helping to maintain Quebec in a status of protectorship. This time is now over.

The problem we face is twofold. How is it possible to let Quebec exert all the powers it needs and asks for to fulfil the programme of reforms demanded by its population without taking the risk of balkanizing Canada if the powers of all the other provinces are unduly increased? The trouble is that presently many leaders of French and English Canada refuse to face the facts as they are. They prefer to believe that some package-deal and horse-trading will in the long run enable the country to overcome the present crisis. They are mistaken. An overhaul of the Canadian constitution and union is overdue. One can hope that Quebec's challenge will help achieve this.

In conclusion, I want to state clearly that the Quebec French Canadians are not waging a war against the rest of the country. They are well-informed enough to realize that their English-speaking fellow-citizens of British Columbia, of the Prairies, of Ontario, and of the Maritimes are not personally responsible for the old situation they want to change in Quebec. Moreover, they have no reason yet to think that the English-speaking Canadians of the other provinces are opposed to their endeavour to settle their own problems and to clean their own house. To achieve these aims, they even need the comprehension of English Canada with which they will have to come to an agreement for building a new Canadian union, taking into account Quebec's national goals and Canada's changing political and economic equilibrium.

Canada is facing, at a moment when the acceleration of history has completely transformed our contemporary world, the major ordeal of her history. To overcome it, English Canadians must revise their former frame of reference. The Quebec French Canadians have already changed theirs in order to adapt it to the second half of the twentieth century. I am convinced that English Canada's young generations will no longer cling to old myths and will meet their French Canadian associates at half way to take up the challenge presented them.

CLAUDE T. BISSELL

Sputnik and the Humanities

I was greatly honoured by the invitation to speak to the Humanities Association of Canada, but not a little disconcerted on finding myself assigned to this special place in your programme. Heretofore on this occasion you have been addressed by distinguished scholars. I can only interpret your selection of an administrator this year as a calculated search for variety, taken, I hope, in full knowledge of the risks you run. As an administrator, a university president is heavily committed to jargon; and as a public orator, to platitudes; and it is well known that scholars in the humanities, rather than be guilty of either jargon or platitudes, will go to any extreme—even to the extremity of dullness.

At some future meeting of the Humanities Association of Canada, you may find it amusing and instructive to investigate the portrait of the university administrator in literature. You might begin with some recent American academic novels, with, for instance, Mary McCarthy's mordant analysis in *The Groves of Academe,* or with Theodore Morrison's more benign portrait in *The Stones of the House,* or with Stringfellow Barr's savage caricature in the most recent of these novels, *Purely Academic.* Mr. Barr, as an ex-university president, writes with a venom that comes, presumably, from personal experience. Here is a passage in which he sets the tone of his comment on the president of his unhappy midwestern college:

President Pomton was a remarkable man. He was perhaps less remarkable than his wife supposed, but he was remarkable just the same. Education was only one of his main concerns, and he gave the impression, not so much of ornamenting the University, as of ornamenting himself with the

HAB no. 25, October 1958. From an address to the annual meeting of the Humanities Association of Canada, 1958.

University. He was the sort of man who would be essentially too big for any job. Neither did he ornament scholarship. Scholarship ornamented him.

I was personally relieved to be told a few sentences later that before his elevation President Pomton had been a Professor of Education.

Another and more scholarly approach to this subject would be to search among some of the great classics for relevant passages. A colleague, for instance, has recently pointed out that there is a passage in Gibbon about the Emperor Diocletian that may have some faint relevance to university administration:

> His abilities were useful rather than splendid—a vigorous mind improved by the experience and study of mankind; dexterity and application in business; a judicious mixture of liberality and economy; of mildness and rigour; profound dissimulation under the disguise of military frankness; steadiness to pursue his ends; flexibility to vary his means; and, above all, the great art of submitting his own passions as well as those of others, to the interest of his ambition, and of colouring his ambition with the most specious pretenses of justice and public utility.

It is rare, of course, that you will find a passage that may have such a direct bearing, but you will find many that deal with the incidental duties of the university administrator. Thomas Fuller, for instance, is one of the shrewdest writers I have discovered on the whole subject of fund raising. I give as evidence this passage in which he talks about the benefactions of a certain Francis Cleark, one of the "worthies" of Bedfordshire.

> He founded four new fellowships; and had he been pleased to consult with the College, the settlement with the same expense might have proved more advantageous; for though in gifts to private persons it be improper that the receiver should be the director thereof, a corporation may give the best advice to improve the favours conferred upon it. But it is a general practice that men desire rather to be *broad* than *thick* benefactors.

I like particularly the distinction between broad and thick benefactors. It goes to the very heart of university financing.

My first task, I realize, is to define and to defend my title. I am sure the title has filled many of you with forebodings, since it is clearly the lineal descendent of our old unhappy friend, *The Plight of the Humanities.* Indeed, William Blissett has recently suggested that *Sputnik and the Humanities* is one of the titles, along with such others as *The Humanities and the Mass Media, The Humanities and Juvenile Drug Addiction,* that should be permanently banned. You will notice the casual use in all these titles of what Millar MacLure has referred to as "that omnipotent conjunction, the fulcrum of more learned articles that you can shake an offprint or a doctor's parchment at." In my title the "and" is not used with any "axial flourish"; I will make no attempt to bring the two nouns into some subtle and complex alignment. "Sputnik" is merely convenient shorthand for referring to the intellectual environment in which we all live—an environment that suddenly pressed closely upon all of us when the Russians launched their first earth satellite. The first effect of sputnik was to place science more firmly than ever at the centre of our civilization. In addition—and this was where sputnik had a direct influence on the universities—it became clear, even to the layman, that great technological triumphs like earth satellites could not be produced by a technological society alone, but depended on the work of pure scientists seeking to uncover fundamental laws of nature. The university, then, both as a manufacturer of technologists and engineers, and as a centre of research, could have a direct and powerful effect on the international race to produce the ultimate gadget, and it should, therefore, be given greater support than ever before.

In recent months, there has been an extraordinary revival of interest in higher education, accompanied by a somewhat less feverish revival of interest in the financial embarrassment of universities. The interest has shown itself chiefly in the area of mathematics and the sciences, but all university disciplines have been beneficiaries. The humanities, and the social sciences too, stand to gain from all this. The real danger of the popular resurgence of interest in science is not that the humanities will suffer, but that all pure learning, whether in the humanities, in the social sciences, or in the sciences themselves, will suffer; and that despite the new awareness of the place and function of research, society will see the educational problem in gross quantitative terms, with the universities reduced to vast production lines. In the fight against this terrifying trend, all disciplines will find increasing common ground.

If they choose their allies and methods wisely, the humanities will, in this seemingly alien environment, find themselves in a position of strength such as they have never known before. It is important that they have such strength, for the opportunities that await them are of a corresponding magnitude.

These opportunities are also a product of the sputnik era—although being of a qualitative nature, they are less obvious, and, for the time being, less demanding than the quantitative ones to which I have just referred. The earth satellite may be the climactic weapon in the race for universal destruction; it may be, on the other hand, the first act in a drama of intellectual struggle. Now that the destructive power of arms is absolute, there exists, according to some commentators, a power vacuum, which will be filled increasingly by the struggle for men's minds, and Canada, as an increasingly important power with no pretensions to be a leader in the armament race, may well play a key role in this civilized struggle. Whether or not this is too benign and optimistic an interpretation of the pattern of events, it is one that, as members of universities, we must believe in, for our whole professional existence is predicated upon it. The intellectual rivalry is clearly apparent in science, for no question exists there of distracting and complicating ideologies. The rules are clearly set forth, and the race is to the swiftest. But the humanities and the social sciences pose a different problem. Competition here might mean the sacrifice of freedom, with literary criticism, for instance, a minor form of political apologetics, and poetry, fiction, philosophy, and history, decorative blueprints of a preordained society. Such, I gather, is the function of the humanities in the countries in the communistic bloc, and there can be no doubt that, in this form, they are sources of power. Our aim is different and more complex; as scholars we cannot resort to indoctrination; our responsibility is to disseminate as widely and as thoroughly as possible a knowledge and understanding of the humanistic disciplines. This is not to deny to the scholar in the humanities the rights that we accord to any citizen to speak freely about matters of public policy. But since the humanities are the least specialized of disciplines, since they are not meant to provide solutions for political, social, and religious problems, the scholar cannot speak as an expert in any of these fields. He is a person, however, who has certainly read widely and has, presumably, thought deeply, and it is not inconceivable that he will have wise comments to make and that he will be listened to with attention. Books like *Culture and Anarchy* and *The Human Situation* are not, strictly speaking, works of humanistic scholarship, but they are books that could have been written only by humanists.

The problem facing the humanities is the same problem that faces higher education as a whole: how can we extend education as widely as possible, without losing both the reality and the vision of excellence. And the problem for the humanities is all the more severe, since traditionally they have been looked upon by the public as the aristocratic studies, the special preserves of an elite. I am convinced that this popular concept is now breaking down, that the old suspicions and antipathies are disappearing, and that the humanities have a new and expansive terrain that they can occupy at will. The danger will be that of taking short-cuts that promise a quick and easy victory. I am going to suggest at a later point in this paper that the humanities embark on a frank campaign of cultural imperialism that will take them outside of the university; but in the meantime it is important that they consolidate and strengthen their traditional position within the university.

Within the university, scholarship must continue to be the chief source of power and influence of the humanities. I use the word "scholarship," and not "research," since the latter has too limited a meaning for the humanities. The term "research" has been taken over largely by the sciences; it suggests a systematic collection and analysis of factual material from which eventually some conclusion may be formulated, often of a minor nature, that will reinforce a theory or an interpretation. Certainly this kind of scholarly activity has its place in the humanities. But it is not the principal concern. It has never been a principal concern of Canadian humanists, perhaps more by accident than by choice: possessing no large libraries and scant manuscript material, we have produced little textual scholarship (upon which research in the humanities often depends), and we have not, of course, attracted from Europe or the United States scholars trained in this exacting tradition. Our particular strength in humanistic scholarship has been synthesis, the taking of the long view, the imposition of ideas on miscellaneous facts and of unity on discordant theories. I am thinking of the work of Northrop Frye in literary criticism, of Barker Fairley in Goethe studies, of Charles Cochrane in the cultural history of early Christianity, and of A. S. P. Woodhouse in Miltonic and seventeenth century studies. To achieve a synthesis, each of these four scholars had to go beyond the strict limits of his own discipline, while keeping that discipline at the centre of his study. All of these books have been interdisciplinary studies, not in the modern foundation manner, but in the traditional manner of the scholar pursuing his subject to its full conclusion.

This kind of study will, one hopes, continue to be a characteristic of the humanities in Canada. It may be that the leisurely pace of our cultural development has saved us from the increasing mechanization of humanistic scholarship. We have, for instance, neither the energy nor the resources to establish the specialized periodicals that flourish so abundantly in the United States, and that make the writing and publication of a learned article an exercise in marketing. Promotion within our universities is not yet based on the length of publication lists; and, in comparison with the MLA midway, the meetings of our learned societies are like Victorian Chautauquas.

In Canada the major humanistic studies have been the result of looking outward beyond this continent to the ancient world, and to modern Europe. I can think of no important studies of American literature by Canadian scholars with the possible exception of E. K. Brown's posthumous biography of Willa Cather, and, until recently, James Cappon's *Roberts and the Influence of His Time* was the only serious work of scholarship on a Candian subject. I speak here, of course, exclusively of literary studies, for the historians have made the Canadian field peculiarly their own. Fortunately, many of our major historians have leaned more heavily to the humanities than to the social sciences, so that the interpretation of our past has not been made exclusively a matter of trade statistics and despatches from the colonial office. But the interpretation will not be complete without the literary historian or critic. Here is an opportunity for the humanist to extend the interdisciplinary method that has worked so well in traditional studies to the cultural environment from which he has emerged. His associates here will be history, which has already taken the lead, and the social sciences, perhaps uneasy associates at first, but indispensable ones if any durable synthesis is to emerge. The association will, I am sure, be good for literary studies. It will remove some of the dangers in a belles-lettres approach to a secondary literature—an approach that leads either to absurd inflation or clever denigration. And it may induce a healthy attitude towards our culture as a phenomenon to be studied, rather than as a past to be dismissed with a nervous self-conscious snicker, or with shrill exclamations of "paltry chauvinism."

I have spoken as if this approach to Canadian studies were yet to be developed. Actually, much has been done, and plans are well advanced for the writing of a literary history of Canada on these broad, interdisciplinary lines. If you would see something of the rich possibilities of such an approach, I urge you to read Roy Daniells' long essay on "Literature" in *The Culture of Contemporary Canada* (edited by Julian Park), in which literary sensitivity and a complex awareness of social and cultural context are delicately, yet firmly, balanced.

I turn now to the problem of extending the power and influence of the humanities outside the university or, more accurately, outside the area of those for whom the teaching and study of the humanities is the major concern. We are not, of course, dealing with two separate problems. The scholar, no matter how austere and withdrawn, is not isolated from society. "We should never forget," writes Whitney Oates, "that every scholar goes into the market place whenever he enters a classroom or mounts a lecture platform or publishes a book." The scholarly book merely needs time to achieve its effects—less and less time in these days when the expensive volume appears overnight in a cheap paperback. The modern ivory tower often comes equipped with the finest long-range transmission devices.

There is no question of minimizing or watering down scholarship in the interests of popularization. It is rather a question of recognizing the legitimacy, indeed the necessity, of supplementary devices that work speedily and exercise a wide influence. The important point is to designate the separate areas clearly, and to determine responsibilities between what might be called the "internal" and "external" divisions of the humanities. They will never be completely separate from each other, but each will have its special needs and will require its special methods.

What then is this external division of the humanities? You will forgive me if I base my remarks upon the department of English with which I still have some tenuous connections. Within the university it includes the practice in writing given to students in the professional faculties, with which is usually associated some introduction to the study of literary masterpieces. In the large universities in the United States, this has for many years been a major industry in which hoards of young instructors are employed, with the inevitable tendency for all this activity to be encompassed under what is, in effect, a separate department, sometimes with the unhappy title of The Communication Arts. This development has not yet taken place in Canada, but similar conditions—namely, the proliferation of faculties and schools, and the enormous expansion of enrolment—may well lead to similar results. The external division of the humanities within the university will, I think, grow tremendously, and in more interesting and challenging ways. I am convinced, for instance, that schools of Business Administration and of Public Administration will turn to the humanities to relieve the tedium of their curricula and to clarify some of the human situations into which most of their problems resolve themselves. So far the only moves have been made by corporations with programmes of in-service training. But the formal professional schools may be expected to follow soon. "We have moved from an era," writes Marshall McLuhan, "when business was our culture to one in which culture is our business. And what has been till recently the business of the university is now becoming the business of the business world itself." Without subscribing to this as a universal truth, we can accept as a useful suggestion the implied collapse of traditional barriers, and the opportunity that is thereby opened for the humanities. What the humanities can offer to the business man and the administrator, in addition to an introduction to problems in human relations, is a training in the grasp of the whole. In the study of the humanities, whether it be a work of literature, a work of art, or a philosophical treatise, one must constantly think of the total work. It is fatal to forget the whole and to become immersed in detail. This is a mental outlook increasingly needed in our society, since the growth of the large organization is demanding of senior administrators a trained capacity for generalization. It is always easy to immerse oneself in minutiae, to avoid making decisions, particularly when one has lost sight of the final end. The humanities are not the only subjects that develop skill in identifying the general picture and the ultimate goal, but they are certainly among the principal ones.

The major part of this external division of the humanities lies outside of the universities. There was a time when communication outside the university was made through the lecture on "Burns," on "Shakespeare," or "The Lake Poets" to literary societies and service clubs. The literary societies have waned, and the service clubs now demand more urgent and pressing fare. But now through radio and television a more relaxed and receptive audience, and one on an enormous scale, is available. Television is not a magic substitute for the teacher in the classroom (used in this way, it is only a means of reducing the cost and weakening the quality of education); but it is a superb device for projecting the university outside. I think that the universities should accept the challenge of television, a challenge to which they have reacted, up till now, with typical caution and unusual lethargy. Here the role of the humanities can be central. They have, for instance, the most diverting subject matter, as the recent success of the New York University television programme on Comparative Literature indicates, and they have, if I may say so, some of the more accomplished performers. A series of lively television programmes could do more for the popular *éclat* of the humanities than any amount of "loose, immodest preaching in the market place." At the same time, the wider diffusion of knowledge and appreciation of great works of literature would do much to raise the standards of popular television programmes. There would be a wider recognition of the fact that the great novelists, poets, dramatists, and philosophers have been endlessly curious about every cranny in life; that they are neither austere nor delicate; and that all experience is their province and nothing is alien to their minds. Familiarity with their work would help popular audiences to detect the phony, to distinguish between what springs out of genuine emotion and what is false and tinselly. The widespread study of the humanities will not breed a contempt of the popular arts. But it will help the public to distinguish between popular art, which is inventive and endlessly variable, and mass entertainment, which is formula-ridden and inflexibly monotonous.

This external division of the humanities has not received any clear organizational structure. Within the university itself we have, as I have pointed out, a hazy division in a department between the scholarly core and the service periphery. The area outside the universities is officially disregarded or is left to the energy and ingenuity of one or two members of the department who may not necessarily be best equipped for these missionary labours. What I would suggest is that the departments in the humanities, and again I am thinking particularly of English, should explicitly recognize this external division and set up a sub-department, which would be related both to the parent department and to the extension division in the university. The members of this sub-department would have the opportunity to see their role in a broad and philosophic way, and to develop mature methods of presenting the humanities, not merely to professional audiences in the university, but to non-professional audiences outside. I am not suggesting a clear-cut separation into two divisions, into, so to speak, the ivory tower and the bandstand, because I think there will always be necessity for a good deal of co-operation between the two. Nor do I think that we need to set up two different kinds of graduate training in order to meet the staff needs of the two divisions. But the awareness of the alternative that would be before a young teacher might bring about some changes in our graduate programme. More emphasis might be given to the general tradition in the humanities, in the manner of the programme at Stanford University.[1] It is a subject worthy of some curious speculation that a new Ph.D. in English should have read all the minor Elizabethan dramatists, and be ignorant of Goethe and Dante. And surely the Ph.D. oral might be dropped. I know of no educational device that can more quickly reduce both student and teacher to idiocy.

Now these suggestions I have been making require a great deal more money since they involve the humanities in a more complex programme of operation. I propose now to make some practical suggestions about the financial implications of an enlarged role for the humanities. In general, the humanists have been the last to recognize that the university is not simply a community of scholars but is also an economic society, where the rules of the market place are not entirely irrelevant. If the humanists are to play this new part that the times demand, then they must be prepared to recognize in a way they have never done before the economic consequences of their responsibilities. They must be prepared to do battle for their rights, not in peevish opposition to other disciplines, but in full consciousness of their own needs. It is particularly important now that they wage this battle, because there is a danger that their whole position may be undermined by the quantitative approach to education, which is the crude concomitant of the sputnik age. In the sudden drive to achieve massive results, there is a tendency to see education in quantitative terms, to talk glibly about the full use of buildings (nobody seems to be interested in talking about the full use of students), and to see the educational problem as one of rapid acceleration. Now this is, of course, bad for all education, but it is particularly bad for the humanities since it deprives them of the only means by which they can realize their ends.

Humanists must engage with more vigour and with a deeper sense of their own involvement in the current educational disputes. I want to emphasize two particular issues. A good deal of attention has been given recently to the cost of educating a student, and the orthodox economics of higher education has it that the education of a professional student or a science student is much more expensive than the education of a student in the humanities. It is confidently stated that it takes two or three times as much money to educate a doctor as to educate, say, an honours student in English, or history, or philosophy. The argument has a simple logic, based as it is on the necessity for elaborate and expensive equipment in the sciences and professional faculties and on the need for a low ratio of instruction in laboratory courses, and, occasionally, on the higher ratio of pay of professional instructors. No one will deny the weight of the argument, given the present structure of the universities. But much of that weight would disappear if humanists placed a proper value on their work. The fact is that the education of a student in the humanities is an expensive business, and if society looks upon him as the cheapest educational product, the humanists have only themselves to blame. They must insist that if an education in the humanities makes small demands in equipment, it makes big demands in human time. It is possible, of course, to use the sprinkler method of education, to set a clever man before an audience of three or four hundred to deliver a series of lectures, and to declare at the end that all have been exposed—painlessly and cheaply—to the higher values. If there were a proper realization of the kind of ratio that should exist in the humanities between teachers and students, much of this apparent difference between the cost of educating various kinds of students would disappear. A similar process of analysis would destroy much of the effectiveness of the argument that the professional schools and the sciences demand technical equipment that is far more expensive than any used in the humanities. The fact is, of course, that the humanities require what is without a doubt the most expensive piece of equipment on the campus, namely, the library. It is also a fact that Canadian universities have been shamefully negligent in providing this kind of equipment. The statistics on Canadian university libraries make dispiriting reading. The largest Canadian university library, the University of Toronto, is twenty-eighth on the list of colleges and research libraries in Canada and the United States, and the next two Canadian libraries rank, respectively, forty-first and sixty-ninth. Moreover, the evidence is that even this position will decline unless some radical change toward the question of accessions takes place. The librarian of a major Canadian university points out that the library's working strength depends on nourishment, and that the counting of volumes during the year shows Canadian libraries have a very low calorie diet indeed. Of 110 American libraries reporting in a group of universities that offer doctoral work, the median intake in 1956–57 was 20,422 volumes. Only Toronto, McGill, and U.B.C. were above this figure, and only two other Canadian universities were above 10,000. I think that if proper attention were given to Canadian university libraries, it would be again apparent that no great difference exists between the cost of educating a student in the humanities and teaching a student in the professional and scientific faculties. Moreover, the building up of our research libraries would have a whole series of salutary effects. It would attract good scholars to the humanities and, moreover, it would persuade faculty that scholarship, like charity, begins at home.

The initiative for strengthening work in the humanities must come from within the universities. It may be that the establishment of the Canada Council will lull us into a false sense of security. The Canada Council is an immense boon to the humanities; for a young foundation it has already shown an unusual flexibility and intelligence in distributing its resources. But we must always remember the Canada Council is at best a helping body, that it has a wide range of responsibilities, and that it cannot take the place of our own energies and activities on the home front. If we continue to acquiesce in large classes in the humanities, if we continue to undernourish our libraries, and if we continue to starve our own graduate schools by sending our best graduate students abroad, then I think we shall have ourselves to blame for the misfortunes that beset us.

I have, in a typical administrative manner, become enmeshed in practical details. It is time to focus on the main argument. The sputnik era has released, and will continue to release, more resources for education, and in these expanded resources the humanities can share. The sputnik era may well be an era of intellectual rivalry and ferment, in which the humanities can join as full partners with the sciences and the social sciences. Within the university, the humanities must continue to give first place to scholarship, and without, they must move into new areas with boldness and despatch. I am convinced that on all sides the humanities have powerful friends and supporters, and that in the coming struggle they have nothing to lose but their own self-doubts and inhibitions.

NOTES

1. Professor A. S. P. Woodhouse has outlined the main ideas of the Stanford programme in "Problems in Securing Staff—The Humanities," in *Canada's Crisis in Higher Education*, 142. "Candidates fulfil the requirements for the doctorate in one of the usual departments, but for the minor in a second department they substitute the new programme in the humanities, and they present a doctoral thesis acceptable alike to the major department and to the interdepartmental committee in charge of the new programme. The work of the programme in the humanities consists of (i), an historical course in the Western traditions, and (ii), basic intellectual and educational problems of the present in the light of the Western traditions (e.g. Conflicting concepts of history and human freedom; the idea of justice as a central theme in Western thought and literature; the idea of a university, its functions in maintaining and modifying tradition)."

A. S. P. WOODHOUSE

The New Role of the Humanities in Canada

As the ground for all further distinctions and inferences three facts must be reaffirmed: first, that the humanities include the languages, their literatures, the fine arts other than literature, which are latecomers to the educational scene, philosophy at least over a large part of its vast territory, and (though it claims a double classification in the humanities and the social sciences) history; secondly, that the humanities thus conceived comprise one of the major groupings of human interests and activities, and, arising therefrom, one of the great divisions of human knowledge; and, thirdly, that the humanities have a creative as well as a critical aspect: they include arts to be practised as well as subjects to be studied. These facts are relevant in a variety of contexts, and first in considering the status of the humanities in Canada today, and the provision made for them.

Though this is pre-eminently the century of science, pure and applied, there is much less reason than there was fifteen years ago to mourn over the plight of the humanities: in this country they command a greater degree of conscious attention than ever before, and very much more in the way of material support. The increased attention is seen in the universities: in the provision of special research funds, in the revision of curricula, especially in the professional faculties, and in the number of able students in arts who are choosing the humanities for their honours and postgraduate work. Outside the universities the interest is more restricted, more fitful, and (it goes without saying) often ill informed. It is one function of this Asso-

HAB no. 28, October 1959. From an address to the annual meeting of the Humanities Association of Canada, 1959. The opening paragraph, printed in the *Bulletin*, has been deleted for this reprinting. The original title was "The Humanities in Canada, 1959."

ciation to speak of and for the humanities to the general public. The task is far from easy. One may know little or nothing of the sciences at first hand and yet recognize at least the magnitude of their discoveries as they impinge upon our daily life and our chances of survival. The social sciences in many of their aspects come home to man's business, which often seems more accessible than his bosom. But with the humanities the only way to gauge their value is to have some genuine experience of their power. All this is a truism. But running athwart it is one substantial fact: the founding of the Canada Council by, or at least with the acquiescence of, the representatives of the people. Even in this era of large expenditures, one hundred million dollars is not for Canada a negligible sum. With its capital endowment of fifty million for arts and letters, the humanities, and the social sciences, and its additional fifty million for building grants to the universities, the Canada Council offers the most tangible evidence that any country could give of public concern for these areas. Unhappily private benefaction has not yet responded to the government's lead: rather, there is a danger that the humanities, especially, may find other sources of aid cut off—but that is another story.

The Canada Council, as everyone knows, was the direct outcome of the Massey Commission's Report. What is less well known perhaps is the preliminary work that was going forward before the Commission was authorized, during its deliberations and in the interval before the Canada Council was founded and in operation. This preliminary work was carried on by three voluntary organizations: the Canada Foundation for Arts and Letters; the Humanities Research Council for the humanities in their educational and scholarly aspects; and the Social Science Research Council. These bodies were able to supply vital data to the Royal Commission on the present state and pressing needs of their respective fields, the two research councils submitting as the foundation documents in their briefs their published reports: *Scholarship for Canada* (in the Social Sciences, 1943) and *The Humanities in Canada* (1947).

Not less important was the spirit manifested from the first by the three independent bodies, and persisting to this day, a spirit not of unrelieved rivalry, but of mutual understanding and respect, which has proved vital and beneficent because grounded on a true appraisal of the facts, general and local. In the wider sense the arts and letters are the humanities in their most creative aspect, and this is the concern of the Canada Foundation; in their critical aspect they are the concern of the Humanities Research Council, whose primary emphasis falls, and properly, on productive scholarship. The common ground of the two research councils is found in their interest in productive scholarship, and also in the fact that, broadly speaking, the humanities and the social sciences share a common subject matter, namely, man in his specifically human activities and aspirations. The now forgotten Mr. Dooley, ruminating on the phrase Christian Science, thought it a pity that Christians weren't a bit more scientific and scientists a bit more Christian. Perhaps one might transfer the remark to humanists and social scientists, and regard the two research councils, with their joint secretariat, as an effort of mutual education. Be this as it may, the spirit of co-operation rather than rivalry has borne fruit in the policies of the Canada Council. Of its expendable income (something over two million dollars annually) roughly one half goes to the support of the arts and letters, and the other half to the support of scholarship, and training for scholarship, in the social sciences and the humanities, again by an equal division between the two.

The third, and I believe the greatest, achievement of the two research councils was to have in operation, when the Canada Council came into existence, working schemes of pre-doctoral fellowships and of grants in aid of research and publication, which the Canada Council could and did take over and expand. I suppose that no one—not even the members of the Canada Council itself—can state with certainty how much the character of its whole programme of aid to the humanities and social sciences has depended on this one fact. What seems quite certain is that in no other country is public support for scholarship in the humanities more nearly adequate than in Canada today.

This being granted, what is the function of the humanities in the general strategy of education and culture? And how, in existing conditions, can that function be best discharged?

There may be better ways of coming at the first of these two questions; but I can think of none better than that advocated by Coleridge in considering any institution—and the humanities clearly are an institution—namely, to discover in history what he called the "idea" of the institution, which included both its nature and its use. And this for Coleridge was no mere piece of antiquarian research, for it was preliminary to the second question, How can the "idea" be made fully operative in the contemporary situation?

What, then, is the "idea" of the humanities? Etymology gives us our starting point, but nothing more: in some way, the humanities are closely related to the life of man. The subjects listed at the outset—the languages, their literatures, the fine arts (other than literature), philosophy, and history—are the humanities as they exist *de facto* today. It is between these two points that we must try to locate and define the humanities. To say that they bear on the life of man is not sufficiently precise. So may biology if it turns its attention to him. We must, then, recognize that they bear on the life of man in his specifically human experiences, aspirations and achievements. But the quest of knowledge, in whatever field, clearly falls under this description, and there is a sense in which every advance may be credited to human experience and ranked among man's achievements. We must further recognize that the humanities find their subject matter in the life of man himself, or at least they find their distinctive focus there. Broadly speaking, history treats this subject matter in particular, and philosophy in general, terms, while literature may employ them both with added elements of imagination and aesthetic pattern. This would seem to be a fairly satisfactory description of the humanities as traditionally conceived—of the humanities, that is, whose common medium was words. With the fine arts, however, there is at the very least a shift in emphasis. They employ other media, and each of these carries its own resources and limitations. Their common ground with the traditional humanities, and notably with literature, would seem to lie in their nature as arts, rather than in the character of their relation to human life. The more abstract the art becomes the more emphatic the difference appears. Nor are the arts alone in their addiction to abstraction: philosophy contributes symbolic logic, and mathematics (which did not appear in our list) avows in many of its branches more affinity with the arts than with the sciences, and puts in a claim to be reckoned among the humanities. Frankly, these questions are beyond my competence, and I mention them only as in duty bound, before turning back to the traditional humanities, or rather to the subjects in our list.

If we admit a degree of utility in the description given, namely, that the humanities find their subject matter, or at least their focus, in the life of man, we are still faced with another problem: how to differentiate the social sciences from them. Historically, the humanities were the as yet undifferentiated *litterae humaniores*, whose tradition goes back to Cicero. For the Renaissance, as for Cicero, these subjects found all they required in the classics of Greece and Rome—that is, in literature in its broadest sense, including poetry and oratory, philosophy and history. In later times, and especially in the last century and a half, two developments have occurred. Increasingly the classics of the modern world have been incorporated in the humanities, with Shakespeare and Milton taking their place beside Sophocles and Virgil, Descartes and Kant beside Plato and Aristotle, Gibbon and Macaulay beside Thucydides and Livy; and not the classics of the modern Occident alone, but those of the ancient Orient as well. And, secondly, the *litterae humaniores*, thus augmented, have achieved a new precision as each of the component disciplines has developed its special and appropriate techniques of study. In this process the social sciences broke away to form a separate category, while the humanities, despite their careful differentiation, have maintained a strong sense of unity and interrelation.

Now, we have implied that the humanities and the social sciences have some common ground, and have suggested that in Canada they have fortunately recognized this fact. The social sciences, like the humanities, find their subject matter in the life of man, only qualifying their interest by the word *social*. But it would be a very unwary humanist who acquiesced in the facile notion that the social sciences pre-empt man in his social relations while the humanities are confined to man as an isolated individual. For man is by nature a social being, and such a restriction is historically untrue, philosophically absurd, and in its effect frustrating. The distinction lies rather in the method which the social sciences have adopted, a method descriptive and even statistical, which they have taken over from the natural sciences. In other words, the operative distinction is found less in the adjective *social* than in the noun *science*. Yet even here it must be recognized that the allegiance is by no means universal or unqualified, and the term itself is in some quarters repudiated in favour of social studies, which really implies some return of these disciplines to the parent stock, the humanities.

In method the humanities themselves are up to a point eclectic. They can employ a scientific method where this is appropriate, as it is in the descriptive study of language; but beyond the descriptive study of language there is language conceived as the art of expression. Again, history rests on a scientific collection and criticism of evidence, but history itself is an art, indeed under certain conditions an important division of literature, and so also is philosophy, at least in its larger and more imaginative constructions. Of the humanities in general it may be safely averred that they cannot rest content with the methods of science but must press on to modes of apprehension and expression that belong rather to art. This is true initially of their creative effort, and derivatively of its criticism.

So far, in discussing the "idea" of the humanities, we have concerned ourselves rather with the prior question of their nature than with their use. That use has been very nearly identical with their place in liberal education. For Cicero the word *humanitas* signified the qualities, feelings and behaviour proper to man—to man, that is, in his specifically human aspect and aspirations. The term was not descriptive alone, but normative, in function: it embodied an ideal, and the ideal in turn defined the end of liberal education and prescribed the means. The purpose, in effect, was to assimilate humane knowledge and wisdom or (as Arnold was to phrase it) "the best that had been thought and said in the world," and thereby to exercise the intellect and refine the sensibility or, in one word, to civilize. And even today, when the sciences and social sciences have claimed their due place in the educational scene, only the humanities avow as their sole aim that cultivation of intellect and sensibility which was the traditional end of liberal education.

No doubt Cicero represented the end of liberal education in less abstract terms: its end was to produce and equip the orator, but for him the orator was the type of the educated man. Even today we judge the effectiveness of liberal education by the power of expression which it confers, and, like post-Ciceronian rhetoricians, sometimes hope to achieve the power by isolating expression and teaching its rules—generally with somewhat meagre results. In the Renaissance the ideal of liberal education operated in a climate of belief and opinion very different from that of Cicero's Rome. The difference lay in the presence and almost unimpaired dominance of Christianity, and the type of educated man was the Christian humanist, the product of a union of the two traditions, which often amounted to syncretism—that is, the absorption of the Graeco-Roman values by the Christian scheme. But, lest we should exaggerate the degree of coalescence, we may remind ourselves that precisely to this period belongs a special use of the English word *humanity* (in the singular as translating *humanitas*), namely, to contrast humane studies with specifically religious or with what was (and is) called *divinity*. Through the long partnership of Christianity and the classics in English education, the sense of this distinction persisted. It is part of the background of Newman's famous formulation of liberal education, in the middle of the nineteenth century, whose end is a trained intellect and refined sensibility, or what Newman called a gentleman. The ideal of the gentleman goes back indeed to the Renaissance, where Spenser made the education of a gentleman the avowed subject of his allegory in the *Faerie Queene*; but Newman's choice of the term on the very eve of the democratizing of life and education brings home sharply to us the problem of preserving traditional values in a changing world.

The world was changing in more respects than this. The gradual secularizing of English thought, which had been going on since the seventeeth century, at last began to permeate education with the founding of the University of London in 1828. A generation later, with the work of Darwin, the rising tide of naturalism threatened to engulf man himself. Society was living on the accumulated capital of Christianity, as it still is today; but no one could call it in the old unqualified sense a Christian society. There were, of course, Christian reactions to the tide of naturalism, but also humanistic reactions, which recognized that man is in nature, but emphasized his distinctively human aspirations and powers, and which appeared alongside the Christian reaction in thinkers like Coleridge and Newman, at some distance from it in Emerson and Arnold, and in a purely secular context, and somewhat unexpectedly, in John Stuart Mill and T. H. Huxley. In all this the nineteenth century is the immediate progenitor of our own age. If in a theological era it was necessary, under the term *humanity*, to distinguish the study of man from theology, which also, of course, dealt in its own way with his nature and destiny, then in an age of dominant naturalism it was necessary to distinguish the study of man in his specifically human aspect from a study of nature that threatened to submerge him. And it is within this area, now duly bounded at both its extremes, that the humanities reside and operate.

I do not mean that they necessarily commit their proponent to a philosophy of humanism in any of its various forms—and certainly not in any sense that would deny the legitimate claims of either theology or the natural sciences, but simply that their area is the specifically human. That is why I was unwilling to accept the title, suggested to me, "The Humanities and Humanism." It is not the business of the humanities to inculcate a philosophy of humanism any more than it is the business of the natural sciences to inculcate naturalism, though with some truth it might be said that the best of all evidence for humanism is the humanities themselves. But, first and last, they are one of the great divisions of knowledge, and their business is the critical exploration of the area that is their own.

We should delude ourselves if we imagined that the role of the humanities was always accurately understood even by those engaged in education. There are some who regard the humanities as the merely ornamental subjects, and their use, to impart a little superficial polish to what are often very rough diamonds indeed. There are others who seize on the notion (true enough if properly understood) that the humanities are concerned with values, and would hasten to ally them with religion or, alternatively, would expect them to supply a sort of secular substitute for it. In this class fall many of the proponents of humanism; and it must be admitted that their approach is not necessarily disastrous if made by a mind of first-class critical calibre, as with Matthew Arnold, Irving Babbitt, and Paul Elmer More, where indeed the diversity of doctrine carries its own antidote. There are others, again, who would direct the humanities to particular tasks, such as the expounding, defending and commending of our Western values (alias the American way of life), or on the other hand to the deliberate fostering of international sympathy and understanding. Some excuse for these and other mistaken views, and for the short cuts which they invite, may be found in the many and pressing needs of our era; but this does not alter the fact that they are mistaken. They are mistaken because they are apt to forget that the humanities are one of the great divisions of knowledge, the division whose subject is nothing less than man in his specifically human aspect and aspirations, that this knowledge demands and deserves impartial critical study, and that the penetrative power of the humanities, their peculiar aptness to cultivate the mind and sensibility, depends wholly on their subject matter and their form, and not at all upon indoctrination undertaken in connection with them, which may well indeed be ruinous to their proper educational effect. This is not the despised doctrine of the ivory tower, but the plainest psychological realism.

By the educationist in a hurry, the humanities are sometimes reproached with drawing so much of their subject matter from the past, the implication being that they are out of touch with the world today and indifferent to it. In this indictment are implicit, I think, two mistakes. The first is a mistake of fact. The history of the humanities during the past century and a half shows a steady appropriation of modern subject matter. But it is not a question of subject matter alone. No one who has studied and taught one of the humanities for any considerable time, or knows the history of his subject, can fail to recognize the constant change in method and emphasis wrought by recent knowledge and by contemporary modes of thought. The second mistake is to overlook an important function of the humanities, and of the humanities almost alone, in the larger strategy of education and culture. This function is the perpetuation of the tradition and such a mediation of the past to the present as will enable the modern man to take secure possession of his cultural inheritance, to evaluate the past in the light of present knowledge and experience, and to judge the present with some awareness of the past.

History, then, has an essential role in the method of all the humanities. To take possession of his cultural inheritance modern man requires at the very least some knowledge of three great shaping traditions: the classical tradition, with its developments and modifications in later literature and thought, the Christian tradition, with its profound insights into the nature of man and its encompassing influence on life and thought in the West, and, finally, the history and philosophy of scientific method. We have spoken of theology and the sciences as lying outside the compass of the humanities, and this, in the context in which we were speaking, is true. But religion and science as they impinge upon the life and thought of man must fall within the purview of the humanities; and students of literature, philosophy and history, of language and of the fine arts, are under repeated invitation to take one or both of them into account. Indeed the history of religion and the history and philosophy of science may well be among the chief additions to the humanities in our century.

We have reached, then, an answer, or a series of partial answers, to the question, What is the "idea" of the humanities?—"idea" including both nature and use. Perhaps we can make some of these answers a little more concrete if we turn our attention for a moment to literature as one of the humanities. I select literature, not to claim for it any priority (though initially *litterae humaniores* were indeed literature in its widest sense), but simply because it is the subject I understand best. No doubt a philosopher, an historian, or a student of any of the fine arts could use his discipline to similar purpose.

Literature illustrates the unity and inter-relation of the humanities: like most of the others it has an affinity with language, for its medium is words; and as it is itself an art it has some affinity also with the arts that employ other media. With the latter it shares such elements of representation, structure and aesthetic pattern as its medium will permit and enable it to embody. With philosophy it shares, through its medium, words, some capacity for speculative thought and expression; and like each of the humanities it has its history and can be shown to have responded to tradition, time and place.

Literature in its wider definition includes whatever is addressed to the general reader—that is, to man as man—and reaches a certain—that is, an undefined but readily recognizable—degree of significance in content and distinction in expression. Literature thus conceived will include the classics of history and criticism and many of the classics of philosophy; it will go further and include *The Wealth of Nations*, *The Origin of Species*, Newman's *Apologia pro vita sua*, and hundreds of other works which may be susceptible of more exact criticism by the philosopher, the economist, the scientist, or the theologian, but are still available to the general reader and negotiable as literature. In this view literature becomes one of the great meeting places of the disciplines (as philosophy and history are, in their own way, others), for if economics, biology and theology lie beyond the humanities, Adam Smith, Darwin, and Newman still find a place there as literature—the literature of knowledge (to borrow De Quincey's phrase) or of thought and opinion.

In its stricter meaning literature is very nearly synonymous with what Aristotle called poetry, and De Quincey the literature of power. Thus conceived, literature is one of the fine arts—the art whose medium is words. It is an imaginative representation of some segment of reality as it appears to man—a representation with its own distinctive structure, capable of provoking thought and evoking and ordering emotion, and of achieving its end in pleasure. Today we should wish to extend the description to include works that were representational only remotely if at all, to make more provision for symbolic meanings, to couple with structure aesthetic pattern, and so to interpret pleasure as to throw the emphasis at once on heightened awareness and on aesthetic satisfaction. This is an example of how the humanities—in this case literature—may modify their definitions and emphasis in response to new knowledge and contemporary modes of thought. But basically the Aristotelian definition remains intact.

There is no time, and fortunately there is no need, to remind ourselves of the vast range of vicarious and ideal experience offered to the imagination by the study of literature. All sorts of secondary benefits accrue in the knowledge gained, but the primary fact is the ideal experience itself. The method, as in any other discipline, must be one of rigorous intellectual enquiry, the aim, so far as possible, "to see the object as in itself it really is." But thus to see the classic is to realize that here truth has met with beauty and with power, here significant content is united with significant form. What commenced as an intellectual enquiry ends, if it is successful, in an experience of unique educative value, since it exercises our intellect and our sympathies, and probably our moral and certainly our aesthetic perceptions: in a word, it exercises and augments our humanity—as Cicero believed education ought to do. Nor is this all. In the experience literature discharges a function allotted to the humanities in the general strategy of culture, the mediation of the past to the present, the preservation of the tradition as a vital part of our consciousness; and it does this so effectively because in the process one of the great achievements of the past becomes vividly present to us. The study of contemporary literature may yield a like experience, but with different secondary results. It will give us new insights into the sensibility of our own age.

This, then, is the way in which literature operates, and *mutatis mutandis* a similar account might be given of the other disciplines in the humanities.

Never before has liberal education at its different levels met with the challenge that faces it today, and never has the role of the humanities been of more essential importance.

The rapid tempo of change which set in with the nineteenth century increases year by year. The discoveries of science and technology crowd in upon us, many of them fraught with unimagined possibilities of power. But power without wisdom intoxicates the thoughtless and may well terrify the thoughful.

The discoveries of physical science can throw little light on the nature of man save as they offer fresh evidence of his adventurous curiosity and his ability to satisfy it. Those of the biological sciences come closer to him as they explore the facts of the animal organism which condition the life and activity of the specifically human. It would ill become proponents of the humanities (which are also a branch of knowledge based on experience) to question the value of new knowledge in any of its forms. But still there is the problem of proportion and a balanced view. Physical science threatens the balance mainly by its claims, perfectly just in themselves, upon our attention. But the biological sciences do so more directly: first, by the restricted view which as science they quite properly take of the life of man; and, secondly, when their adherents, and especially perhaps their disciples in some of the social sciences, suggest or imply that the restricted view is really a total view. Some light has indeed been cast on the nature of man, mainly a light into the dark origins of his impulses and responses. But to define man solely or principally in terms of these origins is to fall into what has been aptly called the genetic fallacy. Again the problem is one of balance and proportion; and long established facts abundantly supported by experience, past and present, do not lose their validity when new facts are discovered, though criticism and adjustment are no doubt continually demanded.

The immense advances in technology are exercising a double influence of a somewhat different character. The sciences, like the humanities, are in their basic nature disinterested, though each may have appropriate practical applications, and the applications of the sciences are technology. The first effect of technology, and the more obvious, is to throw an overwhelming emphasis on material improvements, as in North America today. The second effect is to suggest the unlimited possibility of a planned future by a species of political and social engineering which employs, among other means, techniques of suggestion and control. We like to think of this as a peculiar mark of Communism, but the most we can really say is that there are elements in a true democracy that make strongly against such subjugation. And the preserving of true democracy, which entails the education of the masses generally, and in its principles, is clearly one of our crucial problems—perhaps the most insistent of them all.

Indeed this problem sets the scene for the whole challenge to liberal education and to the humanities today, complicating the issue and intensifying its urgency. True democracy means, among other things, equality of opportunity, and this in turn means vast numbers demanding to be educated and (to put it quite bluntly) requiring to be civilized. There is still force in the alternative that Arnold propounded, "Culture or Anarchy"—though perhaps we should have to add a third possibility, "or Slavery"—slavery to the material advances that man has achieved, to false inferences and analogies which they suggest, and even to the idea of democracy itself if it is misconceived as a levelling out to the average.

Stated in its broadest terms, the task of the humanities in a democratic society is to extend to the many the benefits they have always bestowed on the few. Having established their legitimate place in the educational scheme—a place which Canada seems willing enough to concede—the humanities must do their utmost to humanize and civilize. Their role is the more difficult and the more necessary because in the existing situation they must in some measure act as correctives. They do this by their initial assumptions: that ideas of value are still real and important, that excellence, wherever it occurs, has a claim on our attention and respect, and that, if the victory of democracy is to enjoy its full reward, men must somehow learn to appropriate and adapt to their use the achievements of the ages. By their quiet insistence on quality, the humanities are a corrective to merely quantitative assessment and its accompanying tendency to mistake the average for the norm. By their concentration on the specifically human, and on the highest products of man's thought and art, they offer a corrective to a crude naturalism and to the genetic fallacy. By the simple fact that so many of these highest products come from non-democratic societies, they extend the horizons of the democratic mind and help to correct an uncritical faith in democracy itself.

The standard thus invoked is, I suppose, that of a true humanism, which cannot be established by indoctrination but only by demonstration. The humanities are fully operative as an educational force only when they are regarded, and respected, as one of the great divisions of knowledge, and only when we submit to rigorous critical study their varied subject matters with all the evidence they offer of the dignity and also the fallibility of man. You will be tired of the reiteration of this idea; but it embodies, I believe, a fundamental truth, and one that is often in danger of being forgotten partly because it does *not* come out with complete consistency in the history of the humanities, and partly because the humanities do indeed humanize and civilize and there is always some temptation to identify their results with our own particular beliefs or ideals. The humanities do not furnish a philosophy of life: they do, however, bring to our attention *data* essential to any adequate philosophy of life; and that is all we have a right to demand of them. If we pretend that they will do more, we not only delude ourselves: we put the humanities at a hopeless disadvantage in their contact with the sciences and social sciences: we surrender their claim to be one of the great divisions of knowledge, and with it their power to adjust themselves to discoveries in other fields and to demand that the evidence which their subjects present should also be given full weight.

The task of the humanities presents problems at every level, from the specialized study of the honours course and the graduate school, through pass arts and the professional faculties, to university extension, adult education, and the CBC. But if problems abound as never before, so do the means of solving them. In the advance of scholarship, in the availability of texts, and in the new channels of communication, the humanities have, or may have, their full share. Knowledge is available and, what is scarcely less important, so are the means of following up an interest once it has been kindled.

Instruction at the various levels poses particular problems and requires particular skills. But one principle is, or should be, common to them all. We may sum it up as the primacy of the subject and the necessity of an informed and critical approach to it, or more simply as a determination to see and to expound "the object as in itself it really is." And if this enunciation of principle sounds unduly austere, we may remember the vast range of interest which the humanities embrace, and the delight that every one of us has known in exploring his subject and following the paths to new knowledge which it invites and demands. "What would you give to know about the Argonauts?" said Johnson to the lad who was rowing them on the Thames. "Sir," was the answer, "I would give what I have."

If the humanities are indeed one of the great divisions of knowledge, and one that embraces so much of human interest, two conclusions seem obvious. The first is that interest, which is the beginning of knowledge, should not be too difficult to arouse at any level, provided appropriate means are used. The second is that the only safe and productive basis for popularization is sound and dedicated scholarship. And that (to return at last to our starting point) is why we may congratulate ourselves that the Canada Council is putting the bulk of its aid to the humanities into the support of scholarship and the training of scholars in the making.

F. E. L. PRIESTLEY

The Humanities Association and the University

As far as the University is concerned, it is difficult, I think, to find a directly useful function for the Humanities Association. It is easy to fall, by a rapid but loose association of ideas, into the conviction that there ought to be a directly useful function: the Humanities are undoubtedly important, union is strength, the humanities need strengthening, and so on. But when it becomes necessary to translate the vague conviction into specific terms, difficulties at once appear. The only real means of strengthening the humanities within the university (as distinguished from within the community) are largely in the hands of the administration: what the humanities need is a smaller teaching load and more time for reflection and research, and an improvement in the quality of the teaching and research staff. I cannot myself envision the Humanities Association becoming a pressure group to secure either of these desirable improvements, nor do I believe it should. Nevertheless, the only weaknesses of the humanities within the university spring from these two causes—inadequacy of some instructors, and over-burdening of all—and they are causes the Association cannot deal with.

It might be argued that a national Association will improve the morale of instructors in the humanities. I am sceptical of this for several reasons. In the first place, I have no reason to believe from my own observation that the morale needs improving; no student of the humanities worth his salt has ever felt apologetic about his occupation; any who have been abashed by the greater prosperity or greater notoriety of colleagues in other disciplines have lost sight of those

HAB no. 27, April 1959. From an address to the annual meeting of the Humanities Association of Canada, 1958.

things worth pursuing, and have betrayed their own studies. Secondly, it seems to me foreign to the nature of the student of the humanities to seek comfort in crowds, to rely upon artificial fellowship for outer support. Humanists should not need to huddle together for spiritual warmth.

The present practices in local branches of the Association might be expected to reveal a purpose, if there were any, in the organization. Instead, they reveal rather a dreadful anxiety to find a purpose that isn't there. One member addresses his colleagues—whom in most institutions he sees, talks with, lunches with, meets in committees with, daily—addresses them as if they were townsfolk or a section of general course students, on a subject with which they either have some familiarity, or no desire for familiarity. They are there, not to be converted to an understanding of the importance of their colleague's views—their minds have been made up on that years ago—but because he came, or will come, to their lecture, or he is in their department, or good feeling must be preserved between departments. For this the lecturer and his colleagues pay an annual fee. The general public, if it likes lectures, or is too blind for television, already has a confusing smorgasbord of free lectures at its disposal; in Toronto, for example, each College offers an annual series of free lectures. University College has the annual Alexander Lectures, the Royal Ontario Museum, the Royal Conservatory of Music, the Art Gallery, all offer series—there is a steady flow of visitors of varied distinction, all lecturing.

For those interested in a particular subject, there are Classics Club, History Club, Association of Teachers of English, Alliance française, and so on. For those interested in variety, Toronto has monthly colloquia. (In my day in Alberta, the Philosophical Society and the Faculty Club performed very similar functions, and I suppose still do.)

One might well ask the meaning of the ritual. Are the lectures of the Humanities Association branch to be thought of as a form of communal worship to nourish the enthusiasm of the believers? Are they a mixture of display and exposure, like sermons in a seminary? Are they missionary work directed at the occasional outsider? Are they missionary work directed at us—a sort of post-post-graduate interdisciplinary seminar? To whom are the lectures addressed? For whom do we hold the meetings? For whom is the local branch formed? And, in short, why?

If the meetings were crowded with gentiles, with engineers, economists, statisticians, and others who are convinced that we spend our time cooing girlishly over sentimental verse, pontificating over second-rate novels, or debating over fine points of style, one could see some point to them. If, during only one session a year, a low-browed vulgarian from another part of the campus would rush up to the lecturer, his face transformed with sudden illumination, and beating his breast would cry out in a loud voice, "Forgive me! I never knew till now what the humanities meant," one could even wax enthusiastic. But hardly a gentile appears; the audience is almost certain to be made up of cynical experts judging performance rather than seeking light. The lecturer is tried by a jury of his peers.

In what I have said so far, I have inevitably been thinking mainly of the problems in Toronto. There may be institutions in which the faculty are so starved for lectures or so filled with admiration for their colleagues that they welcome a chance to hear more—I shall be glad to be informed of these idyllic and unspoiled regions. My own observation is that the professor is a distinct species from the busman and prefers other holidays.

Having offered these opinions on meetings of the local associations, with, of course, the proviso that many of the lectures offered are really excellent—but could be offered without the organization—I hasten to admit that I see real purpose in the national meeting, in the national organization, and in the Bulletin. These all keep students of the humanities all over Canada in touch with what is going on, and in touch with each other—I need not elaborate on the value of this. What I was asked to discuss was the role of the Association in the university, and that is what I am trying to discover. In the nation, and in the community, the role is clear; but not in the university as a university. I recognize the impossibility of completely isolating these, but I am doing my best.

I would go so far as to say that the Association not only has no function to perform in the university, but that its function in the community is hampered by too close an association with the university. One of our main claims for the humanities is that they touch life at the ordinary level, that they are every man's concern. So, it may be said, does Science touch life and concern all. But Science touches ordinary life in a secondary way, through its effects, its products; the ordinary man does not himself expect to understand science, nor want to; he waits to be told by experts. It would be fatal to the humanities if this sort of exclusiveness were to enter into their domain. In science, there can no longer be amateurs; in the humanities there should be no complete professionals. Nothing would destroy the importance of the humanities more rapidly than the belief, already present in some quarters, that they belong only to the experts in the universities—that history, for example, is very important to historians, can be written only by duly accredited historians with the proper sort of professional training, and understood when written only by their colleagues; that the duty of professional academic critics is to guide the public to good reading, and to give them ready-made opinions of contemporary literature; that literature in a foreign language exists chiefly for the sake of university curricula. The centring of a branch of the Humanities Association in the university, the dominating of its membership by faculty members, and the tendency for its speakers to be mainly academic, emphasizes this dangerous separation of life and letters, and leaves the ordinary member of the public an outsider. The centre and the main impetus should both be outside, in the community. Many years ago, when I had the pleasure of teaching in Calgary, my wife and I were members of a very lively and interesting literary group of which the Chancellor of this university, Dr. Earl Scarlett, was one of the main organizers and inspirers. This was a model organization in many ways, made up of people who, like Dr. Scarlett, took a deep and permanent delight in literature and felt it as a needed part of a full life. I was invited to join the group, not as an expert (you will readily understand) but as one who shared the interest of the group. Many of the amateurs in the group were, of course, more expert than I, Dr. Scarlett having made a special study of Keats for many years. Unless the local branch receives its impetus from people outside the university, from people like those in the Calgary group, I am very sceptical of what it can achieve.

Finally, since I have cast some doubts on the value of lectures as usually planned, could I suggest anything in their place? Here again we face the problem of the audience and the aim. If our aim is to educate each other—for which there is a good deal to be said—then by all means continue the lectures. If our aim is to educate the lesser breeds without the law, I think we need something different. When the local branch at Toronto first organized, the opening meeting presented a symposium: what are the humanities? This proved a lively subject and I believe an illuminating one for many of the non-academic audience (and many of the academic) who attended that meeting in the first flush of enthusiasm or the height of innocence. But this start was not followed up. There are a number of things that we take for granted that mystify the non-academic. What is the use of textual scholarship? or what is it? Why isn't history settled once and for all? Why isn't there *one* right interpretation of it? What makes a professor think he knows a good play from a bad better than I do? What's the use of Anglo-Saxon? Why does an epic have to be so artificial? And so on. The public tends to be completely in the dark about the nature of our activities, and above all, about the reason for them and value of them. This, it seems to me, is where the attempt at conversion must start.

A. R. C. DUNCAN

An Ideal Programme for the Humanities

To make suggestions about an ideal programme is to talk about what ought to be done, and to talk about what ought to be done is always to lay oneself open to the harshest criticism. On the other hand, if the object of these talks is to promote discussion then I should judge that I have the easiest task of all. If nothing else, I cannot fail to stimulate everyone else to tell me just how utterly wrong my ideas are! I should say at once that I have interpreted my rather liberal instructions in a fairly liberal manner—I am going to talk about an *ideal* programme, and I fully expect large parts of it to be shot down in flames. I am trying simply to provide a talking point. First, I shall very briefly say something about what I understand by "the humanities." Secondly, since the word "programme" can be interpreted as referring to the educational programme in the mind of the educators, I shall have something to say about the sort of ideas which we who attempt to instigate a programme of studies should have in our minds. This will enable me to be rather briefer in the third part of my remarks where I shall talk about the programme of study which might be laid before those who are to be educated. Finally, I have a few suggestions of a very concrete nature about what might be called the administrative details of such a programme. I have tried to construct these remarks so that I move fairly steadily from the highly general to the quite specific.

Speaking in 1956 about the humanities, Professor Woodhouse observed that we shall talk at cross purposes if we are not clear about what the humanities are. He defined them then as "studies bearing

HAB no. 26, January 1959. From an address to the annual meeting of the Humanities Association of Canada, 1958.

directly on the life of man, and on man in his specifically human aspect. . . . the humanities avowedly pursue the ancient ideal, the achievement of general cultivation by means of the acquisition of appropriate knowledge." One could not really quarrel with this, although it is a highly general account. The dictionary is a little more specific, perhaps too specific, for there we are told that the word covers "learning and literature concerned with human culture, as grammar, rhetoric, poetry, and especially the ancient Latin and Greek classics." This is most unfortunate, for grammar and rhetoric are out of fashion, and to put the Latin and Greek classics on a twentieth century programme is to invite a series of remarks about ivory towers and being out of touch with life as it is lived. I am inclined to think that if we asked the average educated man what he understood by the humanities, he would probably say language, literature, the fine arts, history and philosophy. This is the list eventually adopted by Professor Woodhouse in his talk, and I am perfectly content with this as my working list of subjects to be included under the heading of "the humanities." I am prepared to adopt it because these subjects certainly bear directly on the life of man in his specifically human aspect and they are undoubtedly concerned with human culture. There is, I am afraid, no brief way in which I can mark off from the humanities proper those subjects which are now known as the social sciences which also, it may be claimed, deal with human problems. With the exception of history, which is claimed by both groups, I have deliberately refrained from considering the social sciences. The distinction between the two groups of subjects should be made in terms of the methods adopted, but for my purposes it is perhaps sufficient to say that in the humanistic disciplines human problems are viewed as they affect and impinge upon personal life, the life of man as a solitary individual, whereas in the social sciences the same problems are viewed from the standpoint of man as a social being, as one who lives with other persons in community. This is really intolerably vague, but it is, I hope, sufficient for our immediate purposes.

Turning now to the ideas which should be in the minds of those who prepare a programme of studies to be undertaken by students in technical schools and colleges, it seems to me that we might well begin by getting rid of some false ideas which are unfortunately fairly widely prevalent today. In the first place, if you will excuse the shift in metaphor, we must hitch our wagon to a star and not set our sights too low. Under no circumstances must we allow the humanities to be narrowed to the teaching of English with a view to improving the English spoken and written by the average student today. I heard recently a speech by an eminent Canadian business man in which he spoke as if English should be taught in the universities for the sole purpose of ensuring that future business men and executives could write intelligible letters and frame clear regulations. It is true that everything possible should be done to improve the quality of written and spoken English—if we had not abandoned the teaching of rhetoric this would not have been necessary—but ability to write good clear English is a by-product of a grasp of something far more fundamental. It cannot by itself be set as an ideal. Secondly, we must never allow ourselves to imagine that in teaching the humanities what we are aiming at is to produce a kind of top-dressing of ornamental culture on the solid foundations of science and technology. If man could be defined as *essentially* a money-making animal, then we might do so without misrepresentation. In fact, however, the essence of man lies elsewhere and we do well in this modern scientific age to remember, as Professor Woodhouse hinted, that the humanities are the subjects where we come closest to dealing with the very essence of man as a *human* being. We perhaps ought to say more often and more loudly that the humanities are the only possible foundation for any kind of education. They must never be thought of as a top-dressing.

Part of the trouble arises from the abominable word "culture." The humanities are indeed concerned with human culture, but the word culture has become so debased that I have come to feel about it very much what Goering is alleged to have felt. When I hear the word, I want to reach for my gun. The plain fact is that for many people the word "culture" conjures up dreary images of long haired youths listening to Bach and Vivaldi instead of red-bloodedly jiving and skiffling, attending revivals of obscure Elizabethan plays instead of rioting with Elvis Presley, and wandering tight-lipped and white-faced around galleries of paintings instead of enjoying throbbing emotional dramas in glorious technicolour like *Peyton Place.* Worse still perhaps, for many people it has come to denote attendance at various functions which are vaguely thought to be cultural or "improving," functions that one ought to attend whether one enjoys them or not. To be told that one's culture is slipping is socially as great a sin as to have one's slip showing. If in our teaching or our talking about the humanities, we do anything to spread or support this vicious conception, then we fully deserve the fate reserved by Dante in the *Inferno* for those who debase the coinage of language.

Although there are few more detestable phrases in use among educators than "cultural subjects," we must none the less face the fact that as teachers of the humanities we are concerned with human culture, and we do aim, as Professor Woodhouse very rightly said, at producing the cultivated mind. But let us remind ourselves of the significance of the agricultural metaphors which are enshrined in the everyday vocabulary of those engaged in education. In talking about a cultivated mind we are comparing the mind to a cultivated field. A cultivated field has been prepared and treated in various ways, it has been cleared of stones, ploughed, manured, sown, and kept free from weeds. Then, given certain other conditions, it may produce a harvest. The farmer who cultivates his fields has to work very hard indeed, partly against nature which leaves fields with stones in them and allows weeds to grow, and partly in co-operation with nature. What seems to me important in this metaphor is the stress it lays on the hard work which the teacher must be prepared to undertake in doing something to, in changing the nature of, the minds of his pupils. The same point lies hidden in the very word "education" which is not derived, as so many glib would-be Latin scholars assure us, from *educere* to lead out (and on this false etymology they erect an absurd theory of education), but from *educare*, again an agricultural word meaning to nourish or produce, when applied to plants or animals.

I have made these general remarks about culture because on the basis of them I want to make two points which I regard as of the utmost importance in our programmatic thinking. In the first place, in preparing a programme of studies in the humanities for our students we must be prepared to *teach the humanities*. We must be quite clear in our own minds and we must make it equally clear to our students that if any benefit is to be derived from a course of study in the humanities then they and we must be ready to work as hard at them as anyone does at scientific or technological subjects. It is not enough, with the false *educere* derivation in mind, to offer a few bright ideas to the students with the object of eliciting discussion. Discussion is an excellent adjunct to education, but it is worthwhile only when engaged in by students who have first learned something, who have acquired what Professor Woodhouse called "appropriate knowledge." Quite specifically, what we have to fight against is the production of that state of mind which is expressed in the very common phrase, "Oh yes, I took a course in that when I was in college, but of course I've forgotten it all now." This is a very polite, if unconscious, way of saying that the educational process through which the speaker went has been a complete failure. In my experience, people who have had the good fortune to be properly instructed in fundamentals do not make that kind of remark; they cannot and do not need to make it, for what they learned has become part of themselves, their minds were genuinely cultivated and not merely raked over before a top-dressing was laid. Secondly, and this is of equal if not greater importance, if we are to institute programmes of study in the humanities in technical schools and colleges, then we have some real hope of success if and only if we can find and channel into this work teachers of the very highest calibre. Teaching the humanities in a technical school or college may well be very different from teaching them in an arts faculty. The primary interests of the students will lie elsewhere, they will not have as much time to devote to their humanist studies, and their initial background knowledge may be sketchy. They may have done French at school, but they will not have read Racine, Corneille, or any of the great French poets; they may know a little history, but they will probably believe that history textbooks are infallible tables of unassailable truth. To arouse and sustain interest in human studies will make unusual demands on the teacher, and the danger is that if we provide poor teachers the students' resentment may be directed against the subjects, and the whole enterprise will have been ruined from the start. Personally, as one who accepts the basic implications of Plato's "Allegory of the Cave," I believe that this type of work is well worth doing and that therefore we must find means of persuading the best teachers to undertake it. It will not do to leave it in the hands of groping graduate students or of men who are not quite good enough for the faculties of arts. Journeymen teachers we must have, but there must also be more than a sprinkling of something better. This may very well be a touchstone by which we can distinguish between the ivory tower pure scholar and the genuine humanist who wishes to share the benefits he himself has reaped through his own studies.

Returning to the phrase "learning and literature concerned with human culture" and to Professor Woodhouse's human problems, we may now state that our programme of studies must be a programme in which the various achievements and difficulties of the human spirit may be encountered. Generally speaking, there are three main aspects of human experience with which the humanities may be said to be concerned: first and foremost, there is the fact of language or perhaps I should say of languages. Language is not only our major means of communication between human beings but also one of our finest avenues of artistic expression. Language must be studied, not merely as a social or psychological phenomenon, not as an end in itself, but as the means by which one human being can enrich the personal life of another, by which men of artistic genius can throw light on realms of experience known to, but not thoroughly explored by, all of us. In other words, mastery of language is fundamental, and not to put too fine a point on it, this means that grammar and rhetoric (for which the modern word is "composition") must form the basis of all studies in the humanities, whether we or the students like it or not. Secondly, there are the specifically human problems constituted by the fact that we human beings live in a world which contains other human beings with whom we must in some sense learn to "get along." In old-fashioned language this is the sphere of moral problems, where the word "moral" covers not only the study of the difference between right and wrong, but the whole field of personal and historical relationships between persons and peoples. Literature, history, and philosophy are all "moral" subjects in this sense. Through the novel and the essay we see men brooding on the problems of personal relationships; in history we attempt to understand how man has come to be the kind of creature he now is; in moral philosophy we try to discover the basic beliefs in terms of which man lives out his life with other men and the justifications which have been produced for these beliefs. Thirdly, there is the wide and fascinating field of the aesthetic, where we find man attempting to express his sense of beauty or to make permanent, through the medium of words, pigments, or musical noises, these fleeting insights into different aspects of human experience which, when enjoyed, leave one with the sense that human life really is worth living. The importance of the fine arts of poetry, painting, and music is systematically ignored in much of modern education, and yet it would be difficult to suggest anything more essentially human than this vital activity of creating objects whose value and worth lie in what they can do to make human life something more than merely an attempt to get through a series of monotonous days of work.

I can now conclude this section of my remarks by stating that our object in teaching the humanities is to bring the student into contact with what has been thought and felt about the nature of *human* existence, for only human beings have developed the art of verbal communication, have worried and thought about how to get along with each other, and have attempted to express artistically their moments of greatest insight. Above all, we must so teach the humanities that the students come to understand that in the field of fundamental human problems, there are no cut and dried solutions, there is always an essential area of vagueness and uncertainty (this might be said to be a necessary condition of our human freedom), and in consequence that a human being must learn to rely on his own judgment. We must also point out that there is a vital difference between trained and untrained judgment in all fields. Specifically, this means that we must somehow persuade the student to learn how to brood over these problems, how to meditate so that the process of spiritual osmosis can take place between the works he studies and the mind that he is endeavouring to cultivate. No matter how hard a farmer has worked on his fields, if he does not allow time for the laws of nature to operate, his labour will be in vain. Similarly, a willingness on the part of the student to allow the laws of spiritual nature to operate must be postulated. And since he is less likely to understand these laws than he is to understand the laws of nature, this must be explicitly explained.

Coming now to the third section of my remarks, I must ask, what, concretely, shall we attempt to teach? In answering this question, I shall first ask you to bear in mind that our object is not to produce scholars or future teachers, but simply men and women with a sound grasp of the nature of fundamental human problems and potentialities, and then I shall suggest that our programme should contain five parts.

(A) In the first place, just as mathematics is the basis for advance in and understanding of physics, so a study of language, that is, grammar and rhetoric, is the basis for any progress in the humanistic disciplines. The student must know something about the structure of language and the names for its various parts; he must also learn how to put these parts together in a manner which is both effective and artistic. Agreeing that grammar is best studied concretely through the medium of actual texts, and bearing in mind that only through exercise and practice is proficiency to be achieved, I should suggest that certain periods be set aside for pure grammar and composition. The analogy with mathematics might well be explained and drawn out in some detail to students of the physical sciences. In this part of the course the student would cover the sort of ground that is covered in books like Herbert Read's *English Prose Style* or Grierson's *Rhetoric and English Composition.*

I should like now to take a moment to argue that in my opinion what we are aiming at in this part of our course can best be achieved if we also include some study of a foreign language, it does not matter greatly which one, provided that it is one of the Romance or Teutonic languages or their ancestors. I am not suggesting that the foreign language be studied with a view to acquiring facility in speaking it. This utilitarian conception has its proper place but not with the humanities. The subjects which we now call the humanities were largely built up by men who studied Latin and Greek not as speaking languages but as examples of linguistic structure. We might adapt a famous phrase to read: "What do they know of English who only English know?" Even at a relatively elementary stage, in the hands of a good teacher, a student can be taught and brought to understand a good deal of what is meant by linguistic structure and idiom through the act of comparing his own language with another. The exercise of translation possibly does more than any other linguistic exercise ever invented to teach the student how to appreciate subtle shades of meaning and the significance of different ways of saying what seems to be the same basic idea. This can be done partly by giving the student simple exercises in translation and also partly by the teacher himself demonstrating to the student all that is involved in rendering a really complex passage. I doubt very much myself if anything else will more effectively force the student up against what I have called the fact of language. I am prepared to admit that this demands high calibre teaching, but I have already indicated how important I think the quality of the teaching must be in this kind of course.

(B) From language there is a natural transition to what is written in language, namely, literature. Here we face three distinct problems and choices: what kind of literature, shall it be confined to English, and how much of it? As to the kind of literature, I should suggest a careful selection of poems and a fairly large number of contemporary novels. The student must be taught how to read a poem, what sort of principles may be applied in judging a poem, and that it takes time for a poem to make any real impression. Under no circumstances must poetry be taught by anyone who does not know what it is really to enjoy a poem. This may have to be done in high schools, but it must not be allowed to happen when our object is to teach students how to appreciate the humanities. I suggest contemporary novels selected not so much for their sheer artistic worth, although they must be competently written, but because in them the authors are dealing with contemporary human problems, taking some big problem like the relation between men and women, or man and the state, or man and his religion, and showing how the abstract idea works out concretely in particular human lives. The same principle applies of course to drama or to poetic drama where both currents meet. Such novels or dramatic situations can then form the basis of later philosophical discussion of the problems.

There is no reason in a course like this why literature should be confined to English. There exist excellent translations of nearly everything in either the ancient or contemporary languages which we are likely to think worth putting before our students. A play of Euripides, some history by Tacitus, some cantos from the Divine Comedy, a play or two by Racine or Corneille to offset Shakespeare are almost indispensable if the student is to be permitted to enter into his western heritage.

With regard to the age-old problem of the choice between doing a little literary study in a really thorough and fundamental manner and attempting to obtain a bird's eye view of a great area I have no hesitation whatsoever in arguing for a little well done. The student who has learned how to read and to criticise through careful study of a few texts under expert guidance can easily proceed to apply the same principles for himself when he is on his own. The bird's-eye-view man never gets to first base in the study of literature. I should ban anything remotely resembling a survey course. Let the student have a good short history of literature and then he can survey to his heart's content. Again for this work I should plead for the best in teaching. If an original poet or a creative critic is in the neighbourhood, let him be persuaded to do his stint, even if it be slight, with the main work left to the sound journeyman.

(C) From literature, there is again a natural transition to the other fine arts. Here I want to grind an axe and to grind it on the basis of personal experience. As an undergraduate I had the good fortune to be able to take as one of my regular undergraduate subjects a course in the history of art, painting, sculpture, and architecture; in this course we were instructed in the general development of the various forms of art and in the principles of criticism and appreciation; we were made to look at and to meditate over various important works. I have myself no particular artistic talent, but I have no hesitation in saying that this course paid off in terms of later enjoyment more than any other course I have ever taken. I make no claim to be an art critic or a judge of painting, but I am deeply grateful for the heightened awareness to art that was stimulated in me by this course. I should never have achieved this merely by desultory reading or by occasional wanderings in art galleries. What mattered was that we were given systematic instruction and made to work at it. I am convinced that a great many people would have the same experience if such courses were made available. The same, I am sure, is true of music. Again if I may draw on my personal experience, it is one thing to go to occasional concerts and to have a general liking for music, it is quite another thing to have been instructed in how music has developed in the past three hundred years, in how a symphony or quartet is built up, in how to recognise the various instruments and methods used in the modern orchestra. My own interest in music developed very late, and I have never ceased to regret that an analogous course in music was not available when I undertook the study of art. There is no question that one's appreciation and enjoyment of all forms of art are immeasurably extended by even a little fundamental instruction in basic principles. I should therefore argue very strongly for making courses of this type available to our students.

(D) With regard to history, which, in the hands of a good teacher, can be one of the greatest of the humanities, I should suggest that our course fall into two parts. There should be some instruction in how history actually comes to be written, in what philosophers call the logic of or the idea of history. An excellent first step might be taken through a comparison of what the school books say about Richard III with what is revealed in Josephine Tey's *Daughter of Time*. However it is done, the student must be brought to realise the nature of the problem involved when some man takes it upon himself to tell us what happened five hundred years ago, when in the nature of the case all his evidence is second hand. The second part should clearly be the study of certain selected periods or aspects of history. Say a general study of world cultures, the Mesopotamian, the Hittite, the Egyptian, the Hellenic, the European, and the American, or possibly a more detailed study of the origins, causes and results of the French or Russian revolutions, the rise of the U.S.A., or the formation of the British Commonwealth. I speak here very much as an amateur, but in history perhaps we can afford to spread thinner than in the other subjects, but I am open to correction.

(E) Finally, there is of course philosophy. Not every branch and aspect of philosophy is suitable for such a course as ours, and I shall rule out, except for the student's private reading, any systematic instruction in mere history, though I do not rule out the study of important writings from the past. There are two main avenues by which the student in technical schools might be initiated into the study of philosophy. Either through introducing him to the philosophical problems that arise on the borderline between science and philosophy, problems of perception, of the nature and criterion of truth, of the difference between knowing and merely believing or having an opinion about. Or through a systematic study of the value judgments by which the student is accustomed to live his own life. Every human being has his basic values, but few ever have the time or the opportunity either to formulate explicitly or to attempt to justify these value judgments. We may talk about doing the right thing or attempting to lead a good or a decent life, but when asked what we mean by these terms we often get no further than did Socrates' various interlocutors at the beginning of the argument. Taken in close conjunction with what the student is reading in contemporary novels and drama, a course in ethics can very quickly force the student to ask himself very fundamental questions about what it really means to be a human being. Not only does every man have his basic value judgments, but almost every man lives out his life in terms of some overall attitude to the world which may be more or less clearly formulated. Some study of such basic attitudes as materialism, or idealism, or pragmatism would be a fairly natural conclusion to any systematic course of instruction in the humanities.

Finally, after all these various suggestions, I come to what I called the administrative details, how many hours of instruction, at what time of the day, and how much time can the student be expected to devote to the humanities. Again, let me first attack false ideas. We shall have no success at all if we permit the teaching of the humanities to be tagged on at the end of a hard day's work in science and technical matters. The humanities demand as lively and alert a mind as any scientific or technical subject, and on this point we ought not to compromise. Secondly, we must make it quite clear to our opposite numbers among the scientists and technicians that learning how to appreciate a poem or a painting takes time, and that if we do not give the students time for the process of spiritual osmosis to take place then we are acting as absurdly as a mathematician who gave his students one month in which to master the integral and differential calculus. In the ideal programme I should suggest that 20 per cent of the student's time is an absolute minimum if anything of value is to be achieved. Without going into detail, this should work out at two two-hour lecture courses per week, or six full two-hour-per-week courses over a three year period. My own inclination would be to think basically in terms of six full courses, but to divide them and spread them out a little. For the sake of argument, and merely as a suggestion for shooting down, I append a possible curriculum extending over three years at four lectures per week:

Year I—First Term: Grammar and Composition (1); Literature A (2a). Second Term: Foreign language—grammar and translation (3a); Philosophy A (4a).

Year II—First Term: Foreign language—text study (3b); History and Criticism of Art (5a). Second Term: Literature B (2b); History A (6a).

Year III—First Term: History B (6b); The Humanities and the Social Sciences (7). Second Term: History and Criticism of Music (5b); Philosophy B—types of Philosophy (4b).

I have not attempted to specify either the contents or the possible options which should be included for each course as that is clearly the business of the appropriate specialists in consultation with the directing board which should coordinate the whole scheme in detail. It should be noted that in the third year (certainly not earlier) I have suggested a course in which the points of contact between the humanities and the social sciences might be developed and examined. This is partly to placate the feelings of the social scientists and partly because, with the type of foreign language course that I have outlined, it should be possible to deal with the basic principles of grammar and composition in one half-course. This means a total of five full courses divided into parts (2–5) with the addition of what amounts to two half-courses (1 and 7). By way of conclusion I would suggest that an intelligent directing board should be able so to arrange the content of courses that any two given in the same term might be to some extent integrated and correlated. The complete plan might well be explained to the student at an early stage so that he would know where he is going.

PART II

Approaches to Literary Tradition

DONALD SOULE

Comedy, Irony, and a Sense of Comprehension

In view of the confusion which marks so many critical descriptions of twentieth century drama, I think it is worth making some attempt to relate its main characteristics to certain traditional elements of dramatic form. The terms comedy, irony and a sense of comprehension are, I think, indices to this relation and to what seem to me to be the most prominent ingredients of contemporary serious drama.

In the last century, the distinctions between comedy and tragedy have become considerably confused, both in practice and theory. Of course, some confusion has existed, in practice at least, even in earlier, stable dramatic periods, such as the Elizabethan or Greek. Recall for example, the daring use of the comic in Shakespeare's tragedy or in such Greek plays as *The Bacchae*; or, on the other hand, the presence of something close to the tragic in Moliere's *Le Misanthrope* or *Don Juan* or Jonson's *Volpone*. But even in such cases as these, there is no real question as to what the plays are. They are clearly either tragedies or comedies, making dramatic statements appropriate to their type. Moreover, our clear knowledge of what that type is makes it easier to grasp what the dramatist is getting at. It is only in the last seventy-five years that real confusion has arisen; that we have, for example, begun to worry about whether tragedy was any longer even possible. And it is only in that same period that the apparent mixture of the tragic and comic in particular plays has sometimes been so confusing that we felt unable to grasp the true nature of the work, and in consequence have often forced it into some erroneous but more comprehensible mold. The fate of Chekhov's plays in the hands of brisk Soviet or sentimental Anglo-Saxon producers is a case in point.

HAB vol. XIII, 1962–63.

As a small step towards dealing with such difficulties, I would like to begin by reconsidering briefly the comparative natures of tragedy and comedy, and the place of irony in drama.

We must start with a brief clarification of terms. The words "tragedy" and "comedy," particularly in their adjectival forms, have long since ceased to be just formal critical terms. We tend to use them everyday in a variety of loose ways—about train wrecks, cocktail parties, broken marriages, business deals. Unsurprising as this may be, it does mean that we have to be careful about letting these colloquial meanings affect our use of the words in serious criticism. Something sad, for example—or even something catastrophic—is by no means necessarily tragic in the formal or basic sense. Nor is the funny necessarily comic—or vice versa. Nor even—to speak specifically of drama—does the fact that a play ends in death make it a tragedy. All this is perfectly obvious, of course, but it has to be kept in mind in dealing with modern drama.

On the other hand, the terms "tragedy" and "comedy" can be conceived as simply historical. It is quite possible to claim that *pure* tragedy and comedy, in the original Greek sense, ceased to exist at the end of the fifth century B.C. (or, as others would have it, at the end of the seventeenth century A.D.) and that everything since then has been hodge-podge and bastardization. Using the words in this way, we would have to abandon them altogether when speaking of modern drama, for they would be as obsolete and inapplicable as the term "satyr play," for example.

But to do this would be to ignore the fact that certain basic elements of traditional tragedy and comedy have persisted in drama from the fifth century down to the present, and that if we know what some of these are we can more easily detect and understand them in modern plays. In short, if we use the terms not colloquially or historically, but critically—that is, as general but precise descriptions of certain definite elements in form and content—I think we will find them as useful tools for the twentieth century as for the seventeenth.

Since I am primarily concerned with the differences between traditional tragedy and comedy, I would like to outline some of their basic characteristics by means of a series of oppositions. These will be grouped under five subject headings: resolution, area of concern, protagonist, point of view, and effect. I might add that in speaking of traditional tragedy and comedy, I have in mind the great dramas of fifth century Athens, Elizabethan and Jacobean England, and seventeenth century France. I realize that neither the categories of subject nor the range of examples is complete, but I think they will be adequate for my very general purpose.

First, the handling of resolution in comedy and tragedy. It is a truism, of course, that tragedy ends with the downfall of a person of high estate—a king or noble like Oedipus, Agamemnon, Hamlet, Lear, Macbeth. Traditionally, of course, tragedy has meant death at the end, although we should remember that Aristotle, in speaking of tragedy, nowhere mentions death, but only a fall or misfortune. In any case, the end of tragedy is a catastrophe, which is more than mere demise. Tragedy's resolution is final and irreparable.

Comedy, on the other hand, is supposed to end happily. We are all familiar with its traditional conclusion: the couple united, the scheme successful, the fool chastised or corrected. Comedy's resolution, however, is not always one of *unqualified* joy even in the most traditional examples. The nuptials are sometimes darkened, as in *The School for Wives*, or the comic protagonist is even defeated, as in *Le Misanthrope* or *Volpone*. The entirely happy ending is not a necessity. The important fact is that the resolution of comedy points *ahead* to equilibrium—even equanimity—after the final tableau.

To distinguish more accurately between the handling of resolution in the two types, therefore, we might say that in tragedy the finality is absolute, whereas in comedy it is relative. Equilibrium is achieved in the resolution of both, of course, but in tragedy it tends to be an end in itself, in comedy a means to something else. Tragedy states the ultimate fact of death. Comedy presents a kind of working compromise with life—in fact, a *modus vivendi* as opposed to tragedy's *modus moriendi*. The origins of comedy, after all, lie mainly in fertility rites; those of tragedy in the ritual of death and symbolic reincarnation. Comedy's resolution, therefore, represents an accommodation—usually joyous, but not always—to the facts of life. Tragedy is an acceptance of the fact of death, palliated by the suggestion of symbolic survival beyond death. Because death itself is inevitable and immutable, however, in tragedy the battle matters more than the outcome, the question more than the answer. With comedy, it is generally the reverse.

These rough distinctions bring us to the second point of difference: the respective areas of concern of tragedy and comedy. The subject of tragedy is the final powerlessness of man against the forces which rule the universe and against the brute fact of death. This being the case, tragedy speaks in moral terms. Since die we must, death must be given significance if life is to mean anything more than animal survival. We must therefore determine what values are *worth* dying for; something must be found that is more important than death. To this question, traditional tragedy has given slightly different answers in different ages, but all of them can be distilled to the essential conviction that the one thing which is greater than death is the dignity of man himself. This is the truth to which tragedy gives ritual expression —ritual because only in essential and symbolic terms can the defeat of one man represent the triumph of Man himself.

But comedy speaks of winning here and now, not in symbol but in fact. Its subjects therefore are survival and expediency: means, not ends. This is the primary reason, incidentally, why comic plots are on the whole more mechanical and complicated than those of tragedy, for comedy is concerned with the means of survival. Even its laughter is a technique of adjustment. Comedy shows us, therefore, not Man dying but men living.

To sum up, tragedy is concerned with the cosmic and the moral, the incomprehensible and uncontrollable; comedy with the social and expedient, the tangible and manageable. This general distinction is of particular importance in relation to twentieth century drama, as we shall see.

Let us next look briefly at the protagonists of the two forms. The tragic hero, as I have already mentioned, is traditionally of high estate, whereas comedy, Aristotle asserts, is concerned with "characters of a lower type." Nobility is an important attribute of the tragic hero, for the very practical reason that only a man of high estate can create the necessary general level of significance. What is more, his worldly nobility is a necessary means of symbolizing the spiritual nobility of Man.

But the tragic hero should also be, as the *Poetics* reminds us, "a man like us." This does not mean that he must have a "tragic flaw," some particular weakness which causes his downfall. The term "tragic flaw" is actually the consequence of a misunderstanding of Aristotle's use of the word *hamartia*, which means not tragic flaw of character, but more nearly simply error or mistake. The tragic hero's "flaw," in other words, lies not so much in what he is, as in what he does or in what happens to him. Of course, there is some weakness in the character of the tragic hero, but it is just as likely to be an *excess* of strength as a deficiency. Essentially, his weakness is his common humanity, compounded by his inability to recognize that he *is* common. In short, his flaw, if you will, is most often *hybris* of some kind —a pride which makes his downfall a deserved one.

But such pride can also be a characteristic of the comic protagonist, whose fall (when it occurs) is also deserved. The catastrophe is, in both cases in fact, both deserved and undeserved, and the nature of the balance between the two will determine whether it is essentially comic or tragic.

Just how thin the line dividing the comic and the tragic protagonist sometimes is can be shown, I think, by taking a brief look at *Othello*. The story, with only minor editing, could appear this way: A not-too-intelligent Moor, by means of boastful tales of his military exploits, induces a well-born Venetian girl to elope with him. They are sent by a tolerant Doge to Cyprus, where the Moor's ensign, Honest Iago, understandably vexed at being passed over for promotion in favour of an inexperienced young dandy, plays a practical joke on the Moor. He convinces him, on the flimsiest of evidence, that his wife has cuckolded him with the dandy. Enraged—and not troubling to check the facts—the Moor strangles his innocent wife. With the exception of the ending, which may go a bit far for some tastes, we have here the rudimentary outline of a comedy—a comedy in the manner of Macchiavelli or Aretino, perhaps—vicious, but unmistakably comic. Othello ceases to be a tragic hero and becomes the classic dupe—in fact, the *alazon*, the boastful pretender of Aristophanic or Jonsonian comedy. What has happened to him?

The elements of pride and suffering are still present, though of course in a changed mixture. Pride and suffering, after all, occur in comedy too. Can we forget that Alceste suffers, or Arnolphe, in Moliere's comedies, or that Shakespeare's cross-gartered Malvolio or ass-eared Bottom also suffer? The difference lies partly in the relative emphasis upon pride and suffering, guilt and innocence. Most of all, the difference between the comic and the tragic protagonist lies in our response to their pain. The most important factor, in other words, is the degree of objectivity with which the character is presented by the playwright and the degree of detachment in the spectator's response.

Which brings us to the question of point of view. The preceding illustration has perhaps made clear that tragedy presents us with the involved or subjective view of the protagonist and his situation, whereas comedy steps back and views him from a greater distance. In film parlance, we might say that tragedy contains a high proportion of closeups, whereas comedy deals largely in medium and long shots. (Which, quite by the bye, is *one* of the reasons comedy is so rarely successful on the small screen of television.) Because of this closeness of view in tragedy, we are more intensely *aware* of suffering. Watching the action as *individuals*, we become more empathetically involved with the characters, and particularly with the tragic hero himself. No such degree of involvement is found in comedy. Here we are to a greater extent members of a *group* in viewing it, and we see the comic protagonist at a greater distance. He is merely one figure among many: comedy usually has a greater number of important characters. The tragic protagonist, however, is a dominant single figure in a smaller group of characters—many of whom, incidentally, are there primarily as foils to the hero. Consider Ismene in *Antigone*; Creon in *Oedipus*; Laertes, Fortinbras, Horatio in *Hamlet*. In comedy, on the other hand, the dramatis personae are likely to include a wider range of character types, each with some idiosyncratic preoccupation which runs at cross-purpose with the others. In short, the main character of comedy is presented as one element in a primarily social complex, while the tragic protagonist is the dominant central figure in a moral situation.

Another important aspect of the question of point of view has to do with theatrical conventions. (This is a factor which becomes increasingly important in the twentieth century.) Insofar as tragedy tends to induce emotional identification with its characters, it also tends to be, in the general sense, illusionistic. In merging ourselves with the tragic hero, we tend to ignore and move *through* the theatrical terms in which he is expressed to the heart of his concern. This is the primary reason why most traditional tragedy is less realistic than comedy: why it tends to use verse rather than prose, why its acting style is more formalistic than comedy's, why in traditional drama the scenic requirements of comedy are generally more detailed and realistic than those of tragedy. Of course, tragedy makes use of theatrical conventions, but if we look at the ones it most often employs, we find that they are those which tend to generalize, to enlarge the central figure and conduce to emotional identification.

As an illustration of this point, consider the theatrical convention of the single character addressing the audience. In tragedy, this most often takes the form of the *soliloquy*: a character expressing his feelings to himself, without explicit acknowledgement of the presence of the spectator. In comedy, however, this convention usually takes the form of the *aside*—a character speaks, in the presence of other characters, to the audience, or, if he is alone, addresses the audience directly.

In short, tragedy as the more subjective form goes beyond theatrical conventions, using them *implicitly*, while comedy, the more objective form, tends to employ theatrical conventions in an *explicit* manner. As we might expect, the converse of these propositions also holds true: a greater explicit recognition of the conventions of the stage tends to induce a more comic attitude on the part of the spectator: in brief, it "alienates" him. This fact too has considerable relevance to the development of twentieth century drama, as we shall see.

This brings us to the final point of comparison: the relative effects of comedy and tragedy. Here I must be even more cursory. Suffice it to say that both tragedy and comedy accomplish something which can properly be called *catharsis*: a release of certain emotions which have been built up in the spectator in the course of the play. I think that Mr. R. B. Sharpe, in his book *Irony in the Drama* makes a useful point when he says that the emotions which lead to the comic catharsis are "shallower but more violent in expression and less dignified . . . than those of tragedy, but are similar in general nature" and that the ironic devices which stimulate these emotions in comedy are also similar "but less deeply disturbing to the unconscious feelings than those employed in tragedy."[1] I might add that I think it possible that the greater violence, lack of dignity and shallowness of the emotions proper to comedy are perhaps particularly suitable to the emotional tendencies and capacities of a modern audience.

What is more specifically relevant, at this point, however, is that the catharsis of traditional tragedy constitutes a reconciliation to the inevitable and immutable. Pity and fear are alleviated in tragedy, not by the avoidance of disaster at the last moment as in melodrama or comedy, but by an acceptance of it. We experience an emotional, symbolic triumph through vicarious submission to fate or death.

The effect of comedy is quite different, of course. Here our emotions are relieved by a very practical triumph for our side over the disorder of comic aberration. Human reason wins out over inhuman (that is, ludicrous) abnormality. Just as inevitably as in tragedy, disorder is brought under control—not by submission and acceptance, however, but by suppression and correction. The fool who endangers the rational conduct of social relations, the old man or buffoon who stands in the way of the natural union of the young and healthy—both are integrated into the social fabric, or simply ejected from it and forgotten. Man triumphs in the most practical possible way: the world is brought to heel.

These, then, are what seem to me to be the most important points of difference between traditional tragedy and comedy. We must now take a moment to look at irony, the common ingredient of both comedy and tragedy, the *salt* of drama. Here again, we must quickly review a familiar definition or two.

Roughly and simply, irony involves the simultaneous perception of contrasting significances. It can be expressed through words, ideas, actions, characters. Whatever its form, however, it contains three main elements: appearance, reality, and an audience to perceive the ironic contrast between them. We have irony when Iago says to Othello: "Take note, O world,/To be direct and honest is not safe," or when Oedipus discovers that his supposed father, Polybus, has died of natural causes and rejoices that he has escaped the fate the oracle has foretold. In both cases, there is a potent contrast of reality and appearance—of a whole complex of realities and appearances, in fact. A tension is created, in which resides much of the power of art.

In drama, there are three main kinds of irony. First, there is the presence of irony as a basic element of the theatre itself. Hardin Craig has pointed out that drama is three things: action, dialogue, and impersonation. The third of these is in itself an irony. The actor as character is appearance; the actor as actor is reality: the simultaneous opposition of the two creates the constant irony of the theatre. It can be compounded, multiplied and developed by the playwright in countless ways. Consider the speech of Iago cited above: there are in the moment he speaks at least three Iagos: Iago as actor; Honest Iago; and the real villain Iago. The basic irony of the theatrical performance can best be summed up by citing Mr. Sharpe's concise description: "The theatre creates a mood which we call ironic, because of its simultaneous perception of the two concepts of art and nature as at the same time contradicting and harmonious, true and untrue." To this I must add one comment with respect to our present concern. Theatrical irony is likely to be more strongly present in that form of drama which makes more extensive and explicit use of theatrical conventions, namely comedy. The frequent use of masquerade in traditional comedy illustrates this fact.

The second basic kind of irony in drama is that which arises out of the contrast of expectation and outcome—or more accurately between apparent outcome and real outcome. Our perception of this irony requires us to look forward and backward along the story line of the play to see that the outcome which is to occur (or which has occurred) is contrary to the expectations of those involved. Oedipus' declared intention to seek out the criminal in Thebes leads our minds ahead to the real outcome, his finding that he himself is that criminal (a fact which we know from the start) and we perceive the ironic contrast between the two. Again at the end of the play, we look back at the course he has followed and see the inevitable contrast between his original intention and the actual outcome. It is important to note that for this kind of irony to have its full effect, the end should in some degree be foreknown, as was generally the case in Greek tragedy. In forms of drama in which suspense plays an important role (melodrama for instance) this linear irony is less likely to be employed effectively. In the history of drama, this kind of irony is most often and most fully used in plays which are somewhat artificially structured, where there is a sense of inevitability, of some force—finite or infinite, offstage or on—guiding the action to a conclusion unforeseen by the characters.

This force, the reality controlling appearance, can of course be embodied in the play. This is the third kind of dramatic irony, that which involves the ironist as a character, controlling and directing his less perceptive fellows towards unforeseen ends. Thus, of course, we have Iago and Edmund, Volpone and Mosca. Thus too, we should remember, the actor as ironist—as the real force behind the character

—can comment ironically on his own character, as we find comic actors tending to do in both traditional and modern drama. The technique of a character-ironist (or actor-ironist, when it is explicitly used) is primarily comic, partly because it is so obviously didactic. It is comic even when it is used in tragedy. Hamlet, for example, is clearly a comic ironist when he plays upon Polonius or Rosencrantz and Guildenstern. Iago recurs as a relevant example. It is significant that Iago is almost sympathetic, to a modern audience at least, for more than half the play. It is only in Act Four, Scene One, when the audience begins fully to identify with Othello, that Iago's ironic play starts to become really painful. Shortly after this point, incidentally, Shakespeare effectively removes Iago from the play—and plunges from bitter comedy into tragedy.

The final question we must ask about irony is this: Is irony more comic than tragic—or at least more appropriate to comedy than tragedy? I think it is, and for the following reasons. First, the presence of irony in a play disposes us to foresee catastrophe, and thus by natural reaction to steel ourselves against it and minimize it. Insofar as irony is present we tend to view catastrophe more objectively. It may never be downright funny, but it is often bitterly comic. Second, insofar as irony is utilized in a play, it tends to shift the balance of importance between knowing and suffering towards the former. To the extent that we foresee Oedipus' downfall, for instance, we not only view it more calmly but, what is more important, we identify less with his suffering. We are more aware of his *ignorance* and thus more *critical* of him. These are attitudes characteristic of the spectator of comedy. The third reason I feel irony is primarily a comic technique is this: in cases of irony where there is a personified ironist present, we tend to identify with him—at least intellectually, and probably to a great extent emotionally as well (depending, I suppose, on our balance of sado-masochism, among other things). He is, after all, the superior antagonist on the stage. In adopting his point of view, we become, as it were, gods in the theatre, looking down at the blind humanity of the characters. The habitual facial expression of a god, it is hardly necessary to add, is a smile—and a rather complacent one at that. Last: to the extent that we take the detached, essentially comic view of ironists, we become also more aware of the work of the playwright himself (the master ironist) and of the conventions of the stage, including particularly impersonation. Our view moves further and further towards that objective, critical, non-illusionistic attitude which is a prominent characteristic of comedy.

The twentieth century, I might finally remark before leaving the subject of irony, is particularly susceptible to these attitudes. Our sense of the controllability of the world, our preference for knowledge over suffering, our awareness of the prevalence of social manipulation —all predispose us to the ironic view. That irony is a major element in so much of our drama is therefore hardly surprising.

At last our groundwork is laid and we can turn more specifically to modern drama and its relation to traditional tragedy and comedy. This can best be done under two headings: the decline of tragedy in the eighteenth and nineteenth centuries, and what may be called the rise of the new comedy of the twentieth century.

Though it is a much-discussed point, I think it is certainly true that tragedy, in the traditional form at least, is quite dead. One of the most frequently mentioned reasons for this perhaps regrettable fact is that the tragic hero, as found in drama through the seventeenth century, is no longer possible. It is not that playwrights can't create them; they still try from time to time. But we cannot believe in them. With the gradual rise to power of the middle class through the eighteenth century, and the industrialization and democratization of the nineteenth, neither playwrights nor theatre audiences any longer believed that the hero of high estate could be a significant symbol of mankind. The aristocrat had become isolated by social change and had lost contact with the generality of mankind. The Romantics, it is true, tried to create a new kind of hero to take his place, but for a number of reasons their attempts failed. The Fausts and Manfreds made unsatisfactory tragic heroes mainly because they lived in a world of thought and feeling rather than one of action. Each was actually his own world, and a transcendental one at that. On the other hand, another species of Romantic heroes, the Hernanis and Wilhelm Tells, were too committed to simple physical action. They were too optimistic and efficient for evil or fate to have any more than a merely pragmatic significance. In a word, Romanticism created heroes who were either too refined by philosophy or too corrupted by melodrama.

In the latter part of the nineteenth century, dramatists tried to create tragedy with middle-class characters. But it was too late. The intrusion into serious drama of melodrama, and more particularly of social and scientific theory, rendered the creation of a bourgeois tragic hero impossible. The reasons lay not only in the democratization of the audience, but in other areas which should now be examined briefly.

In the latter part of the eighteenth century a change occurred in serious drama comparable to that which took place in Greek comedy between 404 and 350 B.C.: it moved from the public to the private sphere. In consequence, its nature, its form, and its whole significance were altered. With the rise between 1750 and 1850 of domestic tragedy in England, the *Trauerspiel* in Germany, and the *drame* in France, serious drama moved indoors: it ceased to be public and political; it became private and domestic.

The consequence was that the potentially tragic character was isolated and particularized. The characters of these bourgeois dramas lead lives of such limited scope that, despite playwrights' attempts to invest them with general symbolic significance, we cannot feel awe. We feel only curiosity. The characters of traditional tragedy led public lives, which is to say political ones. They lived for other people. The domestic character of nineteenth century drama, however, is a private person with personal problems. To watch him in action is a kind of invasion of privacy: titillating, perhaps, but not tragic.

The rise of realism in both language and staging had much to do with this development. As the nineteenth century progressed, more and more plays were written in prose; in consequence serious drama became more and more prosaic. Prose is traditionally the language of comedy. Tragedy requires poetry, a distillation and ordering of language. When dialogue attempts to imitate colloquial speech, that distillation is lost. The result is a tendency for the level of significance of the action to be correspondingly lowered. Developments in nineteenth century staging also contributed to this process. There was an increasing emphasis on historical accuracy (Lear in Druidic dress, Macbeth in kilts) and upon realistic scenery (the box set, filled with real props to play with and real furniture to sit down on). The emphasis in plays also came to be more and more on the detailed and commonplace. One result, of course, was a loss of economy of means. Too much of the limited time at the playwright's disposal had to be spent taking care of simple physical credibility: motivating entrances and exits, remarks upon the weather, handling dishes, letters and pistols—all the many trivia realism involves. In consequence, there was less time to devote to serious and important things. And so with the characters: they were weighted down by realistic impedimenta. George Steiner, in his excellent book, *The Death of Tragedy*, has remarked that in traditional tragedy "the tragic hero lets his servants live for him."[2] But in realistic drama, the poor hero has to do his own living—in prose, as it were. Finally, such realistic detail has another consequence. It is by implication critical. The more realistically a character is depicted, the more he becomes not general or symbolic, but idiosyncratic. It is his differences from other men that interest us; his particularity, not his universality. This critical viewpoint, as I have mentioned, is more proper to comedy than tragedy. As a result of all these factors, the concerns of realistic drama become more expedient than moral, more worldly than cosmic, more domestic than political, more particular than general—and thus more easily comic than tragic.

The last reason I shall mention for the decline of tragedy is the most important of all: the legacy of Rousseau. Put in considerably oversimplified terms, it involved the destruction of evil. Effectively, Rousseau and the many others who developed this whole view of man insisted that evil in man was the product of schooling and environment. Man is ultimately perfectable. It is immediately clear that with such a view an irreparable tragic conflict between man and evil (much less between man and fate) becomes quite impossible. In the first place, man himself is no longer ultimately responsible. The tragic tension between the deservedness and undeservedness of the tragic hero's fall is thus destroyed. Secondly, moral problems become expedient problems. Thirdly, catastrophe is no longer inevitable and irreparable. And lastly, the importance of the individual is subordinated to that of the group. Such ideas, gradually gaining wider and wider credence, spelled the end of traditional tragedy.

Briefly, then, democracy and privacy, realism and Rousseau, were the main factors which ended the possibility for genuine tragedy. We now arrive at our final consideration: the gradual development, in the late nineteenth and early twentieth centuries, of new tendencies of thought and theatrical practice which pressed playwrights and audiences towards a drama not only non-tragic but specifically comic.

Let us take a moment to look at what actually has happened in drama before we examine why it came about. It may seem surprising to some, but it is a fact that the overwhelming majority of serious playwrights in the twentieth century have worked in the comic vein. They have created a body of drama shot through with irony and bearing a far closer resemblance to traditional comedy than to tragedy. The characteristic form of our time, in fact, is what has been called "dark comedy": a kind of play serious in basic intent, but comic in form and viewpoint.

The process began, I think, with such works as Ibsen's ironic *Wild Duck*, an important landmark for modern drama. Shaw contributed significantly, of course, as did Chekhov—three of whose four major plays, incidentally, he called comedies, whatever Anglo-Saxons may think they are. All these men belonged essentially to the nineteenth century. In the twentieth, the development gathered momentum with Pirandello and his ironic and playful treatment of theatrical illusion and the relativity of truth; Giraudoux, with his graceful, tough comic fantasies like *The Enchanted* and *The Madwoman of Chaillot*; O'Casey's mocking and farcical, yet basically serious social plays, such as *Juno and the Paycock* and *The Silver Tassie*. In poetic drama, there has been Fry's *The Lady's Not for Burning* and Auden and Isherwood's *Dog beneath the Skin*. I have already named a good share of the century's outstanding playwrights, and the plays are in each case typical not exceptional. We must add to the list those playwrights whose work, as I shall suggest, while less obviously comic, contains important elements of comic form and attitude: men like Brecht, one of the most influential playwrights of our time (of whom I shall say more in a moment); Sartre, whose *No Exit* shows comedy in its grimmest and most intellectual form; and Dürrenmatt, whose sardonic plays, *The Visit* and *The Marriage of Mr. Mississippi*, are so typical of the dark comic eclecticism of the fifties. We must also include the various writers of the so-called Theatre of the Absurd—Ionesco, Beckett, Adamov, and others—who, however pessimistic (even nihilistic) in outlook, write plays which are unmistakably comic and farcical. It is more than clear that comedy and irony rule the theatre in our time.

The factors which contributed to the decline of tragedy also contributed, of course, to this phenomenon. But other ideas have arisen—social, theatrical, philosophical—which have caused playwrights specifically to embrace the comic. Let us look first at one or two general social considerations.

The world has grown larger, and at the same time more complex and interdependent. Its population has swollen incredibly, new nations have proliferated, communications have woven a fantastic web of connection over all the world, technology has created a new and intimidating complexity in the work of men. The world has become confusingly, terrifyingly complex. What have been the consequences on man's view of himself and his situation?

One result has been that as the world has grown larger, man has grown smaller. It is a matter of emotional arithmetic. We may smile today at the naïveté of John Stuart Mill and his quantitative social ethics, but the fact remains that we all respond in some degree in a quantitative manner. Emotionally speaking—perhaps even rationally—one man in three-and-a-half billions is less important than one in a hundred thousand. The death of millions of people in the last war, and the imaginative reality of hundreds of millions in the next, have simply reduced the significance of Willy Loman's death—or even Agamemnon's or Lear's.

Any playwright, any theatre spectator, surrounded by such terrific size, is more likely to look upon the individual man as merely a cipher, a tiny *x* in a vast equation. More and more, we tend to see the whole world as the only significant level at which morality can function: the group, that is, not the individual. With the feeling of ineffectuality such size induces in any mere individual, a resigned smile is likely to become the characteristic facial expression, and ironic comedy the characteristic dramatic expression.

It is not just a matter of size, of course. In a world increasingly complex, no man can do everything. Specialization is the mark of our age and our temperaments. The concept of a total man has become virtually impossible to entertain. Yet what else is tragedy predicated upon but this concept? And what else is comedy based upon but the idea that individual specialization and idiosyncrasy are the primary characteristics of humanity, and that reason and reality demand that these aberrations be brought under social control for the good of all? Tragedy has always been concerned with whole individuals; comedy with fragments making up the total unit, society.

Moreover, if each man is only a part, then individual responsibility is correspondingly fragmented and redistributed among the whole. Collective responsibility is what matters. Comedy is built upon this concept. The common social denominator—the audience as mass representing the larger mass—is the comic standard of judgment.

When we do look at the individual character of a play we tend, in an enlarged and complicated world, to be more aware of the fact that he is playing a role. We tend to see him more and more as embodying a social—and by extension an artistic—function. While the character may not be aware that he is only a component part of some theatrical or social construct, we see not only his function, but the total pattern of which it is a small part. Our view has so broadened that he is reduced in significance. Thus, however seriously we may want to take Willy Loman, for example, and however seriously he takes himself, we are still more or less constantly aware that he is a salesman, a minor cog in the economic machine. We are reminded of his dramatic ancestor in the twenties, for example, the comic and pathetic Mr. Zero of Elmer Rice's *Adding Machine*. The machine of which both characters are a cog is a man-made one. If it were not—if it were an awesome, ultimate force like fate in *Oedipus* or evil in *Lear*—perhaps the irony of Willy's or Mr. Zero's situation would be a tragic one. But for most of us in these days of planned economies and social ethics the irony of such characters—however pathetic, serious and regrettable—is not tragic. It is private and comic.

The second source of the comic tendency of our time is technology. It is hardly necessary to describe the phenomenon itself. The essential fact about it, as far as drama is concerned, is that it has weakened the direct connection between cause and effect, between human action and its consequences. When pressing a button or pulling a lever unleashes awesome power, that power completely overshadows the human impulse which started it. The man is hidden by the machine. (I sometimes think that the invention of the pistol was really the first step in the demise of tragedy.) That so small an impulse—a gesture, a slight pressure—can produce so large and potent an action is, I suggest, essentially a comic phenomenon, no matter how terrifying. The detonation of a hydrogen bomb by pressing a tiny button is basically the same, after all, as the film comedian's kicking the door and bringing down the building. The more we habituate ourselves to the indirectness of mechanical means and the discrepancy between action and consequence, the more we become capable of taking only the comic view in life or in the theatre. After all, a man has only two alternatives in working with a machine—he can cooperate or he can fight it. When modern man does the first, he becomes himself mechanical—and thus a character suitable to farce, which is of course largely populated by robots. Most of us say we prefer to fight them (for secretly, we all hate most machines—they are an animal we don't understand). What happens then is best represented in Charlie Chaplin's *Modern Times*, which I feel safe in saying is one of the most significant and representative dramas of the twentieth century. Needless to say, it is sad, it is frightening, and it is riotous comedy.

In habituating ourselves to the separation of human action from its consequence, we have of course disclaimed responsibility for that consequence. (How familiar is the line: "The gun just went off. I didn't mean to *kill* him!") The greater our capacity for construction or destruction, the more jaded and irresponsible we become, until grandeur no longer awes us and horror no longer shocks us. In his 1898 preface, George Bernard Shaw remarks: "We only cry now in the effort to bear happiness, whilst we laugh and exult in destruction, confusion, and ruin."[3] One recalls his own *Heartbreak House* (a comedy), which ends with a bomb and several characters conveniently disposed of. It is a comically expedient resolution and a symptomatic one. Twentieth century drama is full of examples of comic horror, from the drunken farcical ending of O'Casey's *Juno and the Paycock* to Genet's *The Blacks* (which he calls "A Clown Show") and Sartre's serio-comic rationalization of hell in *No Exit*. After all, how can the death of one man be awesome, terrifying, tragic, when we live every day with far greater horrors? It is not simply that the stage is physically too small to contain the monstrous events of our time—though that is a minor reason—but the human mind cannot bear them. How much more sensible, we think, to take the comic view: to look for the incongruity among the terrors, to present the ludicrous pointlessness of destruction, to convert genuine horror into comic grotesquerie? If responsibility is lost, the comic is often the only antidote to the unbearable.

Some of the root causes of modern comedy, then, are found in the inevitable change in the size, complexity and technology of modern society. Others lie in certain developments in the theatre itself in the growth of what might be called a technical theatricalism.

The rise of realistic staging in the nineteenth century tended to focus people's attention more and more on theatrical conventions. In this respect, realism boomeranged. Audiences and playwrights became increasingly aware not so much of *what* was being represented as of the ingeniosities of the *means* of representation. Theatrical writing and viewing became more and more technical. The introduction of electric light and of the dimmer in the nineties had a lot to do with it. So did the development of the cinema early in our century. Those who wanted accurate, detailed representation could go to the movies. In many countries the masses left the theatre for the cinema. With a smaller but more sophisticated audience left it, the live theatre became the place for a less illusionistic kind of drama. The many theatrical "isms" of the twenties were among the results. Impressionism, expressionism, surrealism, constructivism—all represented an extremely art-conscious and experimental approach to theatre.

Theatrical audiences have therefore become generally more aware of a play as an *artifact*. Consequently, of course, they are more likely to view the personae of a play as *characters* rather than as *people*. Plot, in turn, has tended to become not so much a representation of real life occurrences as a constructed arrangement of theatrical happenings. Witness, for example, the frequent use of the Stage Manager character, as in *Our Town*, or the narrator, as in *The Glass Menagerie* or Anouilh's *Antigone*—characters whose function is partly to reassure us that we are watching puppets, as it were, that the dramatic action is finite and well under control. It is no wonder that our view of drama has become so ironic and comic: we are far more sensitive to the irony of impersonation, far more susceptible to the detached and critical view so characteristic of comedy.

I should add, perhaps, that this use of comic formal elements does not mean the playwright cannot be serious. Pirandello's *Six Characters in Search of an Author* or Genet's *The Balcony*, for example, make quite deliberate use of the irony of impersonation and an almost playful contrast between two kinds of imaginative reality, yet deal quite seriously with the question of the nature of reality itself. But the *form* of these plays remains definitely comic.

Finally, the theatricalism so prevalent in the last fifty years has coincided with a general increase in a relativistic *Weltanschauung*. We have come to see the world as a sort of kaleidoscope of complex, contradictory impressions which constantly shift and reveal still other realities behind them. This has been reflected in the theatre not only in Pirandello's work, but in such other plays as Williams' *Camino Real* and Dürrenmatt's *Mr. Mississippi.* When there is no single absolute reality, no absolute truth, no absolute anything, there is little left for the playwright to do but smile and try the best he can to impose some arbitrary artistic or social norm upon the vagaries of existence. The result is primarily comedy.

So the conventions and techniques of the theatre itself have added still further impetus to the shift towards an ironic and comic drama. A third influence has been the emergence of certain ideas about man himself.

The name of Freud must inevitably crop up at this point. With the revelation of the unconscious mind (which Strindberg had already introduced to the theatre before the turn of the century), playwrights felt that perhaps a new mystery had been discovered. It might now be possible to create on the stage a kind of inner cosmos, an internal inevitability, which could restore to drama some of the tragic tension so long lost. Dreams could become dramas, the stage a human mind. But the attempt was doomed, for the whole purpose of the new psychology—and indeed the main effect of these plays by Strindberg, Wedekind, O'Neill—was to clarify the new mysteries and bring them under control. It was discovered in the process that Freudianism was amoral and pragmatic. So the mysteries and near-tragedies of Strindberg gave way to the melodramas of O'Neill (melodrama is always the mark of a dramatist trying to *force* belief in fading absolutes)—and eventually to the platitudes of Hollywood. There remains only Tennessee Williams beating the underbrush of the *id,* looking for tragedy, but finding melodrama and farce. The potential tragedy of the soul has become the comedy of accommodation. We have moved from *The Father* to *Period of Adjustment.*

One last philosophical refuge remained for the significance of the individual: existentialism. I use the term loosely and generally to suggest the idea of man alone, without relation to anyone but himself, in a world full of absurdity, loneliness and violence, preoccupied and cursed with a kind of purposeless freedom. A dark view, but a dominant one in today's drama. It is a view of man as not so much a comic as a farcical figure. In its rational form, it has produced such plays as those of Sartre—*No Exit,* for example, in which the worst that can happen to a man is an eternity of frustration. It is a grim but thoroughly comic view and play.

Recently, the existentialist view has received numerous dramatic expressions. These have been predominantly dramas of an irrational existentialism, and have taken the form of the well-known Theatre of the Absurd. Typical of this group is Eugene Ionesco. He is a writer of serious farce. Convinced of the hopeless absurdity of man's plight, the impossibility of communication, the irrelevance of logic, Ionesco has created a number of bizarre comic statements to this effect. His characters speak with farcical banality yet remain inchoate; they embark on ambitious schemes which come to nothing; they bounce about the stage in equally unjustified terror and elation; they indulge in pretentious spates of logic which mean nothing. Ionesco also makes frequent ironic use of theatrical and dramatic conventions: the pointless recognition scene of *The Bald Soprano*, for example, or the symbolic rape-murder of *The Lesson*. His plays are full of deliberate, ritual theatricalities. These are forms without meaning, however—and that is the point: meaninglessness is the only meaning. Both the ironic form and the farcical effect of such techniques are comic. Ionesco's work, and that of other similar practitioners of this roughly existential drama, display a number of the most important characteristics of traditional comedy: the resolution which points forward to eternal survival, however meaningless; the emphasis on aberration and accommodation; the concern with expedient morality; the adaptability and indignity of man; the deliberate use of violence without pain; the detached view of the inner man. However despairing, dark and distorted, these plays belong to the comic tradition.

This brings us to the last major factor in the evolution of modern comic drama: the sense of comprehension. As we have seen, traditional tragedy depends for its validity upon a dualistic view of the universe. In order for the tragic hero's downfall to have the fullest significance, it must be at the hands of some force which operates at an ultrahuman, metaphysical plane of reality. Only then can man's fate be in the profoundest sense both undeserved and deserved; only then can it be truly inevitable and irreparable. But how many people today believe in a dualistic universe? Very few, I suggest. To the generality of men, whatever their religious or political persuasion, the world is of a oneness. We may not know of what that oneness exactly consists, but that doesn't matter. The fact is that science has explained too many things. We no longer have mysteries; we have problems. And for every problem we have a perfectly conceivable solution, even though it may not yet have received complete and concrete proof. The origin of the universe? The Big Bang or the Steady State theory. The secret of life itself? Somewhere in there among the enzymes and amino acids. The human mind? Speak to IBM, they have already manufactured several quick-thinking morons. These comments are only partly facetious. Of course, I don't really understand about the origin of the universe, or the secrets of life or the human mind—after all, I'm only a specialist. But I *feel*—and I suggest that we *all* feel—that *somebody* does, or that somebody *can*. That is the point. The world may in fact never be fully explained, but we now feel that it can be. We have a *sense* of comprehension. And what can be comprehended can be controlled. Catastrophe can be prevented, inevitability denied, the irreparable repaired. It is perhaps a bleak prospect, but hardly a tragic one.

What attitude can we take under such circumstances? In drama, there have been two main kinds of response in the twentieth century. One is a kind of farcical despair, seen in the work of Ionesco and others I have just mentioned. The other response is to embrace and utilize this sense of comprehension, to say: "We have come this far, let us go on and finish, until *everything* is under control." This point of view is represented by one of the most symptomatic and influential playwrights of the century: Bertolt Brecht.

Brecht's roots are in social realism, that tradition which looks at the world as a finite complex of soluble problems. The universals of Brecht's drama—as indeed of our world—are purely social ones: poverty, power, destruction, logic. In Brecht's plays, the individual is a social cog; the morality is that of the group, even the mass; it bears no relation to the solitary, symbolic total man. Brecht's world is a strongly monistic, materialistic one: everything is comprehensible, controllable, pragmatic. What is more, there are no persons of high estate—except in the ironic sense of capitalists being lofty and destructible. Finally, theatricalism is a conscious and complex instrument in Brecht's hands. To encourage what he calls *Verfremdungseffekt*, whereby the audience (as in traditional comedy) is encouraged to distance themselves from the characters and make social, critical judgments of them, Brecht has used every theatrical convention as explicitly as possible. He says, for example, that actors performing in his plays should make it clear in their work that they are actors presenting the characters, detached from and commenting ironically upon them, at the same time as they represent them. This kind of acting has been long familiar in comedy, as a short look at the work of any good stand-up comedian will reveal. And didacticism, an important element in critical comedy since the time of Aristophanes, is another decisive ingredient of Brecht's plays. In short, with Brecht, as with so many other playwrights of our time, we find again a considerable number of traditionally comic attitudes and techniques: the emphasis on survival and accommodation; the forward-pointing resolution (as in *Good Woman of Setzuan*, for example); a thoroughly social and relative morality; a presentation of the world as comprehensible and controllable; the ironic contrast of lofty sentiments and practical reality; the frequent employment of the actor-ironist; the extensive, explicit use of theatrical and dramatic conventions.

This has been, I know, a very general and sketchy outline of a rather large subject, but it has been meant to suggest rather than prove: to suggest a significant continuity between traditional comedy and modern serious drama; to suggest that the tremendous prevalence of irony in twentieth century plays represents an essentially comic viewpoint and use of technique; to suggest that some of the important occurrences in the recent history of ideas have inevitably pressed the dramatist towards a comic viewpoint, and that the combination of irrational despair and practical optimism characteristic of our day are both likely to result in comedy when they take the stage; and finally to suggest that the proliferation and awareness of theatrical techniques in our time has created a form-conscious drama which must of necessity be primarily ironic and comic. We live, I believe, in a time when comedy, irony, and a sense of comprehension have become the hallmarks of our drama.

NOTES

1. Robert Boies Sharpe, *Irony in the Drama* (Chapel Hill: University of North Carolina Press, 1959), p. 133.
2. George Steiner, *The Death of Tragedy* (New York: Alfred Knopf, 1962), p. 243.
3. G. B. Shaw, *Plays Pleasant* (London: Penguin Books, 1946), pp. 13–14.

C. LOCKQUELL

Notes sur l'intuition comme instrument de critique créatrice

Cette communication ne prétend aucunement définir l'objet indéterminé qu'est l'intuition critique en littérature. Mon propos est forcément plus modeste. Je me contenterai de réfléchir tout haut au problème des relations qui me semblent exister entre l'appréhension critique et la critique créatrice. C'est sans assurance que je vous soumets ces approximations dont le mouvement sera aussi hasardeux que la réalité elle-même qu'elles tentent de surprendre. Ces incursions ne prétendent à aucune rigueur scientifique comme pourrait en avoir l'examen du dossier des structures plus fermes, apparemment, de la critique objective, du dogmatisme dit classique, de l'enquête biographique, des sondages psychanalytiques, de la sollicitation marxiste. ... Il reste qu'entreprendre une justification de l'intuition comme outil critique paraîtra à plusieurs un anachronisme, un retour intempestif au bergsonisme et au surréalisme, vieilles lunes qu'on pourrait croire à jamais éclipsées. Je dois aussi m'excuser de donner quelquefois dans le jargon philosophique — ce qui fera hausser les épaules aux humanistes — et d'avoir trop ajouté foi aux vertus de la digression, ce qui agacera les logiciens.

L'état civil du critique, dans le royaume des lettres, est équivoque. On le regarde comme un métis, le résultat d'un croisement suspect, un créateur manqué, un super-pion. Une chose est certaine; c'est qu'il est soumis aux servitudes interprètes, que son dilemme est redoutable : ou respecter religieusement l'œuvre qu'il veut proposer ou y ajouter une dimension personnelle qui ne s'impose jamais sans quelque lyrisme. Veut-il se donner bonne conscience ? Il prétendra que sa

HAB vol. XIV, fall 1963. From an address to the annual meeting of the Humanities Association of Canada, 1963.

profession est vieille de l'âge de l'intelligence elle-même. N'aime-t-il pas croire que l'activité critique s'est exercée simultanément à l'urgence poétique, qu'elle accompagnait sans cesse les démarches de l'instinct créateur dont elle était le phare et la boussole ? En tout cas, il n'hésite pas à affirmer que dans les contextes culturels les plus évolués, un certain thésaurus critique suscite et modèle toujours telle ou telle transfiguration de l'homme et du monde. Il songe aux générations issues de la poétique d'Aristote, de la Pléiade, de l'art pascalien de persuader, de l'auto-critique baudelairienne, de l'impressionnisme français de la fin du XIXe siecle, des intentions dialectiques du matérialisme, de l' « homo litterarius » de Blanchot ou de Barthes. ... Et comment n'en voudrait-il pas aux créateurs de l'entretenir dans un sentiment d'infériorité ? Pourquoi, à priori et par fonction, serait-il dénué de tout génie et de toute puissance vraiment créatrice ? On n'en finit plus de lui rappeler certaines erreurs de quelques-uns de ses grands patrons : Boileau, Sainte-Beuve, Brunetière, Gide. ... On ne l'estime pas habile à porter des jugements objectivement valables, à peine à communiquer son plaisir. Il est sans cesse menacé du ridicule dont le couvrira la postérité.

Nous sommes bien éloignés de l'autorité arrogante des critiques anglais de la fin du XVIIIe siècle qui se considéraient comme une cour sans appel décidant du sort des œuvres au nom des absolus d'une certaine morale et d'une certaine esthétique. Cette suffisance est impensable aujourd'hui. Une révolution s'est opérée. Naguère, c'est le lecteur qui jugeait l'auteur. C'est maintenant l'écrivain qui morigène le liseur professionnel lui-même. Autrefois, les auteurs, à coup de préface et d'avertissements, sollicitaient les bonnes grâces des amateurs. Le critique ne sera-t-il plus toléré que s'il démarque l'œuvre ou en prolonge servilement la résonance ? L'écrivain d'imagination tolère cependant tout appareil qui met en vedette ce qu'il croit être son originalité; il consentira aux preuves statistiques elles-mêmes, pourvu qu'elles justifient l'inaliénabilité de sa vision et de son écriture. Mais il supportera mal les tentatives de la critique intuitive.

Qu'est-ce que cet instrument ? Disons d'abord brièvement ce qu'il n'est pas. La connaissance intuitive se défie des canons rigides et des normes immuables. Elle tient pour incomplète et tendancieuse, partielle et partiale, l'explication déterministe qui néglige la liberté, les impondérables et les influences occultes. En un sens, elle est anti-cartésienne, elle n'espère jamais des inventaires complets et exhaustifs des causes. Comment ne déplorerait-elle pas qu'on applique trop souvent à une œuvre de l'esprit les méthodes des sciences de la matière ? Elle s'insurge contre une trop grande simplification, un durcissement trop intellectuel de certaines propositions en elles-mêmes vraies, comme : l'opération suit fatalement l'être, le tout n'est jamais ni plus grand ni meilleur que ses parties composantes, l'inférieur ne précontient pas le supérieur, etc. On l'accuse d'être médiocrement intéressée à l'authenticité des sources et des documents, laissant, par paresse ou incurie, cette vérification aux archivistes. Quelle position instable qu'elle se tienne éloignée et des architectures éprouvées de la systématique et du désordre obscur de l'humour noir ! Elle n'est ni historienne, ni philologique, ni idéologique, ni pathologique ... que sais-je encore ? Alors, autant dire qu'elle n'est rien ? Elle n'est rien de définissable, assurément. D'elle on peut affirmer ce que l'auteur des Pensées écrit de la manière d'agréer : « qu'elle est sans comparaison plus difficile, plus subtile, plus utile et plus admirable (que l'art de convaincre); aussi, si je n'en *traite* pas, dit Pascal, c'est parce que je n'en suis pas capable; et je m'y sens tellement disproportionné, que je crois la chose absolument impossible. » Il m'eût donc fallu suivre le conseil et l'exemple de Pascal. Je le suivrai en ceci : je ne *traiterai* pas de l'intuition critique; je tournerai autour.

La critique est multiforme. Quoi de plus instructif et de plus troublant à la fois que la lecture des innombrables commentaires suscités par une œuvre d'art ? Trop de critiques mineurs se croient investis de pouvoirs originaux et indiscutables. Celui-ci pose à l'initié qui vaticine, celui-là joue au guide omniscient. Très peu admettent qu'ils pourraient bien n'être pas autre chose que des liseurs privilégiés par leur culture, leur information et leurs habitus intellectuels perfectionnés. Mais cette connaissance elle-même ne va pas sans inconvénient. La culture peut insensibiliser, tout comme une trop grande sensibilité peut aveugler et amollir. Trop de lumière peut éblouir et non plus éclairer. Par contre, si à l'hermétisme de l'œuvre s'ajoute la complexité de l'explication, le trop clairvoyant vous mène droit au fossé, comme l'aveugle de Breughel ses compagnons.

La critique littéraire, tant en France qu'aux Etats-Unis, traverse une crise majeure. Toutes les Ecoles et toutes les tendances s'y affrontent. On s'interroge sur les méthodes, on élabore de nouvelles théories ou on en rajeunit d'anciennes, on polémique, on lance des anathèmes. Roland Barthes détermine le degré zéro de l'écriture. La littérature s'écrit une apostrophe. Jean-Pierre Richard raffine sur les relations de la littérature et de la sensation et celles de la poésie et de la profondeur. Bachelard, Jean Wahl et Jean-Paul Sartre prospectent les éléments et l'imaginaire. D'autres noms se sont imposés : Marcel Raymond, Albert Béguin, Poulet, Etiemble, Jean Paulhan. Tous s'opposent à la critique dite universitaire, qu'elle soit historique, philologique ou philosophique. Une polyvalence semblable travaille la critique américaine écartelée entre l'optique sociologique d'un Vernon Parrington, la méthode biographique et psychologique, l'intention marxiste et toutes les ambitions de la « New Criticism », d'Allen Tate à Robert Penn Warren. Quelque chose de commun peut quand même se déceler dans ces courants et ces contre-courants : une dérivation de l'intérêt allant de l'œuvre-objet vers l'œuvre-prétexte. Toutes les relations se trouvent justifiées, dans cet éventail. On y étudie les rapports des œuvres respectivement avec le créateur, les diverses contextes, les Ecoles, les modèles et les occasions, les diverses techniques d'écriture. ... Il reste que les jeux de l'intuition ne sont jamais absents de ces démarches et s'ils y sont moins évidents que dans la critique impressionniste et subjective ils y accomplissent un travail de base. Et dans les méthodes réceptives et dans les méthodes sélectives se retrouve l'intuition. La critique des mécanismes de la création — pour une — se fonde sur ses pouvoirs sympathiques. Quand elle tente de recréer l'instant privilégié, elle émet un acte de foi à la théorie bergsonienne de l'unisson. Ajoutons que si elle veut reproduire un « acte », elle entend souvent produire un nouvel acte. Même la critique qui cherche à dégager des essences n'en est pas moins existentielle. Créer des valeurs est devenu une urgence. Par cette ambition, les critiques veulent implicitement se substituer aux philosophes, dont on peut dire, en passant, que le domaine est morcelé par les disciplines connexes des sciences de l'homme. La race des critiques simplement explicateurs est en perte d'influence. Les œuvres dites originales ne sont, de plus en plus, considérées que comme des prétextes — au sens étymologique — à d'autres textes dictés par une autre originalité. A l'intuition qui comprend succède l'intuition qui entreprend. *L'œuvre-originale-point-de-départ*, qui avait été suggérée par quelque circonstance pré-artistique, sert à son tour de matériaux que le critique entend ré-informer, transformer à partir d'une finalité qu'il s'assigne à lui-même. Malraux a justifié un processus analogue en ce qui concerne les arts plastiques. En littérature, le grand exemplaire est peut-être Montaigne.

Abordons notre problème par un autre biais. Supposons que le critique se chante un poème. Son effort consistera à réinstaurer l'expérience initiale qui a induit l'auteur à employer tels mots pour s'exprimer. Sous peine de ne proposer qu'un discours logique, de n'aboutir qu'à des catégories abstraites, le critique doit ou retrouver chez lui une expérience analogue ou en composer une. Il ne saurait apprécier la propriété, la justesse de l'œuvre originale, s'il ne peut mesurer, analogiquement, la propriété et la justesse de sa propre reconstruction. En somme, l'œuvre qui est mesurée par l'auteur mesure d'abord le critique comme lecteur. Mais l'œuvre, dans l'esprit du critique, s'y trouve selon la capacité du récipient. Ce récipient est dynamique, c'est un creuset où s'engendre une œuvre seconde. Il y a déjà altération. Ce nouvel être peut ensuite servir de matière informable. Non seulement le critique voudra parcourir en sens inverse le chemin de l'auteur, mais il inaugurera sa propre route. Il deviendra « auteur », celui qui augmente non seulement la connaissance mais l'être lui-même des choses. Il ne s'agit plus seulement d'étiqueter des significations : le projet est d'en produire de personnelles. Le critique, comme lecteur, peut dire avec Aldous Huxley : « Je suis reconnaissant à l'artiste et à l'écrivain d'exprimer des sentiments que j'ai souvent pu éprouver sans avoir jamais pu les exprimer. » Alors, il est semblable au lecteur ordinaire. Mais comme critique au sens fort, son jugement est un jugement pratique sur une matière praticable. En tant que tel, il peut paraître irrespectueux d'une originalité que lui est offerte par un autre. Cela serait le cas si les œuvres dites originales étaient strictement originales et engendrées par génération spontanée. Mais toute œuvre est un héritage, une tradition collective en instance d'augmentation. On songe à la parole de Paul Valéry : « N'être que soi, quelle pauvreté. » Quand le critique projette sa propre lumière sur une œuvre, il respecte l'infini des potentialités de cette œuvre. C'est pourquoi il est bon que les critiques ne regardent pas la variété des auteurs avec les mêmes lunettes, que certains soient myopes et ne voient que des fragments, que d'autres soient presbytes et ne considèrent que des ensembles plus ou moins flous. L'histoire de la critique nous montre, par exemple, les divers éclairages auxquels on été soumises l'œuvre de Racine, celle de Molière. ... Jusqu'à la fin du XIVe siècle, cette dernière a été reconnue comme inspirée par l'esprit libertin. Puis, on lui a trouvé des résonances catholiques, du moins chrétiennes. Aujourd'hui, elle passe pour athée. La fortune posthume de Racine est également polyvalente. Pour un Gaston Picard, elle témoignerait avant tout d'aventures personnelles. Mauron explique par la psychanalyse certaines obsessions. Pour Goldmann, cette œuvre s'intègre dans une interprétation générale d'obédience marxiste. Il arrive aussi qu'un même critique ne chausse jamais que les mêmes lunettes pour scruter les divers auteurs qu'il étudie. Mauron, encore, ramène à la même perspective psychanalytique Nerval, Mallarmé et, encore, Racine.

Cette critique innombrable nous révèle un inextricable lacis de pistes, un fouillis éberluant de traits. Faut-il nous plaindre de ces divergences déroutantes (ou de certaines convergences) qui nous semblent des sollicitations idéologiques ? Nous pouvons du moins en obtenir des portraits réalisés par une espèce de triangulation à laquelle collaborent (comme les équipes de peintres de la Renaissance à certains tableaux) les critiques. Il n'est évidemment plus question de fidélité à l'original !

Une œuvre est le fait d'une unité d'intention. Mais pouvons-nous affirmer que sa forme soit univoque, statiquement et définitivement déterminée ? En d'autres termes, à partir d'elle, est-il impossible d'établir plus d'un rapport, plus d'une signification ? Examinons un vers de Mallarmé : « Je t'apporte l'enfant d'une nuit d'Idumée. » Que le lecteur soit une femme, il y a beaucoup à parier que le mot clé de ce vers, ou pour parler un langage plus mallarméen, que le sommet de ce mot total sera « l'enfant. » Pour un autre lecteur, ce sera « nuit », ou « Idumée. » D'autres placeront l'accent du vers, en feront porter toute la gravité de sens, sur le mouvement qui le commence : « Je t'apporte l'enfant. » A chacune de ces interprétations a correspondu une expérience personnelle. Mais pour Mallarmé, ce vers devait-il convoyer un sens romantiquement imagé, évoquait-il vraiment l'enfant ? L'enfant de Mallarmé, c'est le poème. L'ambiguïté peut se résoudre. L'auteur d' « Igitur » reconnaît avec humilité qu'il est impossible à un poète de placer, comme il le dit métaphoriquement, des pierres entre les pages de son livre. Le mot n'est pas la chose, n'est pas la transcription parfaite de la chose. (C'est quand même l'effort de la création littéraire de choisir la forme signifiante la plus adéquate, celle qui rend le plus complètement possible l'expérience antérieure.) La perspective marxiste compte qu'il sera un jour possible d'établir une équivalence parfaite du signifié et du signifiant. Il apparaît assez nettement que cette prétention présuppose, en dernière analyse, l'unité homogène de l'intelligence et de la matière.

Autre considération. La littérature est plus que le va-et-vient du signifiant au signifié, l'écrit plus que la transposition d'expériences juxtaposées ou superposées : c'est le passage d'un certain non-être à un certain être. C'est en ce sens qu'il faudrait comprendre Chateaubriand quand, dans ses *Mémoires d'outre-tombe*, il s'écrie, face aux Chutes Niagara : « Qu'est-ce qu'une cascade qui coule éternellement si un homme n'est pas là pour l'admirer et dire admiration ? » En fait, nous passons ici de la notion de forme signifiante à celle de forme constituante. Le langage n'est plus la seule médiation entre deux subjectivités : il est devenu création. Adam confère aux animaux qui passent devant lui leur ultime perfection d'être, en les nommant. Ainsi, le poète constitue un nouveau monde en l'exprimant. A son tour, le critique se trouve en face de l'écrit, et toute proportion gardée, dans la position du premier homme devant la chose. Ajoutons que la multiplicité, l'équivocité, l'ambiguïté des choses mesure la multiplicité, l'équivocité, l'ambiguïté de leur expression. Lisons, à titre d'épreuve, la multivalence de l'hiver telle que sentie par St-John Perse :

> Hiver, bouclé comme un bison,
> Hiver, crispé comme la mousse de crins blancs,
> Hiver, aux puits d'arsenic rouge, aux postes d'huile et de bitume !
> Hiver, au goût de skunk et de carabe et de fumée de bois de hickory.
> Hiver, aux prismes de cristaux dans les carrefours de diamant noir,
> Hiver sans thyrses ni flambeaux !
> Hiver, sans rose ni piscine !
> Hiver ! Hiver ! des pommes de cèdre ! de vieux fer ! des fruits de
> pierre ! des insectes de cuivre !
> Tant de vers blancs d'onyx et d'ongles forts, et de tambours de
> corne où vit la pieuvre du savoir !
> Hiver sans chair et sans muqueuse pour qui toute fraîcheur gît au
> corps de la femme ! ...

Il est indéniable que le critique qui essaie de comprendre, de faire comprendre cet hiver-là, ou qui veut composer son propre hiver à partir de celui de St-John Perse, ne se contente pas des seules ressources de l'intelligence. Celle-ci ne saisit et n'analyse le signifié que dans sa forme spécifique. Mais les richesses concrètes du monde et de l'écrit qui les exprime débordent les frontières de l'intelligence abstractive. Toute œuvre d'art, quelle qu'elle soit, est suggérée par une émotion sensorielle, donc à multiples dimensions, à potentialités indéterminées diversement déterminables, à exploitations indéfinies. La lecture et la création s'opèrent par une collaboration de l'esprit et des sens. Chaque mot recèle plusieurs sensations en puissance. L'opération critique est une collusion de la chair et de l'esprit. Son premier projet est de se replacer et de replacer le lecteur dans la situation créatrice de l'auteur. Et c'est pourquoi, il me semble, l'intuition est un instrument critique excellent. J'entends par là, comme Bergson l'a entendu, un effort presque douloureux de l'attention contemplative pour accomplir une descente bouleversante et difficile à l'intérieur de l'objet, afin de l'épouser profondément, afin de coïncider avec ce qu'il a d'unique et qui, à cause de cela, échappe au langage logique. Mais cette attention n'est pas affaire unique de l'esprit. Si elle est d'abord alerte de l'intelligence, elle est aussi réceptivité de cœur et vigilance des sens. Le but de l'entreprise critique n'est pas seulement, n'est plus seulement d'expliquer l'œuvre par l'expérience antérieure mais de favoriser les illuminations de l'esprit au sens où Rimbaud emploie le terme. Le critique, comme l'écrivain lui-même, doit suggérer l'indicible.

Le critique devrait-il, de toute nécessité, être doté de facultés créatrices semblables à celles du poète ? Il faudrait qu'il les possédât au moins en germe, pour être un « amateur » honnête. Mais pour être un grand explorateur, un découvreur de terres nouvelles, il doit les exercer en acte. Il doit deviner et il doit produire, faute de quoi il ne se distinguerait qu'accessoirement du simple lecteur. La difficulté du critique-lecteur se mesure par l'obligation où il est de se promener à l'intérieur d'un monde créé préalablement et parallèlement à son monde à lui. Il est obligé à des précédés dialectiques ordonnés à la clarification et à la justification de l'œuvre. On peut alors, et à peine, parler de création au second degré. Ce n'est là qu'une intuition de relations déjà existantes. Mais la légitime ambition du critique est d'être aussi « auteur. » Alors, son intuition sera créatrice. Il semble qu'il soit moins difficile au critique d'être créateur à partir d'œuvres contemporaines qu'à l'occasion d'œuvres anciennes. L'entreprise est plus ardue, quant à ces dernières, parce qu'il y faut un plus grand effort de reconstitution, une imagination plus laborieuse des circonstances, un ajustement à des conditions temporelles révolues. Bien sûr, il y a les idées et les sentiments de l'homme éternel ! Mais ne peut-on pas croire, avec Pascal, que ce qu'il y a d'intéressant dans les hommes, ce sont les différences ? Et quelle époque plus que la nôtre est différentielle ? En tout cas, nous sommes mieux sensibilisés à l'inquiétude d'aujourd'hui. Notre littérature n'est pas rassurante : sa fonction n'est d'ailleurs pas de nous donner bonne conscience, mais de nous rendre conscients.

Baudelaire affirmait que tout poète est critique. Nous pourrions, sans paradoxe, retourner cette formule et souhaiter qu'il y eût un poète dans chaque critique. Nous n'en sommes plus à la distinction classique des genres. Et il deviendra de plus en plus malaisé de répartir en catégories étanches les écrivains. Les poètes se veulent métaphysiciens, les dramaturges moralistes, les historiens savants, les critiques un peu tout cela. Sauf celles de la critique dite académique et universitaire, les investigations critiques ne se refusent plus un certain lyrisme. Elles sont de moins en moins asservies aux textes qu'elles sondent. Le dernier livre de Roland Barthes s'intitule : *Sur Racine*, ce qui — le contexte y autorise — peut s'interpréter : « à propos de ... », « en parlant de ... », « à l'occasion de ... ». Et cette manière de réfléchir à la chose littéraire est féconde, puisqu'à Racine s'ajoute Barthes, comme à Mallarmé Jean-Pierre Richard, à Sade Klossowski. ...

Comment résumer ces quelques réflexions que je vous ai soumises en vrac ? Peut-être en soulignant que le critique valable est celui qui à l'intuition qui s'installe dans les productions des autres peut ajouter l'intuition génératrice d'œuvres originales. Autrement dit, le pouvoir d'évaluer ce qui est « fait » doit coexister avec la capacité esthétique relativement à une forme nouvelle.

Je termine en citant deux écrivains, l'un fort décrié de nos jours, l'autre enseveli dans un injuste oubli. « Le bon critique, pour Anatole France, est celui qui raconte les aventures de son âme au milieu des chefs-d'œuvre. » Dans le même esprit, André Suarès déclare : « La critique d'art peut se faire du dedans par un artiste qui fait alors œuvre de son art à l'occasion de l'art et des œuvres d'autrui. »

MAURICE LEBEL

Comment les Grecs concevaient la littérature

Comment les Athéniens du ve et du IVe siècle concevaient-ils la littérature ? Comment le public, les écrivains et les philosophes considéraient-ils la chose littéraire à Athènes aux siècles de Périclès et de Démosthène ? Telle est la question à laquelle je me propose de répondre brièvement dans cette communication.

Cette question mérite d'être étudiée, car, disons-le dès le point de départ, les Athéniens de l'âge d'or ne faisaient pas du tout la même idée que nous de la littérature. Nous sommes portés aujourd'hui à voir l'ensemble de leurs productions littéraires à travers les critiques de l'époque hellénistique et des premiers siècles de l'ère chrétienne. Or, Denys d'Halicarnasse et Plutarque, Longin et Lucien, Hermogène et Dion Chrysostome n'abordent pas la littérature grecque classique comme il convient; ils la jugent en hommes de bibliothèque ou de cabinet qui lisent les textes à loisirs; ils ne songent pas à se placer au point de vue du ve et du IVe siècle qui ont vu naître de grands genres littéraires : le théâtre, l'histoire, la prose oratoire et scientifique, philosophique et morale, l'essai, le dialogue, la biographie, les mémoires, les lettres, la critique littéraire. A l'instar des critiques gréco-romaines, les hellénistes modernes étudient souvent la littérature grecque classique dans le même esprit que leurs confrères analysent, par exemple, la littérature française ou la littérature anglaise classique. Aussi leur arrive-t-il de prêter aux Grecs de jadis des idées qu'ils n'ont jamais eues. Sans doute est-il difficile de se représenter exactement le milieu athénien du ve et du IVe siècle et de juger les œuvres littéraires à la lumière de ce milieu. Mais, sans nous laisser influencer par le pessimisme un peu facile et désabusé d'Anatole France qui a écrit :

HAB no. 33, April 1961.

« J'ai détourné mes yeux du spectacle du monde antique après avoir senti jusqu'au malaise l'impossibilité de bien me figurer les anciennes formes de la vie », essayons de voir un instant comment les choses se sont passées au moment le plus glorieux de l'histoire littéraire d'Athènes.

Commençons par Athènes elle-même, le foyer par excellence de la littérature grecque classique. Du temps de Périclès et de Démosthène, elle ressemble fort à une sous-préfecture, ne comptant guère plus de 30 000 citoyens; sa population totale : esclaves, métèques, étrangers, femmes, enfants, citoyens, ne dépassa jamais 250 000 âmes au ve et au IVe siècle. Périclès, Euripide, Thucydide appellent déjà Athènes « l'Ecole de la Grèce », et Isocrate, qui a défini le premier la culture de l'esprit autant dans l'*Echange* que dans le *Panégyrique* affirme qu'on est Grec beaucoup plus par la culture que par le sang ou la race. N'empêche qu'Athènes fait alors penser à une ville de province, à l'horizon un peu étroit. Plusieurs de ses grands esprits, comme Socrate et Sophocle, Aristophane et Isocrate, ne quittent guère souvent la capitale. On me dira que de nombreux étrangers, et non des moindres, comme les sophistes et les philosophes, aiment y demeurer, car il vaut mieux vivre pauvre à Athènes que riche à l'étranger; la liberté de parole y est si répandue et acceptée ! Mais, malgré l'apport des étrangers et la libre discussion des idées, le monde athénien est relativement limité et conventionnel. Il ne saurait y être question de littérature étrangère, encore moins de langue étrangère ou de langue seconde. Rares sont les livres, bien qu'il y ait des libraires du temps d'Aristophane et que les scribes travaillent ferme sur l'agora non seulement pour alimenter la clientèle athénienne, puis les princes et les tyrans, mais aussi pour faire le commerce du livre notamment avec la Grande-Grèce, l'Asie Mineure et le Pont-Euxin. Quelques écrivains, comme Aristophane et Euripide, Isocrate et Aristote, possèdent une bibliothèque personnelle. Mail il n'existe pas encore de bibliothèques publiques, et très rares sont les citoyens qui peuvent se vanter d'avoir une bibliothèque privée.

La culture est limitée et concentrée. Les écrivains possèdent une connaissance directe et approfondie de leur milieu. Ce qu'ils voient, ils le voient avec beaucoup de clarté et de précision. Ce qu'ils perdent en variété et en étendue, ils le gagnent en concentration. Comme le passé est loin d'être lourd pour eux et que les conflits de civilisation ne les préoccupent guère, ils gardent l'esprit ouvert, et leur attention n'est pas partagée ou divisée. Ils sont connus du public au milieu duquel ils vivent et pour lequel ils écrivent. Ils sont même très près du peuple. Ils n'écrivent pas pour être lus mais pour être entendus. Le public auquel ils s'adressent est avide de savoir, curieux d'esprit et pourvu d'une excellente mémoire; Aristophane lui rappelle des vers cités vingt ans plus tôt. Il est cultivé non pas tant par les livres qu'il lit que par ce qu'il entend au théâtre, aux concours, aux lectures et aux récitations publiques, aux grandes fêtes nationales, dans les cours de justice et les assemblées, sur l'agora, dans les jardins de l'Académie et les promenades du Lycée. De sorte que la littérature grecque classique est une littérature de soleil et de plein air, de place publique et de conversation; de là les innombrables répétitions de mots et de tournures, l'emploi constant de particules et de démonstratifs qui tiennent lieu d'intonations et de gestes, le foisonnement d'expressions familières dans les chefs d'œuvre de la littérature grecque. Aussi la littérature grecque classique est-elle beaucoup plus près du peuple et beaucoup mieux comprise du peuple que ne peut l'être, par exemple, la littérature française classique, qui est avant tout aristocratique, le ton général y étant celui de gens de salon fort cultivés qui parlent comme des livres et dont la langue est une merveille de souplesse, de clarté et de pureté. En un mot, la littérature grecque classique est surtout orale, faite pour être entendue, récitée, chantée, tant il est vrai qu'un Grec ne peut écrire sans se représenter l'auditoire auquel il s'adresse.

Eschyle, Sophocle et Euripide ont composé plus de 300 drames, dont une trentaine seulement sont parvenus jusqu'à nous. Il ne nous reste que le quart des comédies qu'Aristophane a écrites. Des autres auteurs tragiques et comiques, nous avons seulement des fragments. Et pendant deux siècles le peuple athénien aime tellement le théâtre qu'il fait servir presque tous les revenus de la Cité à la caisse du théorique; il ira même un jour jusqu'à sacrifier la sécurité de l'Etat aux plaisirs du théâtre. Aujourd'hui encore, au festival d'Epidaure, on représenta *Le Dyskolos* de Ménandre, découvert en 1957 par Victor Martin, et, pour la première fois aussi, cet été, en 1960, au festival de Dodone, plus de 8 000 Grecs venus des îles et du continent, assistèrent, deux jours durant, comme à une messe, au spectacle d'*Electre*, des *Choéphores* et des *Euménides*. Hérodote lisait en public à Athènes et dans les principales villes de Grèce de larges fragments de ses *Histoires*, où l'historien des Guerres Médiques prend souvent plaisir à bavarder. Si Thucydide a jugé bon d'insérer tant de discours dans son *Histoire de la Guerre du Péloponèse,* — ils sont si nombreux et si importants qu'ils constituent la moelle de son histoire, — c'est que la parole jouait alors un rôle décisif dans la vie publique athénienne. Platon n'écrit pas de livres mais compose des dialogues qui ressemblent souvent à des conversations familières; il parodie les sophistes qui ont créé la prose d'art à Athènes, comme il se moque, dans *Le Ménéxène,* de la manie qu'avaient les Athéniens d'entendre les oraisons funèbres. Isocrate, la Fontenelle de la littérature grecque, qui a tenu école pendant 70 ans et été le professeur de rhétorique des orateurs du IVe siècle, a voulu rendre la prose aussi musicale que la poésie; cette prose, tard venue, est arrivée à son plus haut sommet de perfection en cent ans, de 430 à 330; c'est une prose sans école, pour ainsi dire, sans prédécesseurs et sans successeurs. Socrate n'écrivit jamais de livre — tout au plus mit-il en vers quelques fables ou histoires d'animaux d'Esope —, préférant la parole au stylet, le théâtre à l'assemblée, la ville à la campagne. Xénophon, son disciple, bavarde interminablement dans ses écrits. Il émane donc de la plupart des textes grecs une impression de vie. C'est que les citoyens grecs de jadis consacraient de longues heures à la conversation, et leurs écrits nous ont conservé une parole encore chaude et vivante, un style direct et animé, plein de fraîcheur et de jeunesse.

La poésie, beaucoup plus vieille et plus vénérable que la prose, puisqu'elle remonte à Homère, était faite aussi pour être entendue, récitée ou chantée, presque toujours accompagnée d'un instrument de musique (la lyre, la cithare, la flûte), dont l'air était toujours subordonné au texte. Les poèmes d'Homère, que ceux-ci aient été établis à Athènes par Solon, ou par Pisistrate, ou par son fils Hipparque, étaient déjà connus dans une vulgate populaire en Attique dès le VIIe siècle. Ils étaient d'ordinaire récités au festival des Panathénées. Ainsi Ion d'Ephèse, contemporain de Socrate, récita Homère un jour devant plus de 20 000 Athéniens aux Panathénées. Homère fut pendant plus de mille ans l'éducateur de la Grèce; même après l'avènement de saint Paul et des *Evangiles,* on continue d'enseigner Homère dans les nombreuses écoles de quartier d'Athènes. C'est lui qui fut le principal éducateur du peuple athénien. Platon, dans les deux *Hippias,* par exemple, ou dans *Ion,* nous fait assister à des débats sur les mérites respectifs de l'*Iliade* et de l'*Odysée* ou sur l'inspiration et le talent des rhapsodes, voire sur l'origine de la poésie et la création poétique. Il lui arrive, il est vrai, de chasser Homère de sa *République* idéale, mais c'est seulement au xe livre qu'il le fait, à contre-cœur, les larmes aux yeux, après l'avoir cité et commenté d'un bout à l'autre de son œuvre. Si le divin philosophe le met dehors de sa *République*, c'est pour des raisons de morale, car, à l'instar de Xénophane, d'Héraclite et de Pythagore, il ne peut tolérer la mythologie immorale d'Homère; mais il reconnaît le génie du grand poète épique. Poète à ses heures lui-même, Platon adore Homère. A vrai dire, les Grecs vénéraient tous Homère, qui leur tenait lieu de *Bible* ou de sainte écriture.

Homère est le point de départ, le fondement, le noyau de la littérature grecque. Il est le père et de la poésie et de la prose grecque; en dépit des efforts systématiques de plusieurs philosophes et de plusieurs orateurs pour le détrôner, il a façonné l'esprit et l'âme, l'imagination et la sensibilité des Grecs pendant des siècles. Les Grecs trouvèrent dans l'*Iliade* et l'*Odyssé* de grands tableaux de la vie humaine. Ils le considéraient même comme leur père commun; divisés ou séparés par les dialectes et la rivalité entre les villes, l'amour passionné de l'indépendance et le culte exagéré de la cité aux dépens de la nation et de l'Etat, les Grecs regardaient Homère, cependant, comme une sorte de lien entre les générations successives, comme l'un des principaux éléments de l'unité de la nation. Pour eux aussi le poète est l'éducateur de son peuple, et Homère était un illustre exemple de cette conception générale. La théorie moderne de l'art pour l'art, comme celle de la poésie pure, ne peut s'appliquer à la poésie grecque de la période classique. La distinction entre l'esthétique et l'éthique est assez tardive dans la littérature grecque; ce sont en fait les premiers chrétiens qui enseignèrent aux hommes à apprécier la poésie d'un point de vue purement formel ou esthétique, ce qui leur permit de répéter la majeure partie de l'enseignement moral et religieux des poètes classiques comme étant faux et indigne de Dieu, tout en reconnaissant la valeur de la composition et du style au point de vue scolaire et esthétique. Les sophistes, il est vrai, considéraient les épopées comme une encyclopédie de l'art et du savoir, et Platon lui-même soutenait que la valeur de la poésie homérique était sensiblement amoindrie si l'on arrivait à prouver qu'elle ne disait pas la vérité. Mais il ne reste pas moins vrai qu'Homère, comme tous les grands poètes grecs, est beaucoup plus qu'une figure dans la parade de l'histoire littéraire. Il est le premier et le plus grand créateur et artisan de la vie grecque et du caractère grec. Les poètes tragiques occupent le second rang à cet égard.

Mais dans les nombreuses écoles de quartier d'Athènes et de l'Attique, ce ne sont pas seulement les poèmes homériques que les enfants lisent, apprennent par cœur et récitent; ils s'accompagnent aussi de la lyre en étudiant la poésie et en chantant; ils apprennent à chanter en choeur des hymnes patriotiques et divins qu'ils auront un jour à exécuter publiquement aux fêtes. En plus d'Homère, des hymnes homériques et des poèmes cycliques, qui servent d'inspiration aux poètes tragiques, les enfants étudient Hésiode et Théognis, sans parler des fables d'Esope, des histoires d'animaux, des anecdotes morales truffées de maximes. C'est seulement à la fin du ve siècle et au IVe siècle que les livres scolaires de prose, comme l'archéologie de Thucydide ou le début du premier livre de son *Histoire*, des fragments d'Hérodote, des pages choisies d'Isocrate et de Démosthène, font leur apparition dans l'éducation athénienne. Jusque là l'enseignement était exclusivement fondé sur l'étude de la poésie épique et lyrique; de sorte que les grands prosateurs grecs, d'Hérodote à Démosthène, ont appris à écrire en prose à l'école d'Homère, des poètes lyriques et des poètes tragiques. La récitation de la poésie s'accompagnait de la lyre ou de la flûte. Loin d'être solitaire, elle était plutôt collective et publique. A l'école, dans les banquets, sur les places publiques, on entendait réciter ou chanter, toujours aux sons d'un instrument à cordes, les poèmes de Mimnerme, de Phocylide, d'Archiloque, de Pindare, de Bacchylide et de Simonide qui étaient très populaires à Athènes, dans les villes de Grèce et à la cour des tyrans.

Hélas! il ne nous reste que des fragments de l'immense production de la poésie lyrique, qui fut très populaire de 750 à 450. Elle s'éteint vers 450 avec la mort de Pindare et de Bacchylide; ou plus exactement elle fleurit encore principalement dans les chœurs des tragédies; elle est loin d'avoir perdu sa popularité, comme on le voit dans les dialogues de Platon et dans les discours des orateurs, où les citations des poèmes lyriques sont nombreuses. Mais à mesure qu'Athènes crée son propre théâtre et fait représenter des centaines et des centaines de pièces dont il ne nous reste seulement que des fragments, la poésie tragique est tout ensemble appréciée du public et introduite dans l'enseignement, ne serait-ce que pour faire contrepoids à l'influence d'Homère. Ainsi, vers 430, du temps d'Aristophane, on étudie Eschyle dans les écoles de quartier, Eschyle qui est si près d'Homère, car lui-même a appelé ses drames « des tranches empruntées aux grands banquets d'Homère. » Plus tard, au IVe siècle surtout, qui est le siècle des grands acteurs plutôt que celui des grands tragiques, on étudiera Sophocle et Euripide, toujours pour faire contrepoids à l'influence d'Homère. Fait singulier, Archiloque, Sophocle et Hérodote sont appelés tous les trois les plus « homériques » par les critiques d'Alexandrie et de Rome. C'est qu'Homère est le professeur de la Grèce, le maître incontesté de la haute culture grecque, de la poésie élégiaque, de la poésie didactique, de la tragédie, de l'histoire et de la prose oratoire.

Superbement doués d'imagination et de mémoire, les Athéniens, comme les Béotiens, ressentaient vivement la musique des vers comme celle de la prose. L'air des écoles était, pour ainsi dire, saturé de poésie. Les illetrés étaient rares parmi eux. Ils aimaient le beau, où qu'il fût, en prose ou en vers, au théâtre ou dans les oraisons funèbres, sur la Pnyx ou au tribunal, dans les concours ou aux fêtes. Ils étaient même portés à confondre le beau et le bien, le beau sensible et le beau moral. Ils étaient nourris de poésie et d'art; grâce aux nombreux loisirs qu'ils pouvaient se donner, ils poursuivaient leur culture à volonté et en profondeur, de sorte que, même au Ve siècle, bien avant Philippe et Alexandre, de nombreux Macédoniens se mettent à l'Ecole d'Athènes et apprennent déjà l'attitude.

Mais les philosophes, désireux de protester contre la montée au pouvoir d'hommes nouveaux, d'esthètes dénués de garanties morales, s'élevèrent contre les appâts de la poésie, de l'art et d'Homère, qu'ils rendaient responsables du fléchissement de la morale. Les orateurs, eux, convaincus de l'importance de la parole dans la vie civile et politique, croyaient dur comme fer que le salut était dans l'éloquence. Les philosophes prétendaient être les vrais orateurs; les rhéteurs prétendaient être vrais philosophes. Isocrate et Platon font bande à part, chacun croyant avoir la vérité pour soi set désirant former les jeunes à la vie de citoyen utile. Mais les deux groupes sant unis sur un point: ils font la guerre à la poésie et veulent détrôner le vieil Homère. La prose d'art d'Isocrate vise à remplacer la poésie; la philosophie, qui gagne beaucoup de terrain, veut diriger les âmes au lieu de la mythologie immorale d'Homère. Vers 330, du temps d'Aristote et du discours *Pour la Courronne*, la poésie est réduite à un rôle plus modeste et paraît même moins dangereuse qu'au ve siècle. La prose, l'emportant sur la poésie dans la littérature du ive siècle, tend naturellement à lui disputer aussi le rôle d'éducatrice. Quand Aristote écrit sa *Poétique*, où il est surtout question de la tragédie et de l'épopée, car Aristote n'y parle ni d'Eschyle, ni de poésie lyrique, ni de musique, et il n'aime guère Aristophane; quand Aristote écrit sa *Rhétorique*, où il est surtout question de l'éloquence, de la psychologie et du style; quand il écrit ces deux chefs d'œuvre, l'histoire littéraire se trouve alors réduite à trois grands genres: la poésie épique, la poésie tragique et la prose oratoire, trois genres où les Grecs ont excellé et qui concernent l'art de raconter, de représenter et de persuader. En procédant ainsi, Aristote avait suivi l'exemple de son maître Platon qui avait, trente ans plus tôt, beaucoup réfléchi sur la tragédie, l'épopée et la prose, par exemple dans *Ion, Hippias, Phèdre, Georgias* et la *République*.

La prose grecque, historique, oratoire et philosophique, arrivée tardivement par rapport à la poésie, est devenue une prose d'art en un siècle, de 430 à 330. Elle est extrêmement lucide et précise, nue, simple, directe, concise, compacte; elle charme cependant parce qu'elle est fondée sur le réel et sur l'homme; elle nous plonge dans un bain de réel, elle fait appel à la raison. Quelle consolation de l'aborder après avoir lu un journal d'aujourd'hui! Elle est vivante: elle pose des problèmes fondamentaux et reste toujours en contact avec la vie, elle fait sans cesse la critique de la vie. C'est une prose de plein air, écrite par des gens qui fréquentent le théâtre, l'agora, les banquets, la société. Elle est née du milieu et du tempérament du peuple. Sans modèle, elle est restée aussi sans successeurs véritables.

Par contraste, la poésie, elle, avait la force de la tradition, du précédent, de la convention. Homère a ouvert la voie. Ses successeurs l'ont imité ou s'en sont inspirés. Ils ont écrit des vers, du viiie au ive siècle, pour être récités, chantés, représentés, entendus. Ils ont écrit pour le peuple, pour le grand nombre, pour une fête publique, pour une assemblée populaire, pour un immense théâtre, pour un cercle de connaissances et d'amis. Ils n'ont pas écrit de vers pour eux-mêmes. Ils ne forment pas une clique ou une académie. La poésie appartenait à la société. C'est là qu'elle avait pris naissance, et elle faisait corps avec la société. Elle occupait une place honorable dans cette société. La critique littéraire se faisait en public, au théâtre;

Euripide et Aristophane passent en revue la production dramatique de leur temps. De là aucune nécessité de s'expliquer ou de s'excuser. La confiance du poète et la puissance de son expression découlent précisément de ce rapport étroit qui existait entre le public et le poète. Il n'existe point de fossé, de barricade, entre le public et les écrivains. Socrate assiste aux *Nuées*, Cléon, aux *Chevaliers*. Sans doute tous ne sont-ils pas toujours d'accord. Mais on ne relève pas d'appréhension ou d'hostilité de part et d'autre. Ils sont acceptés; ils font corps avec la cité, dont ils sont considérés comme les éducateurs.

Avant le ve siècle, la littérature grecque est surtout insulaire, coloniale, étrangère; elle comprend principalement la poésie épique et la poésie lyrique. A partir du ve siècle et au IVe siècle, elle est principalement athénienne; elle comprend surtout le théâtre, l'histoire, l'éloquence, la philosophie, le dialogue, l'essai, la biographie, les mémoires, les lettres, la prose scientifique et morale. Les ouvrages de prose s'adressent à des lecteurs, et les auteurs de ces ouvrages s'appellent écrivains, *syngrapheis*. Alcimadas a même écrit un opuscule violent contre les *logon poietai*, c'est-à-dire contre ceux qui faisaient de l'éloquence écrite à la manière d'Isocrate, dont la voix était trop faible pour parler en public. D'autre part, les Grecs ne disaient pas, comme nous, poète épique, poète tragique, mais auteur de vers épiques, *epon poietes*, auteur de vers tragiques, *tragogion poietes*. Le verbe *legein* signifie écrire en prose, tandis que *poiein* signifie dire en vers, faire des vers, tourner des vers, écrire en vers. L'usage de donner à *poiein* le sens particulier de faire des vers remonte aux débuts de la prose grecque. Pour Hérodote, le mot *poietes* comporte l'idée d'auteur de prose et de poésie familière. Pour le public et pour les philosophes, la poésie n'est pas une création mais une imitation. Et les œuvres poétiques, comme celles de Pindare, des tragiques et des comiques, étaient composées par des compositeurs, *poietai*, pour être exécutées publiquement par des acteurs, des chanteurs, des danseurs, des musiciens. Tant en prose qu'en poésie, on ne perd jamais de vue en Grèce l'auditoire auquel on s'adresse.

En résume, la littérature grecque classique, malgré l'artifice de la composition, malgré les répétitions et les formules qu'elle renferme, malgré l'absence de spontanéité de la langue, donne une impression de vie et de contact avec la vie, de conversation familière et de lecture publique, d'intonations nuancées et de style parlé.

JOHN M. ROBSON

Mill and Arnold: Liberty and Culture— Friends or Enemies?

Although John Stuart Mill is frequently praised for his clarity and precision, he often complained about misinterpretation. In one letter expressing puzzlement over a charge against him, he comments: "It is like Matthew Arnold enumerating me among the enemies of culture."[1] The date of the letter (November 4, 1867), suggests that he is referring to *Culture and Anarchy*, and it seems obvious that Arnold's bombardment of the Philistines was aimed at least partly at Mill, and more particularly at *On Liberty*.[2] While Arnold's main purpose was not, of course, to attack *On Liberty*, still the differences between the two works appear to be much more striking than the similarities. But what leads to the making of comparisons at all? One derogatory phrase, "doing as one likes," seems clearly enough a reference to *On Liberty*; some passages, notably that attacking "Our Liberal Practitioners," seem at least obliquely relevant; a few specific matters are treated in both;[3] and there is one direct reference, at the end of a passage taken into *Culture and Anarchy* from "Culture and Its Enemies," Arnold's valedictory as Professor of Poetry at Oxford:

> after hearing Bentham cried loudly up as the renovator of modern society, and Bentham's mind and ideas proposed as the rulers of our future, I open the *Deontology*. There I read: "While Xenophon was writing his history and Euclid teaching geometry, Socrates and Plato were talking nonsense under pretence of talking wisdom and morality. This morality of theirs consisted in words; this wisdom of theirs was the denial of matters known

HAB vol. XXXIV (XII), no. 1, fall 1961. From an address to the annual meeting of the Association of Canadian University Teachers of English, 1961. The author has made some revisions and added notes for this reprinting.

to every man's experience." From the moment of reading that, I am delivered from the bondage of Bentham! the fanaticism of his adherents can touch me no longer; I feel the inadequacy of his mind and ideas for supplying the rule of human society, for perfection.

Culture tends always thus to deal with the men of a system, of disciples, of a school; with men like Comte, or the late Mr. Buckle, or Mr. Mill.[4]

One's sympathies must here be with Mill who, although a *quondam* disciple of Bentham, ally of Comte, and friend of Buckle, had been asserting and proving his independence of systems and schools for over thirty years.[5] In fact, nearly thirty years earlier Mill had written:

In almost the only passage of the "Deontology" which, from its style, and from its having before appeared in print, may be known to be Bentham's, Socrates, and Plato are spoken of in terms distressing to his greatest admirers; and the incapacity to appreciate such men, is a fact perfectly in unison with the general habits of Bentham's mind.[6]

It is not surprising that both selected the same passage for condemnation; it is surprising only that Arnold should have here linked Mill with Bentham.

The question that must arise is: How well did Arnold know Mill's writings? Mill is mentioned some twenty times by Arnold, but only in one passage (in "Marcus Aurelius") does he attempt specifically to deal with one of Mill's ideas.[7] Of the few references to *On Liberty*, one is worth quoting; Arnold recommends the work to his sister as "worth reading attentively, being one of the few books that inculcate tolerance in an unalarming and inoffensive way."[8] Most of the remarks are derogatory, and show little acquaintance with Mill's work or position. As the two men seem not to have met or corresponded, one must conclude that Arnold's opinion, at least until he read the *Autobiography*,[9] was based on the common misconceptions of Mill's mature attitudes.

Seen in this light, Arnold's misconception is easily explained. Known early as an intellectual prodigy and as heir to the Philosophical Radicals of the 1820's, Mill cemented his reputation by the *System of Logic* (1843) and the *Principles of Political Economy* (1848), which, to those who did not read them, seemed but the inevitable fruits of his training. Even readers of *On Liberty* (1859) would see little reason to dissociate him from his early teachers. Mill's own account of activities and mental processes of course colours our view;

from about 1828 on, as he tells us in the *Autobiography,* he had been cutting himself off from sects and parties, and exhibiting his independence in such newspapers as the *Examiner,* and such periodicals as the *Monthly Repository, Tait's Edinburgh Magazine,* and his own *London Review.* But these had a relatively small circulation, and could do little to remould the hard image already accepted by the public. The first two volumes of *Dissertations and Discussions* (1859) made some of these essays more widely available, but appear to have had little effect. He formed no new associations which would clarify his altered allegiance until the 1860's, when he began to attract a band of young disciples, such as Morley, Amberley, and Thornton, and they had little influence till after his death. Even his brief career in the House of Commons helped little, for his election campaigns caused more comment than his speeches.[10] Amongst the working classes his views had a broader circulation,[11] but not one that would make for a better understanding of him by the articulate and influential public. He was known by most as an advanced liberal, or a radical, in the tradition of his teachers, until his posthumous works, the *Autobiography,* the *Three Essays on Religion,* and the incomplete *Chapters on Socialism* clearly revealed the changes in scope and method which mark him off from his early allies. It should also be remembered that he was a semi-recluse from the early 1830's until 1858, and thereafter lived nearly half of each year in Avignon. To all these difficulties must be added the confusion which always characterizes public responses to unpopular opinions such as those advocated so strongly by Mill in his later years. All in all, it is a tribute to Mill's clarity that he was understood as well as he was by those who did not know him or his writings intimately.

It would never do, of course, to see Matthew Arnold's opinions as those of the public. But where would his attitudes towards Mill find origin? Being sixteen years younger, he grew up in a different social and political milieu, as well as under different social and political influences. When comparing them, I think of Mill's comparison of Bentham and Coleridge (separated in age by twenty-four years), as being without and within the tradition of received opinions. In modern jargon, Mill was born and raised outside the "Establishment," Arnold within it. The more important implications of this difference will appear later; here I wish merely to note that the continued assault by the Philosophical Radicals and by Mill upon the Establishment provoked a defence of which Arnold was more aware than he was of the grounds for the attack.

The contrast can perhaps be most easily seen in their fathers: each, in the interest of general utility, conducting an educational *experimentum crucis*; the one humane, the other inhuman; the one creating a community, the other an eccentric; the one working amongst the Barbarians, the other amongst the Philistines. Or the contrast can be seen in their secretarial duties: John Mill was one of Bentham's amanuenses; Matthew Arnold, secretary to Lord Lansdowne. One interesting result of these differences can be seen in their attitudes towards the Universities. Arnold's poignant response to Oxford is well expressed in *Culture and Anarchy*; Mill's forthright attack, especially against Cambridge, is less well known. One quotation must suffice:

> Since the time when the English philosophers gave the law to Europe, England has maintained and added to every other superiority which she possessed. She has advanced immeasurably in Wealth, still more immeasurably in power; civilization has spread to the remotest corner of her territory; the manners of her people have been humanized, their tastes refined; they have outstripped all nations in what most distinguishes a civilized people from barbarians, the power of co-operating for a common object; in the diffusion of reading, of philanthropy, of interest in public affairs, no other people in the Old World can be compared with them. While all these changes have been taking place for the better, in the minds and condition of those whom our two great endowed seminaries do *not* educate, there must be some grievous defect in the training of the classes whom these establishments do educate, to account for the low state of all higher pursuits; of the pursuits which the very existence of universities is but a means to the cultivation of—and in which it is the duty of such establishments to send forth their pupils qualified, some to extend the bounds of knowledge itself, and all to enter into its spirit, and turn it to account for the purposes of life.[12]

Shades of Roebuck and the improvement of the breed! But the passage, written in 1835, was deleted by Mill when in 1859 he reprinted the article on Sedgwick in which it occurs.[13] The university reforms had begun to work: new faces, new ideas, new disciplines were arriving, and in 1863 Mill was able to recommend Oxford, Balliol, and Jowett, although he felt it necessary to add: "Twenty years ago these [universities] were about the last places which I should have recommended . . .; but they are now much changed, and free inquiry and speculation on the deepest and highest questions, instead of being crushed or deadened, are now more rife there than almost anywhere else in England."[14] In other words, the traditional was becoming better by becoming less traditional.

Of course there were more similar than dissimilar elements in the experience of Mill and Arnold; one might cite their common acceptance of Carlyle, Goethe, Wordsworth, and Coleridge as teachers;[15] their common depreciation of intensive moral self-analysis, resulting in each case from torturing doubt;[16] or their common recognition of the essential difference between merely perceiving and actually feeling.[17] Romanticism caught them young, and they seriously tried to swallow life—but they also tried to swallow it whole. Turning from self, they looked for the greater social salvation. Here the comparison really begins: they both saw England as ill, and they both offered remedies. Not Morrison's Pills, but regimens demanding high seriousness and cold cultural baths. What was the Condition of England?

> In the intellectual pursuits which form great minds, this country was formerly pre-eminent. England once stood at the head of European philosophy. Where stands she now? Consult the general opinion of Europe. The celebrity of England, in the present day, rests upon her docks, her canals, her railroads. In intellect, she is distinguished only for a kind of sober good sense, free from extravagance, but also void of lofty aspirations; and for doing all those things which are best done where man most resembles a machine, with the precision of a machine. Valuable qualities, doubtless; but not precisely those by which man raises himself to the perfection of his nature, or achieves greater and greater conquests over the difficulties which encumber his social arrangements. Ask any reflecting person in France or Germany his opinion of England; whatever may be his own tenets—however friendly his disposition to us—whatever his admiration of our institutions and even his desire to introduce them into his native country; however alive to the faults and errors of his own countrymen, the feature which always strikes him in the English mind is the absence of enlarged and commanding views. Every question he finds discussed and decided on its own basis, however narrow, without any light thrown upon it from principles more extensive than itself; and no question discussed at all, unless parliament, or some constituted authority, is to be moved to-morrow or the day after to put it to the vote. Instead of the ardour of research, the eagerness for large and comprehensive inquiry, of the educated part of the French and German youth, what find we? Out of the narrow bounds of mathematical and physical science, not a vestige of a

reading and thinking public engaged in the investigation of truth *as* truth, in the prosecution of thought for the sake of thought. Among no class except sectarian religionists—and what they are we all know—is there any interest in the great problem of man's nature and life: among no class whatever is there any curiosity respecting the nature and principles of human society, the history or the philosophy of civilization; nor any belief that, from such inquiries, a single important practical consequence can follow. Guizot, the greatest admirer of England among the Continental philosophers, nevertheless remarks that, in England, even great events do not, as they do every where else, inspire great ideas. Things, in England, are greater than the men who accomplish them.[18]

Many of the ideas and phrases are recognizably Arnoldian, being echoed, for example, in "The Function of Criticism at the Present Time," and in *Culture and Anarchy*,[19] but they originated from Mill's pen in 1835, two years before Arnold entered Rugby. Here are demands for disinterestedness, curiosity, and comprehensiveness; here is the appeal to the Continent, especially France; here is the attack on machinery, and on sectarian religionists ("what they are we all know").

His attack on the "Hebraists" continued throughout his life. Like Arnold, he anticipates R. H. Tawney in linking capitalism and religion, arguing that the British disregard of the arts

may be traced to the two influences which have chiefly shaped the British character since the days of the Stuarts: commercial money-getting business, and religious Puritanism. Business, demanding the whole of the faculties, and whether pursued from duty or the love of gain, regarding as a loss of time whatever does not conduce directly to the end; Puritanism, which looking upon every feeling of human nature, except fear and reverence for God, as a snare, if not as partaking of sin, looked coldly, if not disapprovingly, on the cultivation of the sentiments.[20]

Even in the supposed textbook of the Philistines, *The Principles of Political Economy*, Mill argues that the tendencies towards accumulation of capital in England have "been greatly aided by that extreme incapacity of the people for personal enjoyment, which is a characteristic of countries over which puritanism has passed." (II, 171; I, xi, 4.) A passage from *On Liberty* is even closer to Arnold's view:

There is a different type of human excellence from the Calvinistic: a conception of humanity as having its nature bestowed on it for other purposes than merely to be abnegated. "Pagan self-assertion" is one of the elements of human worth, as well as "Christian self-denial." There is a Greek ideal of self-development, which the Platonic and Christian ideal of self-government blends with, but does not supersede. It may be better to be a John Knox than an Alcibiades, but it is better to be a Pericles than either; nor would a Pericles, if we had one in these days, be without anything good which belonged to John Knox. (120)

Arnold, recognizing Mill's antipathy for the Hebraists, goes so far as to label "the somewhat degenerated and inadequate form of Hellenism" as "Millism." (Later he retracted most of the pejorative connotations.[21]) Clearly, for both, the prevailing spirit of the nation lacked balance.

The time was out of joint in other ways as well; the *Zeitgeist* (the "Spirit of the Age" for Mill) in stirring men made seemingly impossible demands:

My dearest Clough these are damned times—everything is against one—the height to which knowledge is come, the spread of luxury, our physical enervation, the absence of great *natures,* the unavoidable contact with millions of small ones, newspapers, cities, light profligate friends, moral desperadoes like Carlyle, our own selves, and the sickening consciousness of our difficulties: but for God's sake let us neither be fanatics nor yet chaff blown by the wind. . . .[22]

Thus spake Arnold; while Mill, some years earlier, writing to the "moral desperado," laments the deaths of all the great men of the age, adding:

It is curious that this particular time, in which there are fewer great intellects above ground and in their vigour, than can be remembered for many ages back, should be the precise time at which every body is cackling about the progress of intelligence and the spread of knowledge. I do believe that intelligence and knowledge are less valued just now, except for purposes of money-making, than at any other period since the Norman Conquest, or possibly since the invasion of the Romans. I mean, in our own country.[23]

In such an era, both felt, prose was the best instrument for making poetic truth available to the country. Seeing "how deeply *unpoetical* the age" was,[24] Arnold turned to social, educational, and religious, as well as literary criticism; Mill, similarly arraigning the age, explained at length to Carlyle the need for "logical" rather than "artistic" exposition of truths.[25] But the age would not last for ever; new and better times were coming.

One of the most significant similarities between Mill and Arnold is seen in their belief that theirs was an "Age of Transition." Both felt themselves "caught between two worlds," a past age of calm, order, and unity, and a coming age when again men could rest, obey, and agree. Mill, borrowing his terms from the Saint-Simonians and Carlyle, usually talks of alternate "organic" and "critical" periods; Arnold talks of "epochs of concentration and expansion." The critical period, the epoch of expansion, is one in which questioning, analysis, scepticism, and social turbulence mark the labour pains of a new social organism. Both Mill and Arnold saw themselves as midwives assisting the cumbrous labour of the nineteenth century.

As such they were co-operating with the course of historical change; neither passively attending it, nor frantically opposing it. They were both liberals, but liberals of the future, in Arnold's phrase.[26] So they opposed dogmatism, the dogmatism of allies as well as of enemies. Kathleen Tillotson, in quoting Arnold's remark, "But this is not what we want," calls it "a key to so much of Arnold's criticism," and I would only add, to so much of Mill's, too.[27] For example, in *On Liberty*, he says: "Even progress, which ought to superadd, for the most part only substitutes, one partial and incomplete truth for another; improvement consisting chiefly in this, that the new fragment of truth is more wanted, more adapted to the needs of the time, than that which it displaces." (105–6) To vary my method, I quote a Millian passage from Arnold:

> To try and approach truth on one side after another, not to strive or cry, nor to persist in pressing forward, on any one side, with violence and self-will,—it is only thus, it seems to me, that mortals may hope to gain any vision of the mysterious Goddess, whom we shall never see except in outline, but only thus even in outline.[28]

Here lies the explanation of Arnold's attacks upon "Our Liberal Practitioners," on Colenso, and part of the explanation for his criticism of Gladstone. ("Mr. Gladstone's powers of self-deception are so inexhaustible that he is never insincere."[29]) Offering a word in season, seeing himself as a corrective influence, always wanting the generally good to be particularly good, Arnold offended his allies. "Aliens" are never popular, especially when they examine the oaths of citizenship. Here his similarity in strategy to Mill is most striking: both were sheepdogs to the Liberal flock; no sooner were they convinced that right would triumph than they ran yelping and biting to ensure that the right remained right. Mill describes his practice in the House of Commons thus:

> the idea I proceeded on was that when anything was likely to be as well done, or sufficiently well done, by other people, there was no necessity for me to meddle with it. As I, therefore, in general reserved myself for work which no others were likely to do, a great proportion of my appearances were on points on which the bulk of the Liberal party, even the advanced portion of it, either were of different opinion from mine, or were comparatively indifferent. Several of my speeches . . . were opposed to what then was, and probably still is, regarded as the advanced Liberal opinion. . . . [T]he use of my being in Parliament was to do work which others were not able or not willing to do. . . .[30]

It should be noted, too, that *On Liberty* was regarded as too authoritarian by such advanced Liberals (or Radicals) as Grote and Spencer. One need not go their length, however, to notice the limitations on action justified by Mill in Chapter III, or to see that that chapter is entitled, "Of Individuality, as *One* of the Elements of Well-Being." (My italics.) Similarly worthy of comment is his mentioning among opinions which contain part of the truth, those favourable to discipline as well as to its antagonist, liberty. (107) Like Arnold, he held with Burke's doctrine, "circumstances alter cases," and suited his message to his times.

What truths and what criticisms were most needed in the late 1860's, when Arnold wrote the papers which became *Culture and Anarchy*? The demand for electoral reform, frustrated in the 1850's, and again in 1866, reached a peak reminiscent of, if not equal to, the agitation in the 1830's and 1840's, and for many of the propertied and established classes signalled revolution. For some a revolution by law was the only solution; others, including Carlyle, saw such a legalized revolution as a subversion of all law. But everyone recognized the struggle as one for social equality, and not merely for political democracy. As both Arnold and Mill championed social equality, their different attitudes towards the Condition of England at this time provide an excellent test of their social philosophies.

Some Conservatives, including Disraeli, held Mill partly responsible for the unrest surrounding the Hyde Park riot of July 23, 1866, the riot so roundly condemned by Arnold. Mill, on the contrary, thought that his efforts were alone decisive in preventing the riot from becoming a revolution.[31] Whereas Arnold chastized the middle and upper classes for pusillanimity, Mill went directly to the lower classes with a cry for reason and forbearance. Although he deplored the rioting, he had less fear than Arnold that it would lead to revolution, and judged the temper of the aroused workmen more accurately. Their diagnoses of the condition of the lower classes were different: when Mill argues that a people "in a state of savage independence, in which every one lives for himself, exempt, unless by fits, from any external control, is practically incapable of making any progress in civilisation until it has learnt to obey,"[32] he does not have England in mind; Arnold might well think this an admirable description of the English Populace. It might be said that Mill's more immediate knowledge of the situation inevitably led him to more concrete proposals, while Arnold, in *Culture and Anarchy,* was concerned with abiding tendencies. But with more validity it can be said that Mill's long-range prognosis enabled him to view the current crisis with more detachment than Arnold. In truth, it is not *Culture and Anarchy* that is written for the future, but *On Liberty.* In Mill's eyes, at least, it was not a tract for the times, but a tract for all times. The question of Social Liberty, he says on the opening page, "is likely soon to make itself recognised as the vital question of the future." (65) And a few pages later, he writes, "The majority have not yet learnt to feel the power of the government their power, or its opinions their opinions. When they do so, individual liberty will probably be as much exposed to invasion from the government, as it already is from public opinion." (72) What he feared from the ascendancy of the lower classes was not anarchy, but stagnation. In two revealing letters, written to Charles Eliot Norton in 1868, he argues that social disruption is very unlikely: "The intelligent, who are the politically active part of the working classes, are not impatient; they have a sincere dread of the mass of brutal ignorance behind them, and have consequently set themselves to demand very vigorously a real national education. This they will soon obtain, and it will alter, in an incalculable degree, all the bad elements of the existing state of things."[33] Like Arnold, he had great faith in the power of education to cure the present difficulty, but he looked beyond it to difficulties which education, even "a real national education," would enlarge rather than diminish. Here we approach the heart of the comparison, which can be exposed by a closer look at Arnold's concept of Culture.

Without attempting to define culture—if Arnold couldn't, why should I try?—one can gather the spent shot of his barrage definition: disinterestedness, curiosity, a blending of Hellenism and Hebraism, a harmonious and general expansion of individual and social powers, the triumph of reason and the will of God, the playing of a fresh current of thought upon our stock notions and habits, the supremacy of the best self in individual and nation, sweetness and light. Some of these terms are so obviously part of Mill's programme that they need no discussion: disinterestedness, curiosity, the triumph of reason, the fresh current of thought on our stock notions and habits, the supremacy of the best self in the individual, and light.

When one remembers Mill's allegiance to Goethe's motto, "many-sidedness," and his repudiation of Bentham's concentration on the "business" side of life, his closeness to Arnold in another respect becomes clearer. Of Arnold's four "powers," the power for conduct, the power for intellect and knowledge, the power for beauty, and the power for social life and manners, the first three are recognized by Mill.[34] The fourth is just what he might be expected to omit (although his awareness of it can be seen in the passages deleted from the early draft of the *Autobiography*. But it is of little importance to Arnold: since for him, as for Mill, conduct is three-fourths of life, surely intellect and knowledge would claim three-fourths of the remainder, and beauty three-fourths of the smaller remainder, and (with a flourish of Arnoldian mathematics), social life and manners would be left with but one-sixty-fourth of life. In any case, Mill fully recognized the need for sweetness as well as light, was a dedicated Hellenist,[35] and learned from agonized experience the value of a *harmonious* expansion of individual powers. The *general* expansion of human powers was similarly his passion.[36] Furthermore, since he worked always for social utility, the cultivation of social powers was both method and part of the end for him.[37]

What then would Mill find foreign in Arnold's account? Presumably, the triumph of the will of God, and the reliance upon the best self in the nation. But what does Arnold mean by the will of God? Professor Robbins has competently led us through the mazes of Arnold's "ethical idealism," and found the centre, but there is no

God there. "The Eternal that makes for righteousness" looks suspiciously like (to paraphrase Mill's definition of matter) the permanent possibility of good behaviour. Mill's Manicheanism, if different in formulation, leads to much the same conclusions, for he would have us co-operate with the beneficent but not omnipotent power which cannot be known except pragmatically and hypothetically (and surely Arnold is here at one with Mill). Of course when Arnold talks of "the will of God," he is talking a language foreign to Mill. But strangely enough, when one looks at Arnold's first use of this phrase from Bishop Wilson in *Culture and Anarchy,* one finds the distance between him and Mill not increased by it, but diminished:

> There is a view [of culture] in which all the love of our neighbour, the impulses towards action, help, and beneficence, the desire for removing human error, clearing human confusion, and diminishing human misery, the noble aspiration to leave the world better and happier than we found it,—motives eminently such as are called social,—come in as part of the grounds of culture, and the main and pre-eminent part. Culture is then properly described not as having its origin in curiosity, but as having its origin in the love of perfection; it is *a study of perfection.* (44–45)

And the motto for this view is "To make reason and the will of God prevail." So only the motto is foreign to Mill; the description of the view is clearly appropriate to what Mill would call enlightened Utilitarianism—the pursuit of the greatest social happiness through an individual study of moral perfection. And considering his modified theism, one can easily see that in aiming at social perfection through individual perfection, man is co-operating with a god of limited powers—in fact trying to make the will of that god prevail. Two pages farther on, Arnold even says, comparing this to the other view of culture ("the rendering an intelligent being yet more intelligent") that "in comparison with this wider endeavour of such great and plain utility [the latter] looks selfish, petty, and unprofitable." (47) And he argues that the latter is only a beginning for the former. Perhaps he sees Mill as a supporter only of the latter, but he is certainly wrong. Actually, for both, the best worship is moral; each man must make himself right, and right his actions. Mill's Religion of Humanity is dependent upon Arnold's "morality touched with emotion"—although Mill could never substitute Church for Chapel, Establishment for Dissent.

Surely here lies the real point at issue: must one look to the nation in its "corporate and collective capacity,"[38] that is, to the State, for guidance and leadership? Can the "best self" of the nation lead it out of the wilderness? (To alter the metaphor, and adopt the fallacy of the Canada Council, can the nation, by taking collective thought, add a cubit to its culture?) Arnold does not really present a mystique of the State, but he does not believe in individual bootstrap-lifting, or Samuel Smiling one's way to success. Looking at the various classes—Barbarians, Philistines, Populace, and especially the last—he sees no group able to provide leadership. But he knows that there is a best self in each, no matter how buried beneath transitory desires, cares, and frustrations, and he thinks it possible to give strength and direction to these scattered selves by collecting their voices and adding to them legislative and executive authority. He, like Auden, wants an "affirming flame" from the "ironic points of light." His desire follows his knowledge, of course, in looking mainly to education to cultivate the necessary unity. The feared anarchy arises from a denial of the true scale of moral values: it is hardly surprising that people refuse to follow the best when they are incapable of seeing that it is the best. Only when life is seen steadily and as a whole can behaviour be moral. Reason is essential, but cannot alone create the ordered state; authority must be recognized as authority, before it will be obeyed. And so Arnold looks to traditional and pragmatic sources of authority in State and Church to strengthen and even to initiate a movement that must be ultimately personal and moral. Working in education, and being within the tradition, he does not pay heed, as Mill does, to the distinction between private and public morality. But the question of priority in design must be faced: does he see the State as reflecting individual morality, or individual morality as reflecting the State's? If the latter, then mystique, cultism, racism—all of which have been seen in Arnold's work—are entailed. If the former is correct, however, Arnold is seen as a liberal with a sane view of individual weaknesses. Political arrangements are never easy, and to entrust leadership to stupidity is neither wise nor essentially democratic. And *Culture and Anarchy* is both wise and essentially democratic. Like most of his contemporaries, Arnold feared that the uninformed electorate would remain uninformed, and would never learn to recognize the value of history and precedent; he feared that experience from the past, since it was not their experience, and had not been interpreted by them, would not have presumption in its favour, but would be rejected on class and party grounds. He may seem to be making a speech from the barrel as it plunges over Niagara, but the image is Carlyle's, not his. For him there was still time for wisdom to organize and act, still time for the yeasty remnant to work on the doughy mass. If representatives chose not to reflect class and group interests, if they were not required to accept pledges, if they could act not as delegates but as representatives, then the best self of the nation could be the active self of the nation.

But this is Mill's language again. He saw just as clearly as Arnold the need for wise leadership in a democracy, and, after his early flirtation with more authoritative forms of government than Arnold ever embraced, he embodied in his mature political theory provisions for intelligent and trained planning of governmental activity, with limitations on all the powers of representatives except those exercised in debate and approval of legislation. In fact *On Liberty* can be seen as providing the justification of, and *Representative Government* the means to, continued leadership by Arnold's "aliens" in a democratic society.

The problem is finally not one of leadership, but of authority and sanction. And here Mill's strategy of modifying the good, and his position outside the Establishment, become even more crucial. He always opposed trends towards centralization and paternalism, but his extensive qualifications of the least-government theory have allowed critics to see him as opening the door to state intervention. And a careful reading of *On Liberty* shows that he does not advocate an atomistic anarchy—just as a careless reading leads to the conclusion that he is suggesting a political law rather than a moral principle. He realized, as any perceptive man must, that collective actions acquire a pragmatic sanction. He knew that most individual behaviour is supported by traditional, external, and legal sanctions which, through habit and education, produce an internal feeling of "rightness"; that is, they produce an internal sanction.[39] His apparent rebellion against external sanctions is really against an overplus of unthinking adherence to *any* sanctions. He wants always a free play of thought upon our stock notions and habits. Only individuals accustomed to responding to an internal sanction which they have consciously accepted, and helped to build up, can properly be called moral, and be relied upon to act morally. He does not believe that the internal sanctions of individuals are equally valid, or that external influence is immoral or morally useless. But knowing the power of such influence, knowing the weight of custom and authority, he feared its full extension. Being himself outside "the tradition of received opinions," he did not look to it, as Arnold did, for strength and unity. But he recognized the presence of another kind of received opinion, based on unreasoned adherence to class interests and prejudices, which was most potent among the uninformed electorate just then coming into power. He saw in the future not anarchy, but "Chinese stationariness," conformity, the age of Admass.

It is to counteract this tendency that he suggests that each man should be allowed to do as he likes. Or rather, each man should think and act as if other men are better if allowed to do as they like. This freedom is not a natural right; it is an essential means to morality. Only by mastering one's own actions, in liberty, can man reach the really "blessed" condition described by Arnold as liking "what right reason ordains." (*CA*, 82) Arnold thinks this condition is to be reached only by an active pursuit of the ideal, and so does Mill; but Mill thinks that the ideal must be accepted by full, free, and individual choice, while Arnold feels that the collective wisdom of the race properly selects ideals, and properly enforces their pursuit. One can narrow the gap even further, by recalling that Mill agrees that collective wisdom has a moral right to guide individuals—but finally he holds that even good beliefs and practices, when accepted through external authority, become merely stock notions and habits, and all is to begin anew.

So Arnold and Mill differ not so much in tenets as in prognoses. Their common strategy of "refining relatively good positions," in Trilling's phrase, magnifies their differences, but actually Mill's Liberty is not an enemy of Arnold's Culture, but its ally. At the very least, such is Mill's opinion: "the free development of individuality is . . . not only a co-ordinate element with all that is designated by the terms civilization, instruction, education, culture, but is itself a necessary part and condition of all those things. . . ." (*OL*, 115) But an ally in what cause? Liberty is for Mill not an end, but a means to the greatest happiness of the greatest number, to Utility; however, in

Mill's words, "it must be utility in the largest sense, grounded on the permanent interest of a man as a progressive being." (*OL*, 74) Is not this suspiciously like Culture? And when Arnold says, with Bishop Wilson, "to promote the kingdom of God is to increase and hasten one's own happiness," or, "It is in making endless additions to itself, in the endless expansion of its powers, in endless growth in wisdom and beauty, that the spirit of the human race finds its ideal. To reach this ideal, culture is an indispensable aid, and that is the true value of culture"[40]—when Arnold says these things, is not he approaching Mill's definition of Utility? In truth, Liberty and Culture go hand in hand, and Utility and Culture embrace.

NOTES

1. *Letters*, ed. H. S. R. Elliot (London: Longmans, 1910), II, 93.
2. Cf. Lionel Trilling, *Matthew Arnold* (New York: Meridian, 1955), 236–41.
3. Such as Free Trade, Mormons, the making of wills, and von Humboldt. For almost contemporary attacks on "freedom" and "doing as one likes" which indicate that in *Culture and Anarchy* Arnold is thinking more of Philistines in general, or Liberal catch-phrases, than of Mill, see *Friendship's Garland*, in *Works* (London: Macmillan, 1903–4), VI, 235, 261, 330, 336, 379.
4. *Culture and Anarchy*, ed. J. Dover Wilson (Cambridge University Press, 1955), 126. Hereafter cited as *CA*, with references given in the text.
5. See, e.g., "Whewell on Moral Philosophy," *Dissertations and Discussions* (London: Longmans, Green, Reader, and Dyer, 1875), II, 464. Cf. Mill to Carlyle in Francis E. Mineka, ed., *Earlier Letters, Collected Works* (Toronto: University of Toronto Press, 1963), XII, 128 (22/10/32). The point need no longer be laboured, but it might be pointed out that Walter Houghton, when assembling material to show the rigidity and sectarian fervour of the Victorians, quotes Mill as an exception eight times, Arnold only three, and begins his chapter with a remark by Fitzjames Stephen: "I am falling foul . . . of John Mill in his modern and more humane mood . . . which always makes me feel that he is a deserter from the proper principles of rigidity and ferocity in which he was brought up." Houghton, *The Victorian Frame of Mind*, 161; quoting from Leslie Stephen, *The Life of James Fitzjames Stephen* (London, 1895), 308.
6. "Bentham," *Dissertations and Discussions*, I, 350–51.
7. Arnold argues against Mill's criticism in *On Liberty* of Christian morality as passive: "Marcus Aurelius," *Essays in Criticism, First Series*, in *Works*, III, 377–82.
8. *Letters*, I, in *Works*, XIII, 127 (25/6/59).
9. See the difference between the opinion expressed in "Preface" (1870), *St. Paul and Protestantism*, in *Works*, IX, xxxvii-xxxix; *Letters*, II, in *Works*, XIV, 271 (1871); *Friendship's Garland*, in *Works*, VI, 257 n. (written in 1871); and that expressed in "Preface to the Second Edition" (1874), *Higher Schools and Universities in France*, in *Works*, XII, 100.
10. Cf. D. Brewster, *The Radical Party; its Principles, Objects, & Leaders—Cobden, Bright, & Mill* (Manchester: Heywood, 1867), *passim*.

11. See, e.g., G. J. Holyoake, *John Stuart Mill as Some of the Working Classes Knew Him* (London: Trübner, 1873), *passim.*
12. "Professor Sedgwick's Discourse," *London Review,* I (1835), 95–96. More harsh criticism is found in his two early speeches (unpublished) on the Universities; in "Notes on the Newspapers," *Monthly Repository,* VIII (1834), 525, 591–92; in "Notes on Some of the More Popular Dialogues of Plato," *ibid.,* 89; and in "Civilization," *London Review,* II (1836), 160–205.
13. *Dissertations and Discussions,* I; the passage is deleted from the argument on 98.
14. Letter to Mrs. H. Huth (7/1/63), British Library of Political and Economic Science, Mill-Taylor Collection, Add. Mat. 2, M 520.3. See also the note to the reprinted version (1859) of "Civilization," *Dissertations and Discussions,* I, 200 n.; and *Inaugural Address,* in *James and John Stuart Mill on Education,* ed. F. A. Cavenaugh (London: Cambridge University Press, 1931), 167.
15. It is interesting to note that Mill had a little, but a very little, respect for Newman, one of the other mentors listed by Arnold in his letter to Newman of 28 May, 1872 (*Unpublished Letters of Matthew Arnold,* ed. Arnold Whitridge [New Haven: Yale University Press, 1923], 65–66), and that Georg Brandes (an unreliable commentator) reports that Mill disliked Saint-Beuve (*Creative Spirits of the Nineteenth Century,* trans. R. B. Anderson [London: T. Fisher Unwin, 1924] 199–200. On the other side one can quote Arnold's contemptuous dismissal of Comte, one of Mill's teachers (above, p. 126; and *Letters to Clough,* 74 [8/3/48]).
16. See, for example, Arnold's *Letters to Clough,* 134–35 (1/5/53): "I for my part think that what [John Philpot] Curan said of the constitution of the state holds true of individual moral constitutions: it does not do to lay bare their foundations too constantly." But cf. Trilling, 129.
17. Lionel Trilling, 242, notes the distinction in Arnold's writings.
18. "Professor Sedgwick's Discourse," 94–95 (reprinted in *Dissertations and Discussions,* I, 96–98). Cf. *On Liberty,* in *Utilitarianism, Liberty, Representative Government,* introduction by A. D. Lindsay (London: Dent, 1957), 127 (hereafter cited as *OL* with references given in the text); "The State of Society in America," *London Review,* II (1836), 375; "De Tocqueville," *Dissertations and Discussions,* II, 1; "Guizot's Essays and Lectures in History," *ibid.,* 220; *Principles of Political Economy, Collected Works* (Toronto: University of Toronto Press, 1965), II, 105 (I, vii, 3), 171 (I, xi, 4), III, 754 (IV, vi, 2).
19. "The Function of Criticism," *Essays in Criticism* (London: Macmillan, 1865), 14–16, 21, 25; *Culture and Anarchy* (London: Smith Elder, 1869), 15, 16–17, 18, 31–32, 89, 94.
20. *Inaugural Address,* 191.
21. See footnote 9 above.
22. *Letters to Clough,* 111 (23/9/49). Cf. *ibid.,* 122–3 (7/6/52), and 126 (14/12/52).
23. Mill to Carlyle, *Earlier Letters,* XII, 112 (17/7/32).
24. *Letters to Clough,* 98–9 (early Feb., 1849).
25. *Earlier Letters,* XII, 113 (17/7/32), 153–56 (18/5/33), and cf. *ibid.,* 97 (to W. J. Fox, 3/4/32), 157 (to Fox, 18/5/33), and XIII, 446 (to John Sterling, 1/10/40).
26. *Mixed Essays, Irish Essays, and Others* (New York, 1924), 381.
27. "Matthew Arnold and Carlyle," *Proceedings of the British Academy,* XLII (1956), 146 (quoting from *Letters to Clough,* 146 [30/11/53]). See also *Unpublished Letters,* 33 (31/3/56); *Letters,* III, in *Works,* XV, 93 (25/3/81); and "De Maistre's lettres et opuscules inédites," in *Essays, Letters, and*

Reviews by Matthew Arnold, ed. Fraser Neiman (Harvard University Press, 1960), 218. Cf. Trilling, 12.

28. "Preface" (1865), *Essays in Criticsim, First Series*, in *Works*, III, v. And the epigraph used for this volume (Boston: Ticknor and Fields, 1865) is taken from Burke: "Our antagonist is our helper. This amicable conflict with difficulty obliges us to an intimate acquaintance with our object, and compels us to consider it in all its relations. It will not suffer us to be superficial." (xviii) Comparable passages in Mill include *System of Logic* (London: Longmans, Green, 1906), 446–47 (IV, iv, 6); *OL*, 80; "Coleridge," *Dissertations and Discussions*, I, 402–3, 425; "Corporation and Church Property," *ibid.*, 25; and *The Amberley Papers*, ed. Bertrand and Patricia Russell (London: Hogarth Press, 1937), I, 373.
29. "From Easter to August," Neiman, 368.
30. *Autobiography*, 285–87.
31. *Ibid.*, 289–92.
32. *Representative Government* (introduction, Lindsay), 197.
33. Houghton Library (Harvard), bMS Am 1088, f2v (24/9/68). Cf. *ibid.* (4/10/68).
34. See "Inaugural Address," 191–96; "Bentham," *Dissertations and Discussions*, I, 387; and *Logic*, 620 (VI, xii, 6).
35. In education, although he argues that quarrels between the Ancients and Moderns are otiose, he is generally on the side of the Ancients; see "Inaugural Address," 133, 138 (and *passim*); and letter to Spencer (9/2/67), Northwestern University: "In regard to classical instruction, I do not altogether agree with you that the side favourable to it is too strong; for I think there is a growing reaction to the opposite extreme producing a danger on that side which being the most in harmony with modern tendencies has the best chance of being ultimately the stronger."
36. Cf. Arnold: "First and foremost of the necessary means towards man's civilisation we must name expansion. . . . The love of liberty is simply the instinct in man for expansion." "Preface," *Mixed Essays*, *Works*, X, vi-vii.
37. See *OL*, 164, where Mill argues that only the active involvement of individuals in community and national affairs can result in their "development," in "habituating them to act from public or semi-public motives, and guide their conduct by aims which unite instead of isolating them from one another."
38. A phrase Arnold borrows from Burke; see, e.g., *CA*, 75. In this passage, as elsewhere, Arnold reveals that he is seeing not only the *means*, but also the *ends* in solely British terms. Mill, while devising *means* for the British situation, seldom thinks of Britain when discussing ends. (Cf. Bentham.) Is Arnold more "provincial" (one of his terms of opprobrium) than Mill? (See also *CA*, 94–97).
39. See, e.g., his discussion of motives in *OL*, 69–70.
40. *Culture and Anarchy*, 48, 47. See also 75, where Arnold argues, as Bentham might have, that the State controls "individual wills in the name of an interest wider than that of individuals." In a similar context, on 81, the phrase, the "higher reason of all of them," replaces an "interest wider than that of individuals." See also *Friendship's Garland*, in *Works*, VI, 372 ff.; and Mill, "Inaugural Address," 197–98; and *Utilitarianism* (introduction, Lindsay), 13.

G. M. STORY

Heber the Magnificent: Portrait of a Bibliophile

On October 11, 1833, in his house at Pimlico, Richard Heber, fatally ill with pneumonia, raised himself in bed to scribble a note to Thorpe the bookseller for some rare books, sank back upon the pillows and died. His friend Dibdin has described the private funeral at Hodnet, Heber's principal country estate, attended only by the few friends who were permitted to penetrate the privacy of the old bachelor's last years; and it was Dibdin, too, who led the search for Heber's will, a document discovered three months later hidden behind a library shelf. The will was short, and made no mention of Heber's books. Since he had over a quarter of a million of them, it was a singular omission.

The disposal of Heber's estates was simple; to dispose of the books proved less easy. In addition to the vast library at Hodnet, he had two equally large collections in London, a house at Oxford crammed with volumes from cellar to attic, an enormous collection in Paris, another at Ghent, one at Brussels and one at Antwerp, not to mention smaller collections in half-a-dozen other European cities. The executors very sensibly placed the task of disposing of the books into the hands of Messrs. Payne and Foss, the book-dealers, and sixteen auction sales were arranged, thirteen in London, two in Paris and one in Ghent. At these sales the mighty library to which Heber had devoted his life was dispersed.

Heber's career commands attention for a number of reasons, but chiefly because he was the greatest figure of the golden age of English bibliophilism, that astonishing period between 1800 and 1830 when

HAB no. 32, January 1961.

book-collecting was practised with a passion and a discrimination, and on a scale which has scarcely a parallel in history.

The Heber family came originally from Yorkshire, and by 1500 had acquired the estate of Marton, near Skipton. The Shropshire estate of Hodnet came to the family in the mid-eighteenth century on the death of a cousin, the last of the Vernons of Hodnet. Reginald Heber, the collector's father, succeeded to the property on the death of his elder brother; he resigned his fellowship at Brasenose College, Oxford, and divided his time between supervision of his estates and the living of Malpas, Cheshire, where he rebuilt the comfortable rectory. He was married twice: by his first wife he had Richard (1774); by his second wife he had three children, one girl, and two sons, the eldest of whom, also called Reginald, is variously remembered as the author of a famous Oxford prize poem, Bishop of Calcutta, and writer of hymns.

The Rev. Mr. Heber, a man whose considerable intellectual power assorted oddly with a crusty but endearing conservatism, placed his eldest son, at the age of ten, under the care of the Rev. George Henry Glasse. "Short, fat and benevolent," Glasse was a good classical scholar and a private tutor of brilliance. At his house on the outskirts of London he took in perhaps a dozen boys, most of them the sons of noblemen, and gave them a sound classical education without the rigours of the public schools. Richard, who on arrival had declared to his Aunt Elizabeth, "Lord bless me, I don't know how I shall behave," was very happy at school and responded eagerly to Glasse's expert tuition. To his father he wrote (December, 1784): "I begun to learn Greek almost as soon as I left Malpas and have done the first book of Ovid, the story of Phaeton, Echo Narcissus and Pyramus and Thisbe (which is 110 lines) to construe and say by heart for my Task which I got the first morning before breakfast." With the same breathless zest he threw himself into other activities as well, skating, music, drawing, the spectators' gallery at the House of Commons and, significantly, book-collecting, in which he showed a precocious interest in quality and condition. His father's letters exhibit a mixture of indulgence and vain attempts to restrain his engagingly spoiled son's extravagance: (February, 1786)—"I must not allow dear Richard to be so extravagant in the binding of his books"; (April, 1789)—

I cannot say I rejoice in the importation of the cargo of books you mention from abroad, we had before enow and too many, ten times more than were ever read or even looked into. Of multiplying books, my dear Richard, there is neither end nor use. The *Cacoethes* of collecting books draws men into ruinous extravagances. It is an itch which grows by indulgence and should be nipt in the bud.

But he paid his son's bills, contributed towards the cost of particularly expensive volumes, and on at least one occasion (April, 1784) attended a book-sale to discharge the commission of the school-boy collector for "the very best editions of the classics of all sizes."

In 1792 Heber entered Oxford as a Gentleman-Commoner of Brasenose, provided with an elegant set of rooms overlooking the Exeter gardens and a princely allowance from his father. The result was not altogether what might have been expected in eighteenth-century Oxford at such a College. Heber possessed a genuinely scholarly mind and while still an undergraduate projected the editing of all the Latin poets not included in Barbou's collection; his editions of Persius, Silius Italicus and Claudianus appeared incomplete. He was a distinguished classical scholar, but his interest in out-of-the-way authors and subjects, and his disinclination to publish, restricted his reputation to a small circle: Henry Drury, Dr. Routh, Richard Porson and other scholars among his friends. Meanwhile, at university as at school, Heber displayed the same enthusiasm in other pursuits. Books, partridge and fox were equally his prey. His passion for politics did not abate and he rarely missed posting to London for the important debates in Parliament. Moreover he now began to indulge his fondness for travel, to every corner of Britain and to the Continent. Throughout his life he hated to remain too long in one place, to the alternate exasperation and delight of his friends.

In addition to his Oxford contemporaries and his fellow bibliophiles, Heber's intimate cirle included Scott, Dugald Stewart, Sidney Smith, John Leyden (the future orientalist), Frodsham Hodson (Fellow of Brasenose and Heber's later guide in University politics), Robert Southey, and a score of slightly older figures in the world of politics, among them Canning and the Grenvilles.

The versatility of taste, interest and intellect suggested by these friendships is important if we would understand Heber's activities as a book-collector. At first he confined himself chiefly to editions of the Greek and Latin classics—the conventional field for a bibliophile and one natural enough in a classical scholar. It is remarkable, for example (in view of the scope of this later collecting), to find him at the Farmer sale in 1798 virtually ignoring the early English literature which the old scholar had assembled for his work on Shakespeare. At this sale, or at any rate about this time, Heber met Edmond Malone, the editor of Shakespeare and a notable collector, and their friendship brought Heber into the circle of Steevens, the younger Boswell, Henry Ellis and other English scholars. In Malone especially Heber found a great tutor in scholarly collecting, while from Isaac Gossett, "milk-white Gossett" as he was called from his fondness for books printed on vellum, Heber learned the intricacies of auction-bidding.

It was, however, some time before he became, by the rigorous standards of the age, a great collector. He took his degree at Oxford in 1796 and spent the following years in the pleasures of scholarship, friendship and travel. War with France led to the organizing of a regiment of Shropshire volunteers and Heber, as Colonel, was able to bring his not very efficient troops to a point where they were at least able to fire muskets without causing casualties among themselves. His father's death in 1804 placed the burden of the family estates on him; through efficient management he increased their value. By the end of the first decade of the century, his tastes formed, his collecting experience formidable, his purse amply supplied, Heber was ready to compete as an equal with the most glittering circle of collectors in history.

It was the Homeric age of book-collecting. Malone, one of the last survivors of the scholarly collectors of the eighteenth century, with his barbarous scholar's habit of inlaying rare quartos leaf by leaf to facilitate textual collation, was still dangerous. There was Michael Wodhul, the translator of Euripides, and owner of a fine library of early-printed editions of the classics, elegantly bound by the most famous craftsmen of the day. Rivalling Wodhul as a collector of books in fine condition was James Edwards, who was so ardent a lover of books that he directed that his coffin should be made out of the shelves of his library. Setting a new fashion among collectors was James Bindley, whose superb Elizabethan and Jacobean books bore the inelegant legend: "Bindley, Stamp Office." Even less conventional was the wealthy and eccentric William Beckford. Disdaining any fashion but his own, he gathered a large collection of books as bizarre as Fonthill, the house which Edward Stanley described as "a Cathedral fitted up by a Lunatic Bishop." Beckford's collection, in de Ricci's phrase, was "less a library than a cabinet of bibliographical rarities and freaks, each one a gem of its kind," and curiously like the decadent collections of French bibliophiles around 1900.

Towering over these and other collectors were the great peers of the realm, so many of whom were Whigs that one is tempted to explain this phenomenon of a bibliomaniacal aristocracy by the vicissitudes of a political party. The eldest of them, Thomas Grenville, the bitter political foe of his Tory brothers, retired from public life after a long career as diplomat and statesman and devoted the rest of his life to his primary passion, collecting books and manuscripts. He was a bibliophile in the purest sense of the word, with a sensitive feeling for quality. Early American was his special field, but European literature also attracted him. (His bequest to the British Museum in 1846 was the most valuable it received, apart from the founding gift of Sir Hans Sloane.) Exactly parallel was the career of Lord Spencer of Althorp, the collector-son of a collector-father. He also deserted politics for bibliophilism. Assisted by Dibdin, his librarian, he assembled at Althorp the most beautiful private library in Europe, 36,000 volumes comprising a treasure-house of incunabula and Renaissance books which, in 1892, was purchased as the nucleus of the Rylands Library, Manchester, for £250,000. Lord Spencer's most dangerous rival was the fifth Duke of Marlborough who, as Marquis of Blandford, collected the celebrated library at White Knights, near Reading. Illuminated manuscripts, early printed books, French romances, European poetry, all fell within his field, and he collected them—as he lived—with an extravagance that led to bankruptcy.

Perhaps the most curious of these collectors was a Scottish peer, John Ker, third Duke of Roxburghe. His father had assembled a considerable library of rare books in the early eighteenth century, but the son made no significant additions until after his return from a tour of the Continent. While abroad, he met and fell in love with Christiana, eldest daughter of the Duke of Mecklenburg-Strelitz. Unfortunately, the girl's younger sister was the intended spouse of George III. Since it would not have been proper for a subject of the

British Crown to marry the elder sister of his Queen, the love-affair was broken off and both parties, in the words of a contemporary, "evinced the strength of their attachment by devoting their after-time to celibacy." In the case of the Duke, the result was a passion for book-collecting which he indulged with melancholy determination.

Roxburghe died in 1804; in 1812 his library was put up for sale by auction. The books and the sale are worth describing, for both were characteristic of the taste and spirit of the age.

The Roxburghe Library was a magnificent collection of some ten thousand volumes. It was especially strong in incunabula, French chivalric-romances (in both manuscript and print), early English and Italian literature, Shakespeare and the drama. It contained, among many other treasures, the valuable collection of English ballads known ever since as the Roxburghe Ballads; it was rich in Caxtons and De Wordes, rare Bibles, Shakespeare quartos, and hundreds of other scarce, and sometimes unique, books, most of them in immaculate condition.

The sale-catalogue, prepared with scholarly care by Nicol, the King's bookseller, was issued and at once collectors throughout the kingdom prepared for the contest of their lives. Walter Scott wrote, "The Roxburghe sale sets my teeth on edge," but, his resources strained by the building of Abbotsford, he determined not to compete —a resolution he later broke by dispatching bids through the post. Malone told James Boswell that "absolute beggary would be the consequences to Heber, Lord Spencer and himself." As for Heber, in April he was telling a friend: "I trust we shall strike hard soon, amidst the ruins of the Duke of Roxburghe. I fear there will not be much leisure or opportunity for the exercise of the milder virtues of friendship and forebearance." A week later he was hesitating: "I have serious thoughts of *giving in*, and staying in quiet at Hodnet," adding, "There is something vastly ingenious in balancing the *giving in* by however."

At length the day of the sale arrived, May 12. For two and forty days, with the exception of Sundays only, the voice and the hammer of Evans the auctioneer were heard with equal efficacy in the dining room of the late Duke's house in St. James's Square. The shouts of the victors, and the groans of the vanquished, we are told by Dibdin, the historian of the epic battle, stunned and appalled you as you entered. The throng and press was unprecedented. Attendance at the

House of Lords dwindled to twentieth-century proportions. All the great collectors and bookdealers were there, including, it was whispered, the personal agent of the Emperor of the French, dispatched to redeem the recent defeat at Salamanca.

> A sprinkling of Caxtons and De Wordes marked the first day; and these were obtained at high, but, comparatively with the subsequent sums given, moderate prices. Theology, Jurisprudence, Philosophy, and Philology, chiefly marked the earlier days of the contest. Then came Poetry, Latin, Italian, and French: a steady fight continued to be fought.

At length came English Poetry, and the roar of battle became furious. Heber, with a dash and abandon that astonished his rivals, carried off prize after prize. Still a comparatively young collector, however, he was at length overcome by the combined forces of his antagonists and, like Ajax, retired from the contest, returning only for one glorious afternoon of Dramatic Poetry.

And now the romances made their appearance, led by the unique Valdafer *Boccaccio*. This celebrated volume, the only copy of the 1471 Florentine edition to survive the fires of Savonarola, had been hotly contested by collectors for over two centuries before it was secured in 1740 by the second Duke of Roxburghe for one hundred guineas. Its sale in 1812 provided the most glorious moment in the Roxburghe struggle.

Mr. Evans delivered an appropriate oration over the famous volume, including a dark hint that Napoleon had vowed to secure it for the Imperial collection at Paris. Silence followed the auctioneer's address. All English eyes turned on the supposed French agent, who blushed. "On the right of Mr. Evans, leaning against the wall, stood Earl Spencer; a little lower down, and standing at right angles with his Lordship, appeared the Marquis of Blandford," whose elegance proved the truth of Brummell's assertion that "starch is the man."

> My Lord Althorp stood a little backward to the right of his father, Earl Spencer. The honour of firing the first shot was due to a gentleman of Shropshire, unused to this species of warfare, and who seemed to recoil from the reverberation of the report himself had made!—"One hundred guineas," he exclaimed. Again a pause ensued; but anon the bidding rose rapidly to 500 guineas. Hitherto, however, it was evident that the firing was but masked and desultory. At length all random shots ceased, and the champions stood gallantly up to each other resolving not to flinch from a trial of their respective strengths.

"A thousand guineas" were bid by Earl Spencer—to which the Marquis added "ten." You might have heard a pin drop. The bidding continued. "Two thousand pounds" are offered by the Marquis. For a moment Earl Spencer paused, then advanced one step and bid "Two thousand two hundred and fifty pounds"—to which the Marquis of Blandford added his usual "and ten." For a quarter of a minute Mr. Evans paused, hammer in midair, then down it thundered like Thor's, and the Marquis, tucking the precious volume under his coat-tails, marched triumphantly off with his prize.

The Roxburghe sale was the climax of the book-collecting of the era. The volumes fetched a total of 23,397 pounds; the price paid for the Voldafer *Boccaccio* remained an auction record for the rest of the century. The sale was also, and more significantly, the classic manifesto of the taste of the period, in which (as John Carter has observed), "the effective criteria of the great collectors were not so much literary as physical. The main objectives of the majority were the splendours of early printing and illumination, fine bindings by the great masters, early illustrations, vellum copies, Aldines and tall Elzevirs and the like." They were, in fact, dandies in their tastes, Brummells of book-collecting.

Among these collectors Heber stood out as the marked champion by virtue of his scholarship, catholicity of taste, and passionate absorption in pursuit of rare books. Though he purchased at nearly every sale after 1800, his most active period was in the years following the Roxburghe battle. He had few rivals. At the sale of the Devonshire duplicates, the Stanley, Alchorne, Horne Tooke, Merley, Towneley, Grafton, Tallyrand and Borromeo sales he bought heavily. At the same time he purchased constantly from the stock of the great London and provincial dealers, haunted the humblest bookstall, and would travel a hundred miles to secure a reported rare book. To his fellow-collectors he was a puzzle. Book-collecting on his scale, as opposed to the scholar's search for useful books and the dandy's pursuit of fine books, was something new, and the contemporary anecdotes, not all of them apocryphal, that have survived suggest the wonder of a baffled generation.

Heber had a number of idiosyncrasies. He disliked books with vertical lettering on the spine, as who does not, and he had little use for large-paper copies: they took up too much space on his shelves.

Lack of space, however, did not prevent his owning several copies of many of his books. On being asked by a friend why he purchased duplicates and triplicates, he replied seriously: "Why, you see, Sir, no man can comfortably do without three copies of a book. One he must have for his show copy. Another he will require for his own use and reference; and unless he is inclined to part with this, which is very inconvenient, or risk the injury of his best copy, he must needs have a third at the service of his friends."

"The service of his friends"—Heber's generosity was a striking characteristic, and English scholarship owes him a considerable debt. Alexander Dyce, Chalmers, Sir Egerton Brydges, Ellis, Malone, Boswell, and other pioneer scholars of earlier English literature were given the freedom of a library richer in many fields than the Bodleian or the British Museum. Heber himself, though his published work in the field of English studies was even thinner than in the classics, was a great English scholar; in bibliographical knowledge and expertise he had few equals. Nor did he read only with his fingers. His taste in literature guided the fields he cultivated as a collector; wide as his scope was, through it all ran the necessary intellectual thread of connection which predicates acquaintance with the contents of his accumulating volumes. It was, indeed, the intellectual versatility and catholicity of taste that Heber brought to collecting that, as I have already suggested, distinguished him from his fellow bibliophiles.

The period between 1812 and 1826 was not only that of Heber's maturity as a book-collector but probably the most happy of his life. He was no recluse like Roxburghe. When not in London, he was to be found now travelling in Britain, now on the Continent, now at Hodnet, his splendid country-house, with its gardens and rambling library. Singularly gifted in friendship, he was a familiar figure in the brilliant society of Georgian England. He was one of the founders of the Athenaeum Club, membership in which his friend Sidney Smith at first declined with an excuse too delicious to omit: "the last time we met you helped me very badly to asparagus, no toast and only 3 heads of the vegetable. I don't suppose you meant anything by it, but it had an unfriendly appearance." Heber was also one of the founding members of the Roxburghe Club, that curious society of bibliophiles into which, it was said, entry was more difficult than into the peerage or the Privy Council.

As a patron of scholarship and letters, Heber was a not inconsiderable figure. His support was useful in keeping the *Quarterly Review* afloat; his library, purse, knowledge and influence were freely available to writers as well as scholars. To him Mitford and Ellis dedicated their scholarly works, John Ferrier his once well-known poem, *Bibliomania,* and Dibdin the last of his vast and rambling treatises on collecting. Southey consulted him on literary problems, and half-a-dozen now forgotten works of scholarship benefited from his pre-publication scrutiny. "Heber the magnificent," was Sir Walter Scott's tribute to his equally large-hearted friend, followed by the dedication of Canto six of *Marmion* and frequent references to the collector in those long historical and antiquarian notes by which Scott vainly hoped to supply the interest his poems so conspicuously lacked.

It was during this period too that Heber at length won a seat in the Parliament he had for so long admired. In 1806 he had contested a vacancy for the University of Oxford, but was defeated. The rumour of an impending vacancy in 1814 encouraged his supporters to carry out a canvass on his behalf. His opponent was a man violently opposed to reform, whether legal, municipal, ecclesiastical or parliamentary—so conservative that even the Dean of Christ Church, his sponsor, thought him a little rigid in his views. There was encouraging evidence of support for Heber, so that when the long-expected vacancy at length occurred in 1821 he allowed his name to be put forward.

In the previous contests, Heber had stood as an independent, the position one would expect in a man of his tolerant and liberal nature. It is not easy now to penetrate the complicated and murky affair of the 1821 election, for Heber left the management of the contest to his Oxford supporters. With or without his knowledge, his views appear to have been differently represented to different people, else the cross-currents of university rivalry became entangled with the major political issues of the day. The campaign was organized by Heber's old friend Hodson, superbly fitted for the intricacies of academic electioneering by his long tenure of the chair of casuistical divinity. The contest was short and bitter. His opponent, Sir John Nicoll, an implacable enemy of Catholic Emancipation and Parliamentary Reform, had, at the end of the first day's ballotting, a small lead. The sullen Tories of Christ Church, Lincoln, and St. John's celebrated the anticipated victory with a kind of Belshazzar's feast. But Hodson had his reserves ready. On the second day a slip of paper was delivered at the Senior Common Room of Brasenose, and written on it, in Hodson's hand, was the order: "Let forty B.N.C. men go up and vote." He was obeyed with a military precision marred only by the unsteadiness induced by the College cellar, and Heber's victory was assured. The tactics of Heber's supporters, and those of his opponents, shocked even those familiar with University politics. "I always thought it desirable," wrote Sir John Bosanquet to the collector, "that the election should take place during the absence of the undergraduates, lest the junior part of the University should be scandalized by the bickerings of their seniors, but till I witnessed the uproarious proceedings in Brasenose I was not aware of another reason for preferring the vacation for the assembling of the graver members."

But the scandal was soon forgotten and Heber plunged happily into Parliamentary work. He was assiduous in attendance at committee meetings, and seems to have done useful work on agricultural and financial matters, as well as on the delicate matter of university reform, a question which periodically plagued Parliament because of Oxford's inability to order its own affairs. Other issues, such as Catholic Emancipation and the reform of Parliament, apparently proved more embarrassing. Heber had won his seat against a man who had bitterly opposed both measures. He now discovered that many of his strongest supporters in the University had elected him as an opponent also. Powerful pressure was brought to bear on him to speak up in the House (for example by Copleston, the Provost of Oriel); but whether from a reluctance to engage in bitter debates for which he felt ill-equipped, or from embarrassment at not feeling able to support views which ran counter to his own liberal convictions, Heber felt compelled to resign. In 1826, popular, famous, and at the height of his public career, he left England for the Continent.

And now began the final phase of Heber's career as a collector. His arrival in Europe in January 1826 presented him with the opportunity for which he was born. In a study of the career of Sir Thomas Phillipps, Mr. A. N. L. Munby has pointed out that the state of the book-trade in Europe during the second and third decades of the nineteenth century had no previous parallel and has never been equalled again. "The convulsions of the previous quarter of a century had resulted in the dispersal of many libraries. At the Revolution it has been computed that in the private libraries of France, a nation which led the world in bibliophily, there were thirteen million volumes, ten million of which were destroyed or had changed hands within five years. Though many of these privately-owned books and a larger proportion of the collections of the religious houses found their way into state and municipal libraries, the market was flooded and the shops of the Parisian and provincial booksellers were filled to overflowing." In Germany and the Low Countries the situation was the same, for though the various Napoleonic commissioners for works of art secured many precious volumes for the Imperial collection, not all went into official custody; booksellers' shops here too were crammed, and "it is recorded that the frugal cobblers of Erfurt lined slippers with the products of the monastic scriptorium" and the early presses.

Two men saw their opportunity and seized it enthusiastically. Sir Thomas Phillipps, Phillipps the Deplorable, plunged with frantic abandon on his career as a collector of manscripts; Richard Heber, tired of public life and tempted by the derelict volumes of Europe, advanced boldly in pursuit of rare printed books.

And now the Continent of Europe, at peace since Waterloo, resounded once again to the clash of British arms and feats of British valour. Behold the auction-rooms of Ghent where, in a desperate engagement, Heber of Hodnet wrought havoc! Thence in a flash to Antwerp, locked in mortal combat with the booksellers and collectors of the Low Countries, routing and chasing them from the field. Nor did the English champion rest but, fortified by rents from Yorkshire and Shropshire, he plunged into the fray at Brussels and Amsterdam. In between these epic battles came skilful forays to Frankfurt, Leyden and Leipzig, purchasing, on a vast scale, booksellers' stock and small private collections. Perhaps most remarkable of all was the swift winter campaign in Paris in 1829. There, in the famous auction-room of Silvestre, Sir Thomas Phillipps recorded in his diary: "Met Mr. Heber. He is called Mr. Richard by the auctioneers. He bid for Bede's History, printed in the 15th century, but by some accident it escaped him." It was one of the few items that did escape him. With courage and skill that became legendary he secured the pick of a dozen collections. One after the other, and all together, he defeated the great French bibliophiles and dealers, capping his triumph with the purchase, by private treaty, of a huge library of 30,000 rare books. For five years Heber ranged the collecting-fields of Europe, sometimes in person, at other times through the agency of booksellers.

In 1831 he returned to England. At one of their last meetings in Paris, Phillipps recorded: "Mr. Heber intends to commence a Catalogue of his books, by taking a portion of them at a time, as 1. Class of History, 2. Romances, 3. Theology, etc., etc." It was a formidable undertaking, for Heber's collection (impossible to number exactly) must by now have come close to 300,000 volumes. Simply to assemble them in one place proved impossible, and though a new library built at Hodnet provided shelves for many of the most choice items, Heber was never able to bring together in one place the books stored in England, not to mention the half-dozen libraries he had assembled in Europe. For one thing, the import duty of £6.10s per cwt. on books entering England would have cost a fortune to the owner of collections which would have had to be weighed by the ton—and Heber's estates had by now been strained to the limit.

Moreover, by 1831 Heber was a sick and ailing man, his tall frame emaciated, his speech and eyesight failing, his movements unsteady. He now rarely left his houses at Hodnet and Pimlico, except for brief visits to the booksellers, where something of the old gaiety of spirit would appear. Within two years of his return he was dead and the problem of cataloguing and disposing his collection solved, after a fashion.

The sales catalogues compiled by the firms of Evans, Sotheby and Wheatley for the London auctions, by Citerne of Ghent, and Silvestre of Paris, were arranged not by subject or format or author, but by the houses in which Heber had stored his books. The result is a series of volumes maddening to use, though, from their contents, still an indispensable tool for the historical bibliographer. For in the sixteen shabby volumes is described the mightiest library ever assembled by one man.

To indicate adequately the scope and richness of Heber's library would require a paper in itself. Though he purchased on a vast scale, and in his later years at least bought books partly to preserve them from destruction, he did so with scholarship, taste and connoisseurship. When the catalogues were published they revealed to an astonished world a collection which seemed an epitome of all the great collecting styles of the age, yet possessing also that unity which gives point and meaning to a private library.

Here were the treasures of French and Italian literature, collected on a scale which challenged the Roxburghe Library; classical authors in first and other rare editions which at more than one point surpassed the splendid Spencer Library; Americana and incunabula which suggested the princely collection of Grenville; Bibles in unexampled profusion. In some fields Heber was a pioneer: his Spanish books, for example, were matchless in rarity and richness; and his collection of later Latin poetry and Renaissance humanist works was probably without parallel. Few private libraries have ever contained so many "association" copies: George Chapman's copy of his translation of Homer with a manuscript dedication; Milton's annotated copies of Dante and Petrarch; an edition of Lucian with manuscript notes by Erasmus; the Countess of Pembroke's copy of Sidney's *Arcadia*; Walton's copy of *The Compleat Angler*; Johnson's corrected copy of *The Dictionary*; a Massinger play with the author's textual revisions; Castiglione's *Il Cortegiano* with an autograph sonnet by Tasso on the fly-leaf; a Manilius with textual collations by Scalinger and Bentley; a rare Pliny with annotations by Politian; books from royal collections, in Grolier's binding, and from all the other great private libraries in European history.

The appearance of volume eleven in 1836 revealed that Heber had collected manuscripts as well as printed books: richly illuminated manuscripts; manuscripts of Chaucer, Langland and Dante; the famous Ottenbeuren Horace; a manuscript containing over forty unique Anglo-Norman texts; manuscripts of troubadour poetry and Elizabethan music—manuscripts French, Spanish and Mexican; a whole series of Venetian state papers; papal letters, the private and official papers of Sir Julius Caesar; manuscripts of Burns, Gray and Scott; letters and autographs in profusion.

But the glory of Heber's library was his English printed books. He was not the first collector to cultivate this field: others had built up libraries of Caxtons and De Wordes; scholarly collectors had long been assembling Shakespeare and his great contemporaries. But Heber brought to these collecting fields a passion for completeness and a range of literary and historical interest that had never been seen before. It is doubtful if any collector, before or since, had or has ever possessed so complete a set of Shakespeare early editions. No collector had assembled so many of the great Elizabethans and Jacobeans. But Heber collected more than the obvious authors. He was the earliest collector, if not the first scholar, to grasp the interest and importance of pre-Elizabethan drama. He brought together unique collections of Jacobean masques and Restoration comedy. Few bibliophiles had ever possessed such superb collections of jest-books, song-books and Civil War tracts. Here were books the very existence of which had been doubted, volumes the mere bringing to light of which made obsolete the older scholarly editions and handbooks. The famous fourth volume of the catalogue, which describes the choicest of the English books, took its place as an authoritative bibliographical guide to early English poetry, drama and history. The catalogue as a whole is a monument to a man with a truly Renaissance versatility.

In his lifetime Heber had been the object of gentle derision for his habit of owning more than one copy of the same work. The legend of the magpie collector dies hard. There were some books which Heber (like all collectors) seemed unable to resist, however many copies he possessed already—though the storing of his collection in so many different places made duplication not unreasonable. But the legend of indiscriminate collecting is false. Heber nearly always had perfectly good reasons for possessing duplicates, quite apart from his generosity in lending his books. For example, many rare books survive in imperfect condition: of a dozen extant copies one may lack the title-page, another the preface, a third the colophon. To possess the work complete, therefore, a collector may often need to own several differently imperfect copies. Moreover, of many works Heber possessed not only the first edition but significant subsequent editions as well. In this he was in advance of most contemporary collectors, for few of them realized that the logic of book-collecting (as well as the needs of scholarship) might well dictate a man's possession of, say, the three early editions of *Hamlet*, or a thousand Bibles: the significant first editions of Latin, Greek and Hebrew texts, famous recensions, first translations into English, French, German, Polish, Welsh, and editions famous for their printing, illustration, binding, or association.

The sale of Heber's books by public auction took three years to complete (1834–37); and it was an almost complete failure. The market was flooded and it took a generation to recover from the inundation. For the "cometary period" of English bibliophilism was over when Heber's books were sold, the old collectors were dead or inactive, and the bibliophiles of the next age were either not yet in action, or else provided insufficient competition for so gigantic a dispersal.

Two men only were ready for the sale. The first was Sir Thomas Phillipps, who purchased the bulk of Heber's manuscripts for the great library at Middle Hall. The other was W. H. Miller, "Measure Miller" as he was called from the pocket foot-rule which always accompanied him for the measurement of margins. Through the bookseller Thorpe, Miller was the biggest buyer of the printed books, and from the ruins of the Heber collection were laid the foundations of what later became the Britwell Library, the great collection of rare English books many of which, in our own century, were floated on Henry E. Huntington's Standard Oil to San Marino, California. But so weak was the competition, and so depressed the market, that a collection the cost of which it is idle to estimate sold for little more than 60,000 pounds.

It was a scandal that the great institutional libraries of Britain, or the Government, should have ignored the opportunity to purchase by private treaty from Heber's heirs. The Curators of the Bodleian Library considered the proposal of the Librarian, Dr. Bandinell, but decided against it, and though valuable buys were made at the sale, it cannot be said that the Library rose to the occasion. Sir Frederick Maddan of the British Museum, struggling on a miserly annual grant of 8,000 pounds, was unable to secure more than a handful of choice manuscripts for the national library which existed in the first place only because of a bequest from a private collector. And so Heber's books, assembled painfully with discriminating passion and skill from the European and English book-markets, were once again dispersed. But this time they went forth with the small black oblong which marked their sojourn in the *Bibliotheca Heberiana*, thenceforth to be objects of cherished value.

Herein lies the moral of Heber's career with which I must end. It is supposed by many that the great literary and historical treasures of the past survive through their possession of some magical preservative; that the remorseless grinding of the pulping-mill and the operation of human malice, neglect, ignorance and violence are somehow suspended in the presence of what we have learnt to value in our heritage. The lost plays of Sophocles, and the vanished literature of the middle ages are too remote from most people to bring home with immediacy the tenuous life of texts and records committed to manuscript or print. That so much has survived can in no small measure be attributed to the activities of the book-collectors of the past. "Every great collection in the world," Seymour de Ricci has written, "has been made by men who had foresight enough to secure for themselves, to snatch away from others, objects that they understood to be really significant and desirable." Because it is the ambition of collectors "to find value where there seems to be none, to put a finger on those things which have in them the latent capacity to become valuable and curious," "to preserve what the men of the time refuse in the presence of something newer, and, as they hold, better," "the book-collector is in fact one of the assault troops in literature's and history's battle against the inequity of oblivion."

Bibliographical note. An apparatus of footnotes having proved both undesirable and impractical, I gladly acknowledge generally my indebtedness to the following: for Heber's life to R. H. Cholmondeley, *The Heber Letters* (Batchworth Press, 1950), as well as the usual contemporary sources; for his career as a collector to T. F. Dibdin, *The Bibliographical Decameron* (1817), *Reminiscences of a Literary Life* (1836), and *Bibliomania* (1876), as well as the sales catalogues of the period, often having names of purchasers and prices. Two sets of Sanders lectures have become classics for the study of English book-collecting: Seymour de Ricci, *English Collectors of Books and Manuscripts* (Cambridge, 1932), and John Carter, *Taste and Technique in Book-Collecting* (Cambridge, 1948), and still useful are John Hill Burton, *The Book-Hunter* (1866) and W. Y. Fletcher, *English Book Collectors* (1902). A. N. L. Munby's *Phillipps Studies* (Cambridge, 1951) touches on nearly every aspect of nineteenth-century collecting.

PAUL WEST

Jacob Burckhardt and the "Ideal Past"

Aloof, carping, pessimistic, prophetic and spiritually timid, Jacob Burckhardt, the author of *The Civilization of the Renaissance in Italy*, is not an inspiring figure. He was a dedicated spirit certainly—to sensibility, the living past, decorum, balance, order, hierarchy and conservatism. But, living austerely in two rooms above a baker's shop in Basel, he seems gratuitously medieval; and his view that "things can only be changed by ascetics, men who are independent of the enormously expensive life of the great cities" puts one in mind of Peter and Berenson. He commended the Roman Emperors of the third century A.D. for their unrelenting grip on the masses ("the common people, with their naïve belief in 'the goodness of human nature' "), but maintained that the true saviours of Greco-Roman civilization were the anchorites and ascetics of the Christian church. Without them the Middle Ages would have been, as the twentieth century threatened to become, "a den of murderers." (One is reminded of Berenson's large claims for art without which "our world would have remained a jungle.") All Burckhardt could see was a declining civilization in which the grimly looming masses needed only a saviour—*Führer*—to guide them into carnage and a new barbarism.

It is of course easy to dismiss such fears as the consequence of an excessively withdrawn life: Burckhardt didn't really know enough people as individuals. He preferred the safer, more manageable world of concepts, philosophies and academic routine; a world in which he could, without sensing his own fugitive tendency, contemplate "an ideal past." Such a past soothed the mind which, hating dictatorship, yet preferred the despot to the demagogue. He commended Henry VIII

HAB no. 31, November 1960.

but disparaged Mohammed. He lamented that "Experience teaches us that the human race has over the ages achieved very little of supreme excellence, and will do no better in the future . . ." but (rather aptly) he retained an appetite for miracles, for demonstrations of human free-will.

His book on the Renaissance is an exciting album, an act of wistful homage; and it has tended to fix for us a not altogether accurate image of him. He is the spectator, not the participant; indeed, in seeking in Switzerland an "Archimedean point outside events" he facilitated his attempt to live out his life in serene terms. But from his works on Italy—the study of the Renaissance, his account of *The Age of Constantine the Great and Cicerone,* his Berenson-like guide to the country's art—we are apt to form an impression rather flattering to him. What is negative we have to infer. He rightly estimates Pico della Mirandola's speech on the dignity of man as "one of the noblest bequests of that great age." The titles of his subdivisions would seem to suggest a man of wide and tutored sympathies, as ready for elation as quick to smell out bigotry: he offers "The State as a Work of Art" (much as Croce was to offer history), "The Development of the Individual," "The Revival of Antiquity" (hastening to point out that this in itself could not bring about a new civilization) and even "Society and Festivals" (which he presents with engaging relish). He is constantly on his guard against neat schemes, immaculate plans; he even goes so far as to propose a Carolingian Renaissance and another in the twelfth century. In so doing he manages to pay yet another tribute to the monastic spirit: ". . . monastic scholarship had not only gradually absorbed an immense mass of materials from the Roman writers, but the style of it, from the days of Eginhard onward, shows traces of conscious imitation." And when he uses the word "culture" he means the general way of life of an urbanized people—very much, in fact, what the social anthropologists of our own day intend by the term. He is compiling an image of a state of mind; hence his omission of political events, economic and political institutions and, above all, his reluctance to give facts as one might in an expository lecture.

One's general impression of the man is therefore favourable: scholarly but far from dry; a polymath but not confused; clearly fascinated by the psychology of it all rather than by the dates, the documents of state, or by speculations about ultimate causes. He is concerned to capture atmosphere, texture, temperature, not to attempt a constitutional history of the Italian city-states. All this looks good. There is nothing to suggest intellectual or spiritual meanness, an excessive fondness for lumping people into "the masses," a singular lack of insight into the part played in daily life by charity and unsystematic compromise. But if we turn from these entrancing and entranced, near-Arcadian studies to his *Reflections on History* and the recently-published *Judgments on History and Historians*, another view presents itself.

Oddly enough he had attributed a good deal to the mother-wit, initiative, and human sympathy of the urban upper classes in Italy; these were the people who found themselves managing the transition from prosperity and business enterprise to patronage of the arts. As he says, "It was needful that noble and burgher should first learn to dwell together on equal terms, and that a social world should arise which felt the want of culture, and had the leisure and the means to obtain it." He goes on to speak of "the natural alliance between the despot and the scholar, each relying solely on his personal talent." He seems to be being generous about an unusually fruitful type of relationship; notice his emphasis on initiative and his implication that the dominant class of society cannot but eventually propose moves in a certain direction: the enhancing of life. Where the scholastic philosophers dealt in truth and logic, the humanists busied themselves with ethics. Burckhardt notes the difference but is careful to point out that some of the humanists, acutely aware of their dependence on the whim of a patron, recommended an almost monastic way of life: literary withdrawal, contemplative speculation, the ecstatic inner life fostered by undivided attention to master-pieces and master-works. Ficino, for example, encouraged and subsidized by Cosimo de Medici, set to work on a synthesis of Plato and Christian theology. Burckhardt's comment —and we always do well to watch him closely on the subject of Plato —is revealing:

> Echoes of medieval mysticism here flow into one current with Platonic doctrines and with a *characteristically modern spirit.* One of the most precious fruits of the knowledge of the world and of man here comes to maturity, on whose account alone the Italian Renaissance must be called the leader of modern ages. [My italics.]

It is in assertions such as these, and especially in his use of such vague phrases as the one I have italicized, that Burckhardt dissimulates to the extreme. For he himself, as his volumes of historical comments show, was none too anxious to attempt to foster a similarly modern spirit in himself. Tolerance, the exoteric, the general view of nineteenth-century developments—these he avoids. It is not so much that he believes firmly in the need for an élite and its power to safeguard a hard-won spirit of civilization; his main shortcoming is that he abdicates from the kind of responsibility which we feel intellectuals ought to assume gladly and which only they, in fact, are fitted to discharge. Salvador de Madariaga's phrase, "civic monk," applies more tellingly and more justly to Burckhardt than to Gilbert Murray. It was Burckhardt who could not stomach the increasingly complex and troubled course of his own century; of the psychology of his own time he formed the hastiest impressions, and in the threatening effort of the "masses" to "dwell together on equal terms" even with burghers, he saw no analogy with what he had commended in the Renaissance itself.

Switzerland, his native country, was also the best spiritual home he could have found; this might not have been true of a less fugitive thinker. Studying history at Berlin he drank deeply of the German liberalism of the 1840's; but to Basel he returned, eventually in 1858 to become Professor of History for twenty years, resisting all blandishments to leave (even refusing to succeed Ranke at Berlin), seeing plain the drift of German policy, spotting and hating in their early stages the rise of the common man, of fascism and communism, and devotedly lingering over the records of times less clamorous. The Burckhardt family itself had lost power in Basel: Burckhardts had been burgomasters of Basel, but that privilege was only one of the things that rising democracy, even in Switzerland, swept away. There is something pathetic and irritating in the thought of this dispossessed aristocrat languishing away in that increasingly industrialized city. His lectures at the university must have been impressive; his notes for them certainly are. But, alongside so much learning, so many jeremiads—against "progress," liberalism, industrialism, faith in humanity, even joy. His compensations are exiguous or fulsome: he extols the Catholic Church and Byzantium for safeguarding the European tradition through the age of barbarism; Julius Caesar is simply "the greatest of mortals." Although he could anticipate the special mania that militarism and heavy industry would bring forth in Germany, he could not see the benefits of having a factory civilization or even consider that the hated masses might, like the nobles of Italy in his chosen period, manage to better themselves intellectually as well as physically. There is a lack of chivalry, of charity and mere forthcomingness in this man. One inclines to wonder what he, or for that matter Tocqueville (another pessimist), would have made of the work of Richard Hoggart and Raymond Williams. Certainly their effort to study culture as a general way of life has something in common with Burckhardt's own unbigoted response to Renaissance Italy, or with Tocqueville's open-mindedness in America and Ireland—although that shows to better advantage in Tocqueville's notebooks and journals than when scattered among the polished theories of his major study. In fact, of course, Burckhardt's enthusiasm for Italy is enthusiasm within an enclosed garden; his generous response was the very thing he incarcerated as a gesture well and once made, thereafter to be cherished as a refined feat performed by a beleaguered patrician. His gesture made, he closed up.

Not surprisingly he over-prized art. There is a passage in his *Judgments* in which he chides Erasmus for reasons that cannot but make us think twice about the validity of Burckhardt as teacher:

> In reference to the luxurious tomb of Thomas à Becket and the marble splendour of the Certosa di Pavia, Erasmus preaches the most insipid "charity," saying that the money ought to have been given to the poor and that flowers were sufficient adornment for a saint's grave. (The poor of the time would soon have consumed the money concerned, and we would not possess the Certosa, etc.) Then Erasmus polemicizes against the artistic embellishment of noble graves in the churches generally.

There is fanaticism here. This man, lamenting his own loss of social status, would yet argue art against charity. It may be true that empty stomachs should have something resplendent in their lives, something "most lasting than bronze" that symbolizes something more lasting than anything. Lavish monuments no doubt do persuade the inhabitants of shacks that our stay here is brief and our condition during it irrelevant. But if we are dealing with people as religious as that, then surely they would show an even greater disregard for this world's goods if they could find God in a grain of sand or a dilapidated shack, and then spend the money not on idols but on paint for the shack, to the greater protection of God's gift. There is, perhaps, a wise middle way between over-eating and over-spending on idols, between the sin of self-inflicted penury and the sin of a worship that has to be stimulated by splendours in marble and gold. But these reflections do not fit a Burckhardt; he would never have suggested that although poor people like to leave dingy rooms to enter lavish cathedrals, it is the lavishness of the cathedrals that prevents the rooms from becoming anything but dingy.

Burckhardt's homilies—against getting and spending, the cult of "technical and material greatness," "the total egoism of today's private person," "the inability to distinguish technical and material greatness from the intellectual and moral kinds," "the acquisitive spirit and general haste," "open hatred upon the outstanding person," democracy's "programme involving equality of enjoyment"—are by no means beyond our sympathy but also depend on a fundamentally uncharitable attitude that we might not always suspect. Too often he substitutes for humanity an arid worship of intellect. He condemns materialism not for its inhumanity but for its silliness, its vulgarity, its link with the majority. He blames people not for selfishness but for being selfish about intellectually unworthy objects. (Julien Benda inherited something of this attitude; Benda, as T. S. Eliot says in his essay on Irving Babbitt, had "a romantic view of critical detachment which limits his interest." The same is substantially true of Burckhardt.)

I think I have said enough to show that Burckhardt was a romantic: self-obsessed and incapable of the middle way. He commends the "subjectivity of the intellect" which in the sixteenth century "was so vigorously astir in all new things and produced such strong personalities." But he doubts "whether our time is favourable to primary, creative *geniuses* . . . whether the gathering of knowledge does not stand in the way of higher productivity." Democracy, he says, "stands outside anything intellectual." He is writing in the third quarter of the nineteenth century; all the same he is not displaying the clear-minded objectivity he commended in the Renaissance humanists. The truth about him begins to emerge; he has strange longings to live in an epic age; not only does he look fondly back to Tacitus' reports of German atavism ("they celebrate Tuisto, a god born of the earth, and his son Mannus as the origin and founders of their race") but asserts that "A valuable possession of a people is its first heroic epic. In addition to daily life there at least exists an ideal past. . . ." And here, strangely similar to the atavistic outbursts of Charles Kingsley and J. G. Frazer, is a passage of Burckhardt idyll:

> Camoens is accustomed to dealing blows to Mohammedans and Malabar Indians, problably fighting one against ten. No dust from the road whirls in his poem, but the salt of the sea; it is life on shipboard, sinewy, severely simple, fine-blooded, replete with martial fervour to the point of extreme fanaticism. It, too, is austere. Nothing but the roaring of the sea and the clangour of arms is audible.
>
> He repeatedly voices profound complaints about his nation's harsh, austere insensitivity to poetry; it is still wholly caught up in acting and acquiring and is not yet ready to listen. And yet he expressed its feeling clearly and completely at a time which still tolerated true feeling. And only today, when people talk much more about poetry, would he be completely lost; the cities would either ignore him or seize upon his palpable imperfections and finish him off.
>
> Camoens still satisfied the best of his times and of his nation. There is no longer any satisfying the best of *our* times.
>
> *Os Lusiades*, the Lusitanians! It is the whole glory of the nation. . . .

Explanation yields to a sudden transport and that to a wail followed by what surely is meant to be a virile exclamation to himself. The yearning for heroic simplicity is obvious; it amounts to the inward pastoral and evokes, for us, D. H. Lawrence, Pound, and Pater. There is no doubt that we have come a little further along that road leading from contact with primitive nature to contact with too many things of our own devising. (One is reminded of, for instance, the Canadian summer-shack habit: a reversion to primitive type.) Burckhardt, writing in the fairly late nineteenth century, is sketching out his own Waste Land. But he is also indulging in the kind of gratuitous "martial fervour" that occasionally prompts the military (as at such times as the Suez affair) to go and bomb something for sheer spiritual ease. A milder version is Frazer's scholarly pastoral: "No one who has seen the calm water of the Lake of Nemi, lapped in a green hollow of the Alban hills, can ever forget it. Diana herself might still be lingering by this lonely shore, haunting the woodland wild." But Frazer, piecing together his scattered deity, also relished the human comedy—as do E. M. Forster and Gilbert Murray. What Frazer and Burckhardt have in common is a weak sense of both social texture and of individual psychology. Burckhardt knew little of people but that did not discourage him from condemning the excessive (as he thought) individualism of his time. The trouble is that he defined as excessive individualism any move not allowed for by his aristocratic notion of society; so any reform making for increased liberty where none was before is excessive. In fact he condemned according to a rather simple faith in categories—those unfailing annullers of people as persons. At least Frazer stuck to his gods.

Burckhardt berates the same phenomenon, "excessive individualism," in the Renaissance. It developed from the subjective pursuit of worldly ends: "The individual first inwardly casts off the authority of a State which, as a fact, is in most cases tyrannical and illegitimate. . . ." This he found true of scholars, humanists, rulers, nobles, and papacy alike. There were exceptions; in some men "a clear and unmistakable tendency to strictness in matters of religion and morality" was paramount. But his account of his own age finds no exceptions; the wording is very similar: ". . . today's private person . . . wants to exist as an individual and asks of the community only the greatest possible security for himself and his property, for which he pays taxes amid sighs and sighs. . . ." He is really distinguishing between a vigorous and an idle self-seeking, neither of them (in his eyes) half as desirable as what is to be found in antiquity:

> . . . the complete individual in antiquity is, above all, polites (part of the state) to a degree of which we now in the present mode of connection between the individual and the state, have no idea. Whenever one breaks with the poleis (polis) or when it is lost, it is a tragedy every time.
>
> Finally, today's "educated" men are firmly resolved to make a bargain, with whatever power, for their existence at any given time. There is an enormous veneration of life and property. There is a mass abdication, and not just on the part of the rulers!

He might well talk of abdication; his own utopia and ideology are plain: "fine-blooded," patrician, civic, conformist. He may offer us a glimpse of some middle way between anarchy and sheer line-toeing; but he says that the individualism of the Renaissance came about through "historical necessity." We might have thought his ideal one of stoical, alert citizenship; he certainly anticipates some features of behaviour in the welfare state and the lonely crowd. But he approves of individualism and originality only when they do not threaten to upset the social order to which he is emotionally attached. He may, as some have said, anticipate the existentialist concern with self-creation; but his sense of the dynamics of that process is enfeebled by snobbery. How ironic that this expert on the age of voracious humanism should have learned so little from it about the art of being reasonable.

But at least, if not an outgoing type of humanist, Burckhardt was an accurate prophet of destructions both physical and intellectual. It was in 1896 that Ernst Troeltsch, with distressed elation, informed a theological conference at Eisenach: "Gentlemen, everything is tottering!" That everything included traditional views of consciousness, time, factuality and political theory; and the topplers of the old edifices were themselves uneasy. For the spirit of inquiry is in itself no edifice; and most men need an edifice or system to live by. In place of lip-served certainties the topplers, with much show of logic, set paradoxes, anomalies and hypotheses bound to bewilder or be misinterpreted.

The world-picture changed; much seemed lost, much discovered. But what was discovered seemed of little compensatory value: people like to change their way of being wrong only if the new way confers the old sense of security. But, if we consider the record only briefly and roughly, the new world-picture is obviously one of uncertainty and relativity: Planck and Einstein evolved new determinisms that brought with them new, inevitable dangers; the Cubists and Schoenberg revised established schemes of portrayal and harmony; Pareto showed that democracy is incompatible with equality; Max Weber diagnosed the mentality that would follow the Hitler-*shamans*; Durkheim established the principles of social incoherence in terms of *anomie*; Freud exposed hidden parts that Jung affiliated together; Bergson and Gertrude Stein posited the continuousness that cannot be ordered, divided up and still less labelled; and Marx evolved a political theory both powerful and invulnerable. Middle-class liberalism and positivism were discredited by the scientific, or scientific-seeming, methods of sociology; for once hopeful guesswork in political theory was not enough. And the consequence was irrationalism or a rather frantic reliance on science: infatuation with Marx, then an equally exaggerated repudiation once the "Great Depression" was over. The unsteady allegiances of Shaw and Sorel exemplify the disorientation of the time.

Much of this disintegration without synthesis Burckhardt anticipated and condemned, reflecting how the mind's ingenuity and gullibility would outstrip its atavistic needs as well as the capacities of human nature. We may not approve of his fugitive response, but we cannot altogether deny the accuracy of the insights on which he based his slowly monopolizing gloom.

G. MARCOTTE

D'une littérature nationale

De plus en plus fréquemment, lorsqu'on me parle de littérature canadienne-française, j'ai envie d'aller prendre l'air. Car j'ai l'impression qu'on ne me parle pas de livres, d'œuvres, mais d'une sorte d'entreprise de propagande culturelle qu'il faut mousser à tout prix, pour la plus grande gloire de la nation canadienne-française. Parfois même il me semble qu'on invite les écrivains à produire à seule fin que les éditeurs puissent éditer, parce que l'édition doit être florissante dans tout pays qui se respecte. Je ne vois pas, par exemple, qu'on se soit étonné, scandalisé, de l'extrême pauvreté spirituelle et littéraire de la grande majorité des œuvres d'imagination parues au Canada français depuis un an. Mais on s'est beaucoup inquieté de la diminution du nombre des nouveautés. C'est qu'il nous faut une littérature nationale, à tout prix, quelle que soit la qualité des œuvres qu'elle comporte. Tant mieux si c'est bon — on ne va pas jusqu'à souhaiter expressément une mauvaise littérature —, tant pis si c'est mauvais, l'essentiel paraît être que le Canada français puisse jouer un rôle voyant, à fois à l'intérieur de ses frontières et sur l'échiquier mondial des littératures.

Cette volonté — qui est en même temps un aveu d'inquiétude — n'est pas exclusive au Canada français, mais elle a atteint ici un degré de virulence qu'on rencontre rarement ailleurs. Que je sache, le Belge, le Suisse, le Sénégalais, ne sont pas préoccupés outre mesure du problème d'une littérature nationale. Le Canadien français, oui. Et depuis fort longtemps. Depuis Crémazie, qui désespérait de voir le Canada devenir autre chose, au point de vue littéraire, qu'une simple colonie, jusqu'à certains jeunes poètes d'aujourd'hui, qui parlent de « canadienneté » et de « québécitude » comme si la littérature cana-

HAB vol. XIV, fall 1963. From an address to the annual meeting of the Humanities Association of Canada, 1963.

dienne-française pouvait se trouver dans deux ou trois néologismes. Mais celui qu'il faut citer, c'est le plus sérieux et le plus logique de nos critiques, Monseigneur Camille Roy, qui écrivait, au moment où commençaient de paraître au Canada quelques œuvres écrites en bon français :

> Faisons donc ici, écrivait-il, une bonne littérature canadienne; et cette littérature sera le prolongement nécessaire des vertus de notre langue française, et elle en sera aussi comme un rempart solide et respecté. Faisons cette littérature aussi nationale que possible, c'est-à-dire aussi chargée que possible des choses et des pensées et des sentiments de chez nous, et elle portera ainsi au grand jour, en plein soleil, les fleurs de la notre vie; faisons-la aussi artistique que possible, et elle montrera que notre parler n'est pas celui de colons barbares, mais qu'il est plein des harmoniques de la plus belle langue du monde; faisons-la militante, appliquée à défendre le verbe gardien de la foi, et elle s'érigera jusqu'à la hauteur du plus généreux apostolat.

Personne aujourd'hui, sans doute, n'oserait proposer un semblable programme, car la notion même de littérature, dans notre milieu, est devenue moins simple, elle a échappé, notamment, aux engagements un peu trop précis que voulait lui assigner le bon Monseigneur. Mais je crois déceler, dans maintes déclarations récentes, des aspirations analogues aux siennes. Cela, il me semble, mérite un peu d'examen, car le national, en art, est un ingrédient assez particulier. Comment, dans une aussi petite nation que la nôtre, dans un monde où les échanges culturels sont si rapides qu'on assiste véritablement à la naissance d'une littérature internationale — « A guerres mondiales, littérature planétaire, » écrit Roger Caillois —, comment se présente et se justifie le désir d'une littérature nationale ? A quel besoin correspond-elle, et quels services peut-elle rendre ?

Abordons la question par son aspect le plus superficiel, celui de la propagande. On désire que le Canada français ait une littérature nationale, et que cette littérature soit appréciée à l'étranger, afin que notre nation obtienne une petite place aux Nations-Unies de l'art. On attend avec impatience l'œuvre forte, éclatante, neuve, qui attirera sur le Canada français l'attention du monde entier. Mais aussitôt nous nous heurtons à certaines difficultés, à certaines équivoques. Car il ne suffit pas qu'une œuvre soit de qualité pour obtenir le succès qu'on espère. C'est presque une lapalissade, mais on ferait bien de la prendre au sérieux. Les œuvres canadiennes-françaises qui ont obtenu le plus grand succès en France, ces dernières années, sont *Les enfants qui s'aiment* et *Autour de toi, Tristan*, de Claire France, deux romans médiocres, très inférieurs à *Poussière sur la ville* d'André Langevin et au *Temps des jeux* de Diane Giguère, qui sont passé à peu près inaperçus. Voyons un exemple plus récent : *Le Charivari*, de Robert Goulet, qui avait d'abord été publié aux Etats-Unis, sous le titre de *The Violent Season* et y avait remporté un grand succès, qui se répétera peut-être en Grande-Bretagne et en France. Or, sur un sujet analogue, Yves Thériault avait donné une œuvre beaucoup plus forte et vraie, *Les Vendeurs du temple*, qui n'a fait aucune carrière internationale. L'édition est un commerce, et il ne faut pas s'étonner que ses lois diffèrent considérablement de celles de la littérature. C'est une conjuration de hasards et d'influences, ou peut-être l'intervention imprévisible d'un grand écrivain français — comme celle de Sartre en faveur d'Aimé Césaire — qui fera que la littérature canadienne-française percera le mur du son. La qualité même de cette littérature n'est pas directement en cause. Qu'Alain Grandbois, par exemple, ne soit pas connu à l'extérieur de nos frontières, ne change rien au fait qu'il est un des grands poètes français de ce siècle.

Sur un plan plus profond, plus nécessaire, une littérature nationale a pour fonction de faire entrer dans la conscience internationale ce qui caractérise la collectivité dont elle est issue. La littérature a beau être devenue, selon le mot de Roger Caillois, « œcuménique, » elle n'en cesse pas pour autant d'accueillir les différences de sensibilité, d'imagination, de vision du monde, qui se font jour d'une nation à l'autre. Et même, écrit Caillois : « Un peuple ne confère à sa littérature une portée mondiale qu'au moment où il cesse d'habiller sa propre culture de vêtements d'emprunt pour tirer, de l'épaisseur de ses préférences, de ses misères et de ses vertus, le seul style capable de les exprimer complètement. » Mais les exemples cités tout à l'heure démontrent qu'il n'est pas toujours facile de faire comprendre ces préférences, ces misères, ces vertus. On peut, avec quelque raison, attribuer cette difficulté à notre littérature elle-même, ou plus profondément à ce que le Père Gagnon appelle « l'indétermination de notre géographie intérieure ». Notre géographie extérieure, même, nous l'avons à peine dite, et nous sommes encore étonnés quand nous rencontrons chez le Suédois Erik Lindegren de flamboyantes images d'hiver — un hiver semblable au nôtre —, et chez le Russe

Boris Pasternak une célébration de l'automne qui pourrait, qui devrait peut-être avoir été faite par un de nos poètes. Mais, malgré tout, il me paraît que la littérature canadienne-française a entrepris d'affirmer sa différence, qu'une histoire assez nouvelle s'y raconte — celle d'un exil, ou d'un drame d'isolement —, et qu'elle n'a pas été comprise. Je lis la préface d'Alain Bosquet à son anthologie de la poésie canadienne, et j'y vois toutes sortes de considérations sur le nationalisme canadien-français, le vocabulaire particulier (c'est-à-dire les canadianismes) de certains poètes, mais rien qui indique la présence, dans cette poésie, d'une interrogation commune. De même, la préface de Pierre Emmanuel au recueil d'Anne Hébert, *Le Tombeau des rois* : « On peut faire, écrit-il, l'expérience des déserts de l'âme à Québec aussi bien qu'en Arabie pétrée », c'est-à-dire : lisez la poésie d'Anne Hébert comme si elle venait de n'importe où, il ne nous chaut absolument pas qu'elle soit née dans la Province de Québec, où il y a des gens qui gèlent en hiver et brûlent en été, et parlent français contre tout bon sens. Par contre, il est assez significatif qu'on ait cru nécessaire, aux Editions du Seuil, de faire précéder le roman d'Anne Hébert, *Les Chambres de bois*, d'une explication donnée par M. Samuel de Sacy. Que se passe-t-il donc ? Il y a encore du vrai dans la remarque de Crémazie : « Ce qui manque au Canada — écrivait-il, avec un humour qu'on aurait aimé retrouver dans sa lourde poésie —, c'est d'avoir une langue à lui. Si nous parlions iroquois ou huron, notre littérature vivrait. Malheureusement nous parlons et écrivons d'une assez piteuse façon, il est vrai, la langue de Bossuet et de Racine. » C'est-à-dire que nous sommes, à la fois, trop près et trop loin de la France. Les canadianismes qui enchantent Alain Bosquet dans la poésie de Rina Lasnier, ne sont que d'anodines décorations, auprès des bouffées de langage neuf qui nous accueillent dans la poésie d'un Aimé Césaire. En somme, nous manquons d'exotisme. Nos meilleurs poètes et romanciers s'expriment bonnement en français, comme tout le monde. Pis encore, et cela vaut surtout pour nos poètes, ils paraissent exprimer les mêmes thèmes, les mêmes préoccupations, que leurs contemporains français. Lisez *L'Anthologie de la poésie nouvelle*, de Jean Paris : vous y verrez que des poètes comme Yves Bonnefoy, André du Bouchet, Roger Giroux, mettent en œuvre un drame de l'absence dont on retrouve aisément les échos dans la littérature canadienne-française. Tout beau, nous voilà enfin à l'heure de Paris.

Mais attention, cette rencontre apparente cache une profonde dissemblance, et l'absence n'est pas ressentie de la même façon à Montréal qu'à Paris. L'absence du poète français contient, si je puis dire, la présence niée, disparue, tandis qu'au Canada français elle est au départ, sans souvenir et sans tradition de présence. Aujourd'hui même, et bien que notre littérature et notre conscience collective aient fait d'étonnants progrès, l'écrivain canadien-français est forcé de commencer, d'inventer. Et ce qu'il invente, c'est moins de nouvelles formes littéraires que les premières formes de l'existence. C'est cela, je pense, que le lecteur français, si intelligent qu'on le suppose, ne réussit pas à comprendre quand il aborde notre littérature. Il imagine, consciemment ou non, que la littérature canadienne-française sera la littérature française, avec un léger coefficient d'exotisme. Il admet difficilement que l'aventure qui se poursuit ici, en français mais en terre américaine, doive se trouver, dans son existence concrète, des fondements nouveaux. Il y a là une source de malentendus énormes, et qui n'est pas près de se tarir. En fait, elle ne se tarira vraisemblablement que lorsque des œuvres canadiennes — à la faveur de quelles circonstances, je ne sais — auront imposé, avec une puissance tout à fait exceptionnelle, une vision nouvelle du monde; et alors le lecteur étranger pourra jeter un regard neuf sur une littérature neuve.

Enfin, dernier aspect de la question, et sans doute le plus important, le rôle d'une littérature nationale dans la collectivité même qui la produit. On admet aisément aujourd'hui, contrairement à Monseigneur Camille Roy, qu'il ne s'agit pas d'un rôle d'abord militant. La littérature, dans ses rapports avec la collectivité, n'a pas à combattre, sauf cas particuliers; sa fonction est d'élucider, d'amener au jour les puissances obscures qui sommeillent dans l'inconscient collectif, et, ce faisant, d'ouvrir la voie au possible. La littérature canadienne-française a commencé d'accomplir cette tâche, et l'on peut soutenir qu'il est impossible de comprendre notre nation sans avoir consulté sa littérature. Dans l'ordre de la constatation, la littérature a précédé constamment, dans notre milieu, les disciplines dites scientifiques; c'est elle qui la première, avec le *Bonheur d'occasion* de Gabrielle Roy, a découvert au Canada français un véritable prolétariat économique et culturel; Claude-Henri Grignon dans *Un Homme et son péché*, Ringuet dans *30 arpents*, on décrit le manque à gagner spirituel d'une certaine classe paysanne bien avant que des historiens entreprennent de dénoncer le mythe « agriculturiste »; et ce qu'il y a de valable aujourd'hui dans le mouvement séparatiste — c'est-à-dire une volonté d'affirmation collective —, nos poètes l'exprimaient déjà il y a plusieurs années, alors que dans les autres milieux intellectuels toute pensée nationale était résolument dévalorisée. Assurément, la littérature a également contribué à entretenir des mythes périmés; mais aussi bien c'était sa fonction de les exprimer, au sens étymologique du mot, c'est-à-dire de les presser comme des citrons, pour en faire sortir tout le jus, et à cet égard des œuvres comme *Menaud, maître-draveur* de Monseigneur Savard et *La Chesnaie* de Rex Desmarchais, dans leur exaltation malsaine du particularisme canadien-français, n'ont pas été inutiles. La littérature n'est pas un mode d'accouchement de tout repos, et livre, plus souvent que ne le voudraient les esprits sages, des monstres à trois yeux et à cinq bras. Il faut savoir lire la littérature; et de cette lecture, dans une collectivité, les critiques sont en grande partie responsables. Or on ne peut pas dire qu'au Canada français, ils se soient montrés particulièrement lucides et vigilants. Peut-être, aussi, leur demandait-on plus que ce qu'ils pouvaient fournir : déchiffrer une littérature qui n'a pas encore, dans la grande majorité de ses œuvres, atteint le stade esthétique, exige les moyens du psychologue et du sociologue, plus que ceux de la critique littéraire traditionnelle.

Je viens de prononcer le mot « esthétique, » et peut-être s'est-on étonné qu'il ne soit pas intervenu plus tôt dans ces considérations. C'est que le national n'épuise pas le littéraire proprement dit, et peut-être même l'inclut-il avec difficulté. Sans doute il n'est pas inutile à une nation de posséder — pour employer le langage du commerce — des œuvres belles et fortes, célébrant la gloire et la diversité de l'existence; son niveau culturel en est haussé d'autant. Mais alors ces œuvres, si elles portent la marque du milieu humain qui les a vu naître, ne se définissent plus en premier ressort par le national. Faulkner, St-John Perse, Shakespeare, Goethe et Mayakowski exercent sur moi leur emprise, non pas d'abord parce qu'ils sont américain, français, anglais, allemand, russe, mais parce qu'ils posent à l'homme universel les questions de toujours, dans un langage qui, par delà les particularités linguistiques, peut devenir celui de tous. D'où l'impatience que je manifestais au début de cette communication. On parle peut-être trop de littérature nationale, au Canada français, pour qu'il soit aisé d'y parler littérature. On y parle peut-être trop de l'homme canadien-français, pour qu'un humanisme véritable impose enfin ses formes.

E. W. MANDEL

A Lack of Ghosts: Canadian Poets and Poetry

Most criticism of Canadian poetry has been concerned with one major puzzle: how is it possible for there to be a distinctive Canadian poetry? The question lends itself easily to some silly answers, like the one given by Lighthall in his introduction to *Songs of the Great Dominion* when he tells us that if we listen to the poets in his anthology we may catch something of the great Niagara falling, a remark which recalls Paul Heibert's superb parody of literary critics and Canadian poets, *Sarah Binks*: "Unschooled, but unspoiled," says Heibert of the sweet songstress of Saskatchewan, Sarah Binks, "this simple country girl has captured in her net of poesy the flatness of that great province." Obviously, if we are going to look for the distinctiveness of Canadian poetry, we will be tempted to find it in geography or sociology; we will want a poetry which in some way reflects or defines the particular and distinctive place and time in which it originates. But even if we avoid the worst excesses of this kind of criticism, there are still certain traps in it which can trouble the most skilful and wary reader.

I am not saying that there has never been such a thing as a Canadian poem which defines or evokes the atmosphere and quality, the very shape and form of the life of a particular place. This would be the most patent nonsense to anyone who has read, say, Louis Dudek's *East of the City*, a good deal of Raymond Souster's poetry, or the Vancouver poems of Earle Birney. There are such places as A. M. Klein's Montreal, with its curiously oriental streets, its Jewish candy stores, and its French-Canadian politicians; or Fred Cogswell's Mari-

HAB vol. XVI, no. 1, spring 1965. Adapted from a lecture given originally in the Ontario College of Art series "Almost One Hundred Years."

times with their dreary roads, their shacks, their grim-faced, sex-crazed Puritans; or even Reaney's Stratford, with its maiden aunts, its janitors and Victorian houses, its musty parlours, and its grim-faced, sex-crazed Puritans. There's Anne Marriott's prairie graveyard, and Miriam Waddington's remembrance of things past in Winnipeg, and Charles G. D. Roberts' Tantramar marshes. I am saying, however, that it is very difficult to discover in what a particular poetic reality consists. "Our experience," remarks Francis Sparshott, "is of a single personal life, and of a single social life. We are conscious of no such discontinuities as would justify the claim that the personalities of our selves and our societies cannot be characterized. If they cannot be briefly described, this is only the more reason for supposing that in works of art their flavour may be caught, since a work of art is obviously related in multiple ways to the other phenomena of its time."[1] This is also the reason for feeling that the flavour of social reality is something more than mere natural description or representation. Poetry of place and time is peculiarly deceptive. More often than not, it is as conventionalized as the more general or abstract forms which lack its particularity. After all, what we recognize as particular or detailed is very often precisely what we have been called upon to see in a purely conventional way.

I suspect that here we have a reason for the continuing concern of our critics with the problem of a distinctive Canadian poetry. Above all, it seems important to say that if ours is a valuable poetry it is not derivative or imitative. Ironically enough, this very desire for an original poetry is a product of the colonialism which it seeks to escape and is itself a sign of the provincialism which we would like to pretend we have long grown past. It may sound a good deal more satisfying to some people to be told that Roberts' potato fields are real live Maritime potato fields rather than a romantic landscape in the mode of Wordsworth or Keats. But in the end, it is not Maritime potatoes which endure, nor on the other hand, is it the Wordsworthian romantic mode which is provincial. The potatoes are provincial, nothing more so; the romantic mode is part of the developing structure of Western thought, part of the whole civilizing process which we call culture and which we feel transcends the boundaries of Nova Scotia.

In order to meet these objections, that in so far as our poetry is local it is provincial, and that in so far as it is not local, it is derivative, our critics have been put to some peculiar contortions, and the history of Canadian poetry as a result reads like a most curiously involved page in literature. From Lighthall on, we have had the persistent notion of some kind of dichotomy in Canadian poetry between the purely local and the general, literary, or universal, depending on how grand you want to make literary tradition sound. In the important and influential criticism of A. J. M. Smith, this becomes a distinction between the native and cosmopolitan traditions of Canadian poetry. In John Sutherland's answer to Smith, it becomes a distinction between the American and English influences on our poets; among contemporaries, like Raymond Souster, it is the difference between realistic and formal or academic poetry. I myself remember once trying to work out this distinction in purely critical terms as the difference between imitative and creative art or between some kind of realism and symbolism or expressionism.

I think it is important to put aside the theory of a dual tradition, to admit at the outset how very much our poetry has been influenced by the poetry of England and the United States, and especially to get rid of the notion that we must somehow cut ourselves off from all civilizing traditions in art. We cannot quite escape, it is true, from the feeling that somehow everything once began at a certain point here in Canada and that we are new, untouched, virgin, pure, untainted by the older, corrupted civilizations of Europe. But this view, which finally works itself out as a myth of a new Eden and a new paradise, is actually one which the Americans have made better use of than we have. Our own myth, which is only just beginning to take shape as we discover the shape of our own poetry, is something rather different and works the opposite way to the American. But this is something I'll come to a little later on. Just now, I would want to insist on the powerful and continuing influence from abroad.

The four major impulses of Canadian poetry—the work of the Confederation poets, the New Provinces Group in Montreal in the thirties, the poets of the forties and fifties, and the so-called Toronto group of myth-making poets—all were generated, as we have been reminded more than once, by powerful currents of poetic ideas coming from outside of Canada. In the first instance, among Carman, Lampman, Scott, and Roberts, what was operating was an eclectic version of romanticism, a mixture of Wordsworthian pantheism, Shelleyian myth-making, Arnoldian melancholy, and the pre-Raphaelite extension of Keats through Tennyson and Swinburne down to the aestheticism at the end of the century. Among the Montreal poets of the thirties, Smith, Scott, and Klein, in particular, the impulse for a revitalized poetry came quite obviously not from anything within Canadian poetry but from the effect of Eliot on English literature, in particular his re-reading of Elizabethan and Jacobean dramatists, his juxtaposition of diverse traditions and attitudes, his bold experiments in diction, and his extension of the aesthetic of Pater and Wilde into the methods of French symbolism and irony. In the forties and fifties, the major impulse was American rather than English. Beginning first as a mild contact with the new poetry of the imagists, it came on with full force in the impact of Pound, Williams, Olson, Fearing, and Creeley on poets like Souster, Dudek, and Layton, though Layton, of course, likes to claim for himself grander ancestors: Shaw, Nietzsche, Lawrence, Jeremiah, Isaiah, and God. And finally the myth-makers: diverse as they are, they owe something at least to Edith Sitwell, Robert Graves, and George Barker, though they too, with a gesture as grand as Layton's, claim more impressive forbears: the whole of English literature, a triple-headed goddess of some old Celtic story, and what looks like the entire Egyptian scripture in its most esoteric version.

All this must sound, I realize, like a meaningless listing of names. Influences, you will say to me, explain no more than does environment. But there are some peculiar points worth noting about this list. First, it shows a special and oblique relationship to the development of English poetry itself, moving, like that poetry, from romantic impressionism to myth-making through the medium of new and more concentrated uses of imagery and diction; second, it shows an increasing awareness of and sophistication in the purely literary and traditional aspects of poetry: its direction is from the representational to the abstract; and third, it reveals an increasing awareness of its own pattern of development. By the time one reaches the poets who claim all of literature for their province, one has reached the peculiar state where Canadian poetry too is something to be looked at seriously to see what it in fact has to offer the young poet. There has been little, if any, interaction among Canadian poets over the long range, and yet at any given time they were obviously aware of each other and of what they were doing. No one, of course, is willing to say that his poetic father is William Wilfred Campbell, or Charles Heavysege, or Oliver Goldsmith, let alone Theodore Goodridge Roberts, or Alexander McLachlan. But now, for their own purposes, the poets have begun to insist on a peculiar shape or development in Canadian poetry. Leonard Cohen sees himself as in some way a relative of Klein and Layton. Alden Nowlan writes as if not only Fred Cogswell and therefore Edgar Lee Masters, Edward Arlington Robinson, and William Morris are his poetic masters, but Raymond Souster as well. And Reaney muses over his interest in the "dear bad poets" of our past. Strange and surprising links appear which make sense of what seemed to be disparate and discrete developments: A. J. M. Smith, we are told now, begins to sound more like Carman than like those metaphysical poets of the seventeenth century whom he would like to think he resembles. Irving Layton begins to appear as a late romantic. Klein, who was once so attractive because of his esoteric lore and Talmudic wit, becomes domestic and cosy, almost, one hesitates to say, as quaint as, well, if not Drummond, then at least Marjorie Pickthall. Certain names from the long-forgotten past suddenly leap out with new significance: Isabella Valancy Crawford, for her radically metaphorical narrative poetry; Mair, because he wrote a poetic drama; O'Grady, because his narrative is the first of what begins to look now like a long line of narrative or semi-narrative poems, ranging through Goldsmith, Duvar, Pratt, Marriott, down to Reaney's *Suit of Nettles* and Louis Dudek's *Europe* and as yet unpublished epic, *Atlantis*.[2]

The present rewrites the past. It becomes impossible now, as I said at the beginning, to read the nature poems of the Confederation poets as simple description, merely because we are now aware of one of the major movements of Canadian poetry, as Reaney puts it, "from things outside personality to a place somewhere inside personality."[3] So far as I am concerned the entire history of Canadian poetry is contained in a paragraph which Northrop Frye wrote about Bliss Carman, a paragraph which could not have been written before the poetry of E. J. Pratt, as Frye himself makes clear:

The first stage in the development of a romantic poet's mind is normally a sense of the unity of that mind through its variety of impressions: this in turn is likely to be projected as some form of pantheism, which has its advantages if properly developed, as Wordsworth shows, but the disadvantage of adding vagueness to monotony if it is not. Carman's conscious mind stuck at a broken down and corny version of Emersonian oversoulfulness: his editor, with a touch of distaste, speaks of "his elaborate theory of Unitrinianism—spirit leading; mental guidance, physical fulfillment—the full revelation of the doctrine of Personal Harmonizing." I don't know what all this means, but it sounds in more than one sense too awful for words. . . . On the other hand, Carman's poetic sense told him, as it told Isabella Crawford before him and Pratt after him, that the most obvious development of a romantic landscape poet is towards the mythological, towards making his emotional impressions into a *dramatis personae* of forces at once human and natural. Carman's formative influences were late Victorian, and he follows Swinburne, Morris, and Rossetti in enamelling nature with primary colours and peopling it with the pagan gods of the turning year, "Our Lady of the Rain," the dying gods Adonis and Attis, nymphs and fauns. And while his conscious mind called for songs of the open road and getting in tune with the infinite, his real poetic imagination became increasingly brooding, lonely, and haunted . . . .[4]

From landscape as a metaphor of the mind itself to the mind as a landscape animated with living beings: this, in the microcosmic career of Carman, is the history of what Canadian poetry is worth preserving. And, it bears repeating, its direction is not outward to things as they are but inward to "a place somewhere inside personality." To take another example: the same progression Frye discovers in Carman can be shown in Lampman, where we find a movement from poems like "Heat" and "In November," in which the external world is an equivalent for an inner state, to a poem like "The City of the End of Things" with its unholy trinity, its "grim idiot at the gate," its curiously prophetic vision of a fully-automated city, empty of all human life but clanking about in its endless round, a vision unmatched, I think, in Canadian writing unless in Grove's frightening account of a similarly demonic machine world in *The Master of the Mill.*

Sociology finally has been replaced here by something quite different, and the geography we are concerned with is, if Canadian, not one which you are likely to encounter anywhere between Regina and Winnipeg, north of Toronto, or even in Quebec. In a moment, I am going to examine that geography more closely, as a means of defining what Canadian poetry is, but first there is one objection to be put aside.

I am aware of the fact that some readers of Canadian poetry will still insist that the potato fields of the Maritimes are really there, and if they're not, they ought to be. They will point to the poetry of Raymond Souster and say, "but this is precisely the Toronto I know." To this I can only reply that Raymond Souster and others will certainly convince us that they are writing about places which we know. But this is by no means all they are writing of. On closer examination —and I have argued this point elsewhere—Raymond Souster's Toronto turns out to be a most curious city. It is inhabited by cripples, whores, beggars, beaten animals, old and dying men. All of its intellectuals are eunuchs; all of its women prostitutes; love, at the very best, is something stolen in secret corners and desperate moments; at what used to be Sunnyside, a roller-coaster takes off from its tracks and flies out across Lake Ontario, and at Casa Loma even stranger things are happening. This demonic city is observed by a poet who is at one and the same time villain-rogue-fool and doctor-saint, while outside, beyond the suburbs, there is a green world in which trees ask budding questions and become beautiful girls to be embraced by an athletic sun. You can call this realism if you like, but to me it sounds as mythic as those underground worlds which Earl Birney's miners inhabit or those curious and endless patterns of the waves which so fascinate Louis Dudek.

From the point of view of the modern myth-making poet like James Reaney, all of Canadian poetry tends to fall into a pattern which is the geography of the human mind, the "place somewhere inside personality." It is this geography which I want to look at now. It can be defined by isolating the recurrent images of Canadian poetry as these leap into prominence in the light of recent concerns and recent obsessions.

The most striking of the several recurrent images in Canadian poetry is that of the lonely voyager through the wilderness. In its most concentrated form, we find it in Douglas LePan's "Country Without a Mythology." In P. K. Page's "Stories of Snow" we can see how the traveller-image is modulated into other keys and how it finds expression in contemporary terms. One of the most interesting things in Miss Page's poem is the story within the story framework which is repeated in images of enclosure (the whole poem, in a sense, takes place inside a glass bowl). Things inside things finally become, in the poem, an image for the goal of the journey: inward to someplace behind the seeing eye, which is itself a pun upon vision and selfhood. In still other versions, the traveller becomes Roy Daniells' "Anthony" in the sonnet sequence "Deeper into the Forest"; rather obviously, he is E. J. Pratt's Brébeuf among the Hurons; or again, Ron Bates' sea-wanderer, Ulysses; most strikingly, he is the old, proud king of A. J. M. Smith's parable, who will sing "to the barren rock" the "difficult, lonely music" of the heart.

It is worth asking just how often doors close in Canadian literature, how very often Canadian literature gives one the sense of an enclosed room or the image of a back turned or eyes turned inward.[5] Here the theme of the voyager through the wilderness connects in another set of images with the theme of isolation or loneliness. Among the romantics, the parallel is obvious enough, though one finds it as well in modern writers like P. K. Page and Patrick Anderson whose poetic worlds, according to Milton Wilson, are "extremely insulated," "anaesthetic," "glass tight," "centripetal," and "half-empty."[6] I think here of the melancholic romantic brooding by the marshlands in *Tantramar Revisited* or the same man by the sea in *Low Tide on the Grand Pré,* and of how these two connect with the wanderer in the forest in Lampman's *In November.*

An early version of the image of the lonely voyager through the wilderness, and an important one because it takes up some of the major threads of the pattern, is a prose one, Frederick Philip Grove's *Over Prairie Trails.* Ostensibly an account of seven trips between two Manitoba towns, the book has a fascinating pattern which suggests that Grove's interest is in something quite different from mere reporting. At the centre of his book, in fact, a remarkable transformation takes place: a blizzard becomes an ocean. Here Grove reminds us of another variation upon our central image, that is, the poet who is swimmer, afloat or drowning, or boatman, besieged by the waters or safe from them. Recently, Milton Wilson remarked on the number of drowned poets we find in our poetry, and he gave us a fairly inclusive list: from Roberts' Shelley in *Ave* to D. C. Scott's *Piper of Arll,* to Klein's poet at the bottom of the sea in his poem "Portrait of the Poet as a Landscape"; the list includes such various other drownings as Miriam Waddington's John Sutherland, Dorothy Livesay's Raymond Knister, and Irving Layton's swimmer in "The Cold Green Element."[7] But this neither exhausts the possibilities nor opens up all the connections between swimming, drowning, and other images.

In both *Tantramar Revisited* and *Low Tide on the Grand Pré,* the lonely brooding figures are finally overwhelmed by the tide of memory and grief; Scott's Piper of Arll drowns on a ship to which he is carried after he is dead, the theme being apparently that fatal possession which kills what it wants to possess. Isabella Valancy Crawford writes more than one mysterious canoe poem, and in a particularly striking one the canoe sings of an immortal love which is killed by those who try to hunt it down. LePan's canoe traveller doesn't drown but he seems, at the end of the poem, about to meet a more dreadful fate. F. R. Scott has a very fine poem about a meditative figure by the lake, not unlike the brooding melancholics of the earlier poets, who, gazing into the waters which have for him a hypnotic fascination, hears the rains of the great flood. He concludes with memories of Mount Ararat, which suggests that, after earlier having tricked us into thinking he might be a kind of fish, he is really another Noah. In Roy Daniells' newest book, interestingly enough, we find a Noah who survives the attempt of a zoning committee to cancel his boat-building permit. E. J. Pratt, of course, gives us ships which are sunk by icebergs, whales, and other ships, and also a remarkable cat swimming about in an ocean of Canadian liquor. Earle Birney, who used to see his poetic characters as mountain climbers or airplane passengers, now presents us with Orpheus-like miners in the underworld or Captain Cook, Leander, and Byron on or under the sea, and Margaret Avison, who is likely to surprise us by equating the poet with a tennis player or a super-market shopper, also tells us, "For everyone,/The swimmer's moment at the whirlpool comes."

Our lonely voyager has finally turned into a poet-swimmer-boatman whose journey is not simply through the wilderness but into an oceanic world. This curious, composite figure finally takes complete and coherent shape in Jay MacPherson's book entitled *The Boatman,* in which all the associations of voyagers, sleeping giants, swimmers, boats, and even fishermen, are gathered together in one place.

However the Canadian poet chooses to express this pattern, whether through images of drowning, voyaging, climbing, or descending, its immediate significance seems clear enough: he is not content with surfaces or with mere description; he seeks to penetrate to some secret world where some final secret will be at last unlocked.

From the point of view of its images, then, Canadian poetry can be seen as developing a deepening perception of the nature of inner reality. Its pattern is the pattern of a movement from an external wilderness to the wilderness within and finally to some sort of conquest of this inner world. The wilderness takes shape first of all as a natural monster, then a social monster who, we discover, at least if we have read the preface to Irving Layton's *Balls For a One-Armed Juggler,* is the beast inside ourselves, finally confronted, at last acknowledged for what it is, and therefore telling us what we are and what we might become.[8]

This concern of the poet with an inner reality and the nature of the self has aroused the very considerable scorn of some of our more militant sociological critics. They ask: what has this concern with private sensibility and individual guilt or suffering to do with the structure and nature of our society? What does it tell us of the relationship of man to man or of the urgent and critical problems of social evil? What has it to do with the social realities of our time: the dehumanization of the individual, the soullessness of an industrialized, collectivist society, the destructive effect of mass communication in the hands of a huckstering commercialism? Or with the deeper, perennial conflict in society between manners and morals, life and custom, reality and illusion? These, we are told, have been the great and abiding concerns of novelists and poets in other ages and other places, and among the greatest, such awareness has gone hand in hand with a sense of the individual and his personal tragedy, but without the shattering loss of perspective which attends the dislocation of social reality.

This sort of criticism, which you will find as a general comment on modern literature in the writing of Sir Charles Snow and as particularly urged against Canadian literature is strong stuff, but I am convinced it is wrong-headed and it can be answered. I think there are the most pressing reasons to argue that it is only in, and precisely in, the poet's search for himself, which may be his "literature," that our society can finally become aware of itself and that it is therefore the very pressure of our ignorance of ourselves which has driven the poets to their search. Earle Birney remarks in a recent poem, "It's only by our lack of ghosts, we're haunted." Anyone without ghosts, without memory, without tradition, is haunted indeed. He inhabits an empty house: ignorant of his past, he is ignorant of his present too. Nothing shapes his life. He is unformed, immature, disturbed, underdeveloped, in short, neurotic, even, Lord help us, psychotic. If one wanted to pursue this kind of Freudian analysis of the Canadian character, he could find ample material for it in our poetry. He could, for example, compare Roberts' patriotic ode "Canada" with Earle Birney's much later ironic ode, "Canada: A Case History." In the first, he would find a sleeping giant whose connection with the older European tradition turns out to be a dream of bloody shores and dead soldiers. In the second poem, he would discover that the sleeping giant has grown into a juvenile delinquent with latent symptoms of schizophrenia. "What happened?" we ask. "Where did we go wrong?" The answer would appear to be the simple Freudian one: we are a people who have never discovered ourselves because we have refused to look into what we really are. And this, in fact, is the answer one of our novelists gave some time ago. Frederick Philip Grove, in a passage which E. A. McCourt is fond of quoting, remarks on our ignorance of ourselves:

> The Canadian public is ignorant, cowardly and snobbish; it is mortally afraid of ideas and considers the discussion of first principles a betrayal of bad manners. . . . [Canadians] are supposed to be born explorers; but they have not yet heard that the human heart and soul are perhaps the only corners in this universe where unexplored and undiscovered continents are still abounding.[9]

That we have to go there is the persistent theme of an American novelist who has the most immediate and demanding reasons possible for his insistence. James Baldwin, who knows something of the darkness of the human heart, writes,

From this void—ourselves—it is the function of society to protect us; but it is only this void, our unknown selves, demanding, forever, a new act of creation, which can save us—"from the evil that is in the world." With the same motion, at the same time, it is this toward which we struggle and from which, endlessly, we struggle to escape.[10]

Both Grove and Baldwin point to the same fact of our history: our past really isn't empty; rather it has been marked by a visionary collapse, the collapse of ancient cultures and traditions into triviality, frivolity, superficiality, vulgarity. What we have lost as a consequence, the sense of who and what we are, it has become the burden and task of the poet, the modern poet, to rediscover. Our haunted past, then, which is our haunted present, is the distinctive concern of Canadian poetry. Like Fredrick Philip Grove in the novel, the Canadian poet is in search of himself, and it is this search which makes him a modern man and a modern poet. We ignore him only at our own peril.

NOTES

1. *The Structure of Aesthetics* (Toronto, 1963), pp. 269–70.
2. Reaney, of course, has tried to make sense of a "narrative tradition" in his articles on Crawford and on "The Canadian Poet's Predicament." Frye draws attention to the narrative tradition in his oft-quoted article in *Gants du Ciel* but elsewhere too: in his introduction to Pratt's *Collected Poems* and most recently in his conclusion to *A Literary History of Canada.*
3. "The Canadian Poet's Predicament," *Masks of Fiction* (Toronto, 1962), p. 117.
4. "Letters in Canada: Poetry, 1952–1960," *Masks of Fiction,* p. 104.
5. ". . . withdrawal becomes a more characteristic response than commitment. The representative images are those of denial and defeat rather than fulfilment and victory." Robert L. McDougall, "The Dodo and the Cruising Auk: Class in Canadian Literature," *Canadian Literature,* XVIII (Autumn, 1963), 11.
6. "Other Canadians and After," *Masks of Poetry* (Toronto, 1962), p. 126.
7. "Klein's Drowned Poet," *Canadian Literature,* VI (Autumn, 1960), passim.
8. "Because he is a prophet, the poet must take into himself all the moral diseases . . . so that from them he can forge the wisdom his tortured fellowmen need to resist the forces dragging them down into the inhuman and bestial." Preface to *Balls for a One-Armed Juggler* (Toronto, 1963), p. xx. Frye's concluding essay in *A Literary History of Canada* suggests a connection between images of a hostile or indifferent nature, images of the killing of an animal, and "the riddle of unconsciousness." It might be interesting to discover to what extent Canadian poets equate landscape with "low society" or "body" or with Watson's "Canada of the Unconscious."
9. "The Plight of Canadian Fiction?—A Reply," *UTQ,* vii (1937), 459–60.
10. "Everybody's Protest Novel," *Notes of a Native Son* (New York, 1955), pp. 20–21.

GUY SYLVESTRE

Un Continent littéraire à découvrir

C'est, pour nous, Américains, celui de la littérature comparée. Les diverses littératures américaines fournissent pourtant, en ce domaine, une matière presque inépuisable. Mais nous n'avons pas encore exploré ces terres vierges. Ces quelques remarques n'ont d'autre but que d'attirer l'attention des universitaires — professeurs et étudiants — sur ce domaine de la littérature comparée qui nous offre d'innombrables sujets de thèse possibles.

De même qu'on peut, d'une certain manière, faire remonter l'histoire des lettres ibéro-américaines aux lettres de Christophe Colomb et de Hernán Cortés, aux chroniques de Díaz del Castillo et de José de Anchieta, aux poèmes de Juana Inés de la Cruz et de Ercilla y Zúñiga, on peut dire que l'histoire d'une certaine littérature canadienne commence avec les récits de Jacques Cartier, de Samuel de Champlain et de Marc Lescarbot, les lettres et les écrits de Marie de l'Incarnation et les *Relations des Jésuites*. Mais toutes ces œuvres de pionniers n'étaient que des prolongements en terre américaine de littératures européennes au moment même où ces dernières atteignaient leur maturité avec un Cervantes, un Camoëns et un Montaigne.

Si ces œuvres étaient, en grande partie, inspirées par les réalités d'un monde nouveau — aux yeux des Européens, du moins — elles appartenaient néanmoins aux littératures des mères-patries, et on ne peut les considérer, à proprement parler, comme les débuts de nouvelles littératures autonomes (dans la mesure où l'on peut parler d'autonomie en littérature). Aujourd'hui encore, le cordon ombilical n'est pas totalement coupé, et tant que les républiques du sud, les Etats-Unis et le Canada auront des langues communes avec l'Espagne,

HAB vol. XII, no. 2, winter 1962.

le Portugal, l'Angleterre et la France, leur autonomie culturelle ne sera jamais complète, même si la souveraineté politique leur est acquise. Il suffit, pour s'en rendre compte, de constater que quantité d'œuvres sont lues des deux côtés de l'Atlantique sans qu'il soit nécessaire de les traduire. Cette double appartenance est un des caractères communs à toutes les littératures américaines — à la seule exception de la littérature folklorique indigène — même si la dépendance des anciennes colonies à l'égard des anciennes mères-patries va diminuant. Un autre caractère qui leur est commun leur vient de ce que la majorité de leurs écrivains cherchent à exprimer dans une langue déjà constituée outre-mer — même s'il s'y ajoute des apports linguistiques locaux — des faits, des réalités, des manières de voir, de sentir et de penser qui, dans une certaine mesure, leur sont propres.

Que les littératures américaines aient un public en Europe comme les littératures espagnole, portugaise, anglaise et française en ont un en Amérique, est un des atouts les plus puissants que les nations occidentales aient en main pour faire s'épanouir une civilisation atlantique qui, en gestation depuis trois siècles, n'a pas encore réussi à prendre nettement forme, comme autrefois la civilisation méditerranéenne. On ne peut pas dire que les nations occidentales aient encore réussi à exploiter cet atout. Ni que les écrivains, tant américains qu'européens, aient su mettre en lumière les éléments essentiels de cette civilisation en formation. Nous en sommes encore à la période des tâtonnements et nous ne nous connaissons pas encore assez bien pour savoir où nous allons les uns et les autres. Car, s'il y a communauté de langue entre les républiques du sud, les Etats-Unis et le Canada, d'une part, et l'Espagne, le Portugal, l'Angleterre et la France, d'autre part, il y a entre les diverses nations américaines — sauf entre les républiques espagnoles et entre les Etats-Unis et le Canada de langue anglaise — des barrières linguistiques trop peu souvent franchies. Si le facteur geographique joue certes contre nous, il nous reste la possibilité de traduire et de publier dans les autres langues parlées en Amérique un plus grand nombre d'œuvres représentatives des diverses nations du monde nouveau. En tout cas, l'immense domaine encore vierge de la littérature comparée nous est ouvert.

Je ne suis pas assez au fait des littératures ibéro-américaines pour savoir s'il existe d'importantes études de littérature comparée portant sur les meilleures œuvres espagnoles et portugaises, mais je sais qu'il y a des études intéressantes à faire, et qui n'ont pas été faites, pour comparer les diverses littératures américaines en espagnol, portugais, anglais, et français, entre elles, comme à celles des anciennes mères-patries. La moisson est abondante, il ne manque que les ouvriers. De telles études n'ont même pas été faites entre les deux littératures nationales du Canada. Nous n'avons qu'à battre notre coulpe.

Sur le plan culturel, anglophones et francophones restent, non pas ennemis certes, mais étrangers. La vérité est que les échanges culturels entre les deux groupes ethniques sont rares et discontinus, et que les Canadiens anglophones connaissent mal la littérature canadienne de langue française, comme les Canadiens francophones connaissent peu la littérature canadienne de langue anglaise. Il y a sans doute des traductions, mais relativement peu nombreuses, et cette ignorance réciproque est due non seulement à la barrière linguistique, qui ne devrait pas en être une, mais aussi au fait géographique qui, au Canada, est d'importance primordiale.

En plus des caractères communs déjà mentionnés plus haut, toutes les littératures américaines ont encore en commun ceci que la plupart de leurs écrivains, dont la formation intellectuelle était le plus souvent européenne, ont souvent cherché, parfois réussi et parfois failli, à exprimer des événements, des faits géographiques ou historiques, des impressions, des sentiments, des idées et des aspirations conditionnés par un milieu aux dimensions nouvelles. Cela est encore plus vrai des Américains du Nord que de ceux du Sud. Mais les Américains du Sud ont été plus marqués par la présence, et par l'apport, de civilisations indigènes avancées dont la contre-partie n'existait pas au nord du Rio Grande del Norte. Les Anglais et les Français se sont installés dans d'immenses territoires où ne vivaient que des tribus nomades et peu évoluées, qui furent d'ailleurs vite réduites à l'impuissance. Nous n'avons pas, non plus, en Amérique du Nord, de littérature ni d'art pré-colombiens qui puissent être comparés, à ceux du sud. Et, dans les temps modernes, les tribus indigènes qui vivent dans les réserves des Etats-Unis et du Canada n'ont donné au nouveau monde aucun écrivain important. Il y a bien, aux Etats-Unis, une littérature et un art noirs, mais les noirs sont eux-mêmes des importés, et cela est une autre histoire. Il reste que les littératures de l'Amérique du Nord sont, d'une certaine manière, plus purement européennes que celles de l'Amérique du Sud — ce n'est pas là un éloge mais un simple constat

— et nous n'avons jamais eu au Canada ni *Araucana*, ni *Uruguay*, ni *Los Tymbiras*. Nous n'avons célébré que les hauts faits des conquérants et des explorateurs venus d'Europe. Il y a donc là un principe de diversité qu'il faut signaler à côté des analogies.

Les diverses littératures américaines ne se sont pas toutes développées simultanément ni au même rythme. Les colonies espagnoles ont donné très tôt à l'Espagne un Garcilaso de la Vega et un Juan Ruiz de Alarcón, tandis que ni les treize colonies anglaises d'Amérique ni la Nouvelle-France n'ont donné d'écrivain important à l'Angleterre ni à la France avant le siècle dernier. Il n'y avait pas encore de littérature canadienne que déjà existaient, en plus des écrivains ibéro-américains déjà mentionnés un José-María Heredia, un Andrés Bello, un Fernández de Lizardi, un Antonio Narino et un Esteban Echeverría, pour ne nommer que ceux-là. Les premiers écrivains canadiens qui comptent étaient les contemporains de Domingo Faustino Sarmiento, de José Hernández, de Bartolomé Mitre et de José Marmol. Notre premier écrivain important, François-Xavier Garneau, est né plus de trois cents ans après Garcilaso de la Vega et Juan Ruiz de Alarcón. On sait qu'il y avait une presse à Mexico dès 1536, mais l'imprimerie ne fit son apparition aux Etats-Unis qu'en 1639 et, au Canada, qu'en 1752. Au Canada français, elle n'apparut qu'en 1764, à Québec, et il fallut attendre le milieu du dix-neuvième siècle pour la voir se répandre dans le pays. Depuis la fondation de Québec en 1608 jusqu'à la conquête anglaise en 1763, la Nouvelle-France n'a produit aucun écrivain — j'excepte les quelques écrivains français qui sont venus s'établir au Canada et qui n'étaient pas Canadiens de naissance. Pour assister à la véritable naissance d'une littérature nationale au Canada, il faut attendre le milieu du dix-neuvième siècle, avec François-Xavier Garneau, Philippe Aubert de Gaspé et Crémazie. La littérature américaine anglaise avait pris son essor un peu plus tôt, grâce à Thomas Paine, Washington Irving et William Cullen Bryant et, au moment où naissait une littérature canadienne, les Etats-Unis donnaient au monde Emerson, Thoreau, Poe, Hawthorne et Melville. La littérature anglaise au Canada est née à la même époque, si on la fait débuter avec Thomas Chandler Haliburton, Charles Sangster et William Kirby. C'est aussi à la même époque que les lettres brésiliennes s'affirmaient grâce à Antonio Gonçalvés Dias, Antonio de Castro Alvés et surtout Machado de Assis.

La littérature hispano-américaine est donc beaucoup plus vieille que les autres littératures du nouveau monde. Les colonies espagnoles étaient d'ailleurs plus peuplées que les autres à l'origine, et, encore aujourd'hui, les républiques espagnoles constituent le groupe linguistique le plus puissant après le bloc anglo-saxon. Aussi, l'immense avantage d'études de ce genre en Amérique est qu'elles n'exigent la connaissance que de deux ou trois langues. Avec la connaissance de l'anglais et du français, on peut comparer des œuvres des deux littératures du Canada, et même comparer ces dernières avec des œuvres des Etats-Unis. Avec la connaissance additionnelle de l'espagnol, on peut s'ouvrir les portes de toutes les littératures américaines, sauf la littérature brésilienne et certains folklores indigènes. Il faut donc espérer que les études de littérature comparée attireront certains de nos universitaires qui enseignent ou étudient les lettres. Il y a là tout un continent littéraire à découvrir. Il ne manque que les explorateurs.

PART III

Writers and Their Works

WILFRED WATSON

Tarquin, the Master-Mistress, and the Dark Lady: The Role of the Poet in Shakespeare's Sonnets

I want to consider what Shakespeare implies about the role of the poet in the *Sonnets*. Whatever arrangement Shakespeare intended these to have, they fall into three main groups: 1/19; 21/126; 127/152. Possibly there is some misgrouping of sonnets in the Thorpe quarto. I suggest that Thorpe's placing of these three main groups is correct. I would further suggest that Thorpe's location of Sonnet 20 is correct. This sonnet requires 1/19 as a preliminary, and the key-passion it refers to is demonstrably the subject of Sonnets 21/126. If the placing of Sonnet 20 is correct, an important observation can be made, namely, that in Sonnets 1/19 Shakespeare regards the poet (and himself as a poet) in a general light but that in Sonnets 21/126 he is not writing about poets in general but about himself *as a particular sort of poet.*

Let us examine the supposition that Sonnets 1/19 are prefatory to Sonnet 20. The first sonnet in Thorpe's quarto—"From fairest creatures we desire increase"[1]—develops the paradox that not to procreate approximates beauty to famine and death. Sonnet 20—"When forty winters shall besiege thy brow/And dig deep trenches in thy beauty's field"—deals with the paradox of being young in one's child's flesh when one's own flesh is old. Sonnet 3 deals with the paradox that the practice of virginity destroys its own image. Sonnet 4 deals with the paradox of not using one's beauty and so wasting it. Sonnet 5, with

HAB vol. xv, no. 2, autumn 1964. From an address to the annual meeting of the Association of Canadian University Teachers of English, 1964.

the paradox of flowers distilled, and so on. It is rather chill stuff, until we notice that all of these paradoxes are part of a larger paradox, namely that beauty, if it is to persist in spite of the destructive process of time, must become part of that process—it must, to use a once-fashionable tag, "in the destructive element immerse," for, as Sonnet 12 says, "nothing 'gainst Time's scythe can make defence/ Save breed, to brave him when he takes thee hence." There is an intensification, as if something were happening. It is. If Thorpe put these first sonnets into sequence, he had a nice sense of climax.

What happens occurs partly because of the introduction of a conflict between Beauty and Time, but chiefly because of a sudden and unexpected focussing upon the role of the poet. Shakespeare characteristically sees Time as a Tarquin, ravishing beauty, but even more characteristically sees himself as beauty's traditional poet defending it not from a position of strength but from one of weakness. It is this fact I am sure which makes Sonnet 18 a favourite anthology piece though I suspect that sometimes its irony is sensed rather than intellectually understood. The lines "But thy eternal summer shall not fade" are brave, but they are already compromised, at least in Thorpe's sequence, by Sonnet 11, by Sonnet 12, and by Sonnet 14, even before the opening question of Sonnet 16:

> But wherefore do not you a mightier way
> Make war upon this bloody tyrant, Time?
> And fortify yourself in your decay
> With means more blessed than my barren rhyme?

Sonnet 11 has observed that "If all were minded so"—that is, minded to remain unreproductive virgins—"the times should cease /And threescore year would make the world away." It is an unlikely eventuality, witty rather than probable. But it is sufficient to put the conventional claims of the poet to immortalize beauty into perspective. In the final couplet of Sonnet 18 Shakespeare balances brave words against an equally extreme scepticism to arrive at a first approximation to truth: "So long as men can breath, or eyes can see, / So long lives this, and this gives life to thee." What is adumbrated in this first group of sonnets is a theory of the function of the poet: the poet can supply beauty with a sort of conditional lastingness, but the fact is stressed that *lines* of verse depend upon *lines* of flesh. The function of the poet is to help beauty to breed, an ancillary function though not unimportant. To put the matter in rounder terms, poetry is to help life to be more living; it becomes part of process in order to intensify process. Today when art criticism is extremely prolific in devising theories of art as process, this theory of Shakespeare's is not, at least in substance, surprising. In defence of this theory of art I would say that it is a working theory because it gets poems written, pictures painted, plays written and produced—if it turns the artist into a sort of "activity-centre ant," it at least provides him with a role and it is not sterilizing, like the "weave a circle round him thrice" approach of those who would turn the poet into a god and stifle him in an amber of ritual dread. But as a matter of fact as far as the *Sonnets* are concerned, Shakespeare dismisses it. At least I think we can infer this, if the sequence of sonnets in Thorpe's quarto from eleven to twenty is in Shakespeare's order. I think it must be. For Sonnet 19, positioned where it is, is a performance of genius. It is a piece of acting; the poet rages against Time, "Devouring Time, blunt thou the lion's paws,/ And make the earth devour her own sweet brood; / Pluck the keen teeth from the fierce tiger's jaws," etc. He threatens Time, "But I forbid thee one most heinous crime." His threat diminuendos to a plea, "O, carve not with thy hours my love's fair brow." And he ends the sonnet with a pompous affirmation: "Yet, do thy worst, old Time! Despite thy wrong, / My love shall in my verse ever live young," which is both a truth and also, considering what has been said before about the immortality conferred by the poet, a rather empty one. If Sonnet 19 were positioned before Sonnet 11, it would contradict or weaken the argument for breeding with which the sequence begins. If it were to precede Sonnet 18, we should find the assertion of that sonnet, ironical as it is, insincere. If it came before Sonnet 14, it would contradict in a very clumsy way the conclusion of Sonnet 14, which prognosticates of the non-procreative beauty, "Thy end is truth's and beauty's doom and date." A further possibility remains, either that we are to read these sonnets without connection or that Sonnet 19 belongs in one of the other groupings. I shall proceed to show why neither of these suppositions can be maintained.

Sonnets 1/19 are structured by a very tight genetic[2] wordplay on the word *increase,* in the sense of horticultural increase—the first line of

Sonnet 1 announces the genetic pun word: "From fairest creatures we desire increase." Shakespeare's use of genetic wordplay, so much part and parcel of Counter-Renaissance literature that almost no one today takes notice of it, is significant, various, and fertile in the extreme. We may note here that this sort of paronomasia makes possible the creation of new forms at the very moment in English literary history when Counter-Renaissance fragmentation was destroying old ones. Even in Lancelot Andrewes' the "crumbling style," the *arena sine calce,* sand without chalk, style, is modified enormously by the powerful cohesiveness of genetic wordplay. With the genetic pun on *increase* in Sonnets 1/19, the emphasis is on form rather than meaning for even though a novel theory of poetry is developed we are inclined I think to be most of all interested in the formal way in which *increase* in Sonnet 1 shifts via *succession* in Sonnet 2; *husbandry,* Sonnet 3; *legacy,* Sonnet 4; *distillation,* Sonnet 5; *usury,* Sonnet 6; *get* in the sense of beget, Sonnet 7; *concord* (occurring in the phrase, "true concord of well-tuned sounds,/ By unions married"), Sonnet 8; *unthrift,* Sonnet 9; *repair,* Sonnet 10; *store, print,* Sonnet 11; *breed,* Sonnet 12; *husbandry,* Sonnet 13; *pluck, fortune,* Sonnet 14; *engraft,* Sonnet 15; until, in Sonnet 16, which I have already cited at length, "But wherefore do not you a mightier way," the paronomasia swerves from *lines of life* to *Time's pencil* to the poet's *pupil pen* to the *eternal lines* of Sonnet 18, and finally, with characteristic Shakespearean decrescendo to the *lines* that Time's *antique pen* draws on *love's fair brow* in Sonnet 19.

Formally, this genetic pun on *increase* resembles the genetic pun on *do, deed, done* in *Macbeth* with its inexorable step-wise progression from Macbeth's "If it were done when 'tis done" to the enormity of "Confusion now hath made his masterpiece! / Most sacrilegious murder hath broke ope/ The Lord's annointed temple," for though it hasn't the sonorous plangency of the *Macbeth* paronomasia, it does move in clear, distinct, step-wise fashion. But it also resembles the great genetic pun of *Measure for Measure,* where measure as trick and measure as law are manipulated endlessly through every shift of dialogue until measure becomes mercy and mercy is seen as the "law of law" and also as an expedient to perfect the law, for as we have noted the genetic pun on the word *increase* reconciles or at least relates the two opposites, life and poetry. Indeed the pun on *increase* compares usefully with other important Shakespearean puns, those on *ecstasy* in *Hamlet, service* in *Othello, nothing* in *King Lear,* and on *mark* in *Antony and Cleopatra.*

But though the pun on *increase* has some striking formal values, it is also a linkage of meanings. From this complex we can see clearly that Sonnets 1/19 contain not only a persuasion to procreate but also a disclaimer about the eternalizing power of the poet. It is the latter meaning which is blocked out by the most intense formal values, for these occur when the genetic pun crosses over from an injunction about life to an insight about art. To observe this, is merely to say that the sonnets about the poet's power or rather about his weakness have most stress. We cannot reasonably argue that Shakespeare didn't intend this effect since his intentions are only patent in his emphases. It would seem then that Sonnet 19 is correctly placed, for of all this group of sonnets it achieves the most telling formality and hence the most intensity. It caps Shakespeare's doubts about the poet with downright ridicule. Plainly then Sonnet 20 with its new theme is adversative to Sonnet 19 and to the series Sonnet 19 completes. I suggest that there is not a complete break, but Sonnet 20 introduces a "but." What this "but" prefaces is our next consideration.

That there can be no new meaning without a new form is a truism of modern art theory, but it is also likely that there can be no new form without new meanings. The genetic pun was especially adapted to the practice of this two-sided principle. Genetic wordplay can be as much a heuristic as a structural or organizing device. In the second group of sonnets in Thorpe's quarto, Sonnets 21/126, the noticeable feature of the long genetic paronomasia on *passion* is not so much form as its proliferation of meanings. But though the form of this wordplay is not obvious, I think it can be demonstrated.

Instead of a clear, stepwise progression, this new genetic pun proceeds to produce a series of kennings for the pun word, *passion.* Each of these sonnets contains a kenning for that "passion" which, Shakespeare tells us in Sonnet 20, has for its master-mistress a male paragon Nature, believe it or not, intended for a woman. But if Sonnet 20 is facetious, the subsequent development is quite the reverse —sometimes the generated kennings are of great beauty, as for example that in Sonnet 22, where Shakespeare speaks of passion as the "seemly raiment of my heart," or as in Sonnet 23, where he refers to the "dumb presagers of my speaking breast." Occasionally the genetic pun will exfoliate, in a given sonnet or group of sonnets, into a series of variations and inversions. This sort of thing happens in Sonnet 97, where the emotion of absence is called a winter and its inversion, "the pleasure of the fleeting year." Shakespeare develops the contrast stated: "What freezings have I felt, what dark days seen!/ What old December's bareness everywhere!" And, he continues, lest the literalist mistake his metaphor, to specify what he intends: summer and its pleasures wait on the gratification of the alienated passion. This sonnet, 97, "How like a winter hath my absence been," reminds us of the metaphoric stretch of Shakespeare's mind, but it can also serve to remind us that usually when Shakespeare is developing material by means of genetic wordplay, metaphor is likely to go hand in hand with punning.

At first approach we may look upon this second group of sonnets as a sort of comprehensive treatment of emotion. Curious about how these poems came to be written, we may speculate that Shakespeare gave himself the task of setting down day by day the various states of emotion he was aware of. In Sonnet 22 we find him exploring the emotion of tender possessiveness,

> O, therefore, love, be of thyself so wary,
> As I, not for myself, but for thee, will;
> Bearing thy heart, which I will keep so chary
> As tender nurse her babe from faring ill.

Sonnet 35 shows possessiveness modulating into an emotion of mixed reproach. Sonnet 55 gives expression to an emotion of conscious pride. In Sonnet 124 we discover Shakespeare probing the emotion which underlies moral courage, the psychological strength we exhibit when we resist disapproval of a social or political group: "If my dear love were but the child of state, / It might for Fortune's bastard be unfathered."

Shakespeare in these sonnets was becoming aware of the inner experience of a poet almost entirely committed to the theatre. They are then both log and sketchwork. True there is little externality to these sonnets, but we needn't expect much simple observation of men or of nature, for Shakespeare limits himself to self-examination. Two techniques for dealing with emotion can be seen developing in these middle-group sonnets—techniques important for the sense of living life with which the dramatist invests even the woodenest character. The first of these techniques comes right out of the catenary, kennings-wise pun on *passions*: there is an exploration of emotional experience, developed as a series: I feel, I burn, I turn chill, I have a sense of autumn in my soul, I have a sense of hot June lapsing into autumn, I freeze, etc. With this serial development goes emphasis upon emotion as growth and decay, upon the rising/falling, swelling/lapsing of emotion. But if in the plays emotional acceleration/decelerations render the Shakespearean character life-like, something else is needed to give it first intensity, the term the Pound/Lewis/Eliot school of criticism gives to matching of meaning and form. There must be in the emotion itself both a livingness and an artful rigidity and these must work together. The second technique for exploring emotion we find in the sonnets involves an emotional duality every actor must master. It is summed up in the old theatre tag, "acting is re-acting." One reacts to something happening on the stage; that is reaction; but also one acts towards the reaction to come. We see an example of this in *King Lear*: "What's he that hath so much thy place mistook / To set thee here?" Lear asks. Kent of course is in the stocks. But this duality can occur in lyric poetry—Donne's "For Godsake hold your tongue" has this action/reaction quality. Here the reaction is clear enough. Donne is retorting to critics. When however this reaction quality occurs in Sonnet 104, the effect is mysterious. "To me, fair friend, you never can be old," Shakespeare begins, as if addressing the master-mistress. The reaction quality is very specific in the next line: "For as you were when first your eye I eyed / Such seems your beauty still." The beautiful generalizations ensuing would seem to pluralize the person addressed, and change the force of "first your eye I eyed" to make it agree, partly singular, partly plural, with the phrase in the sonnet's last line, "beauty's summer," which is not certainly singular, nor plural, but could be a group, a crowd or even at a stretch something like *la jeunesse*, to whom the French actor J.-L. Barrault addressed himself. These two techniques, which work so well in the plays, dominate the second group of the sonnets. Emotion, the accelerations and decelerations of the soul, is made the sign of life itself. Yet this life is caught in a network of art. The joint effect is both vivid and strange. The fabric of emotions supported is real enough even if the master-mistress functions merely as coat-hanger.

A few pages back I suggested that the large group of sonnets following Sonnet 20, the master-mistress sonnet, is related to the preceding group in the ratio of preface and main discussion. I suggested that Sonnet 20 marks a shift in emphasis. I have been explaining how the prefatory group of sonnets develops a genetic wordplay linking together life and poetry as part of process, and how the longer group of sonnets develops a genetic wordplay on the term *passion*. What I now want to determine is the relationship between the master-mistress and an equivalent entity in the prefatory group. That the master-mistress is the poet's muse can readily be established once we have recognized that the sonnets of the second group are interconnected by genetic wordplay. There is then no impediment to taking the correspondent of Sonnet 20 to be the same as that of Sonnet 38, who is addressed as the "tenth Muse, ten times more in worth/ Than those old nine which rhymers invocate." The master-mistress then is Shakespeare's muse. Muses can of course be nothing much more than coat-hangers—let us compare the master-mistress nevertheless with Shakespeare's muse in the prefatory nineteen sonnets. The word is not used in Sonnet 14 though here the poet explains that his inspiration derives from the eyes of the nubile beauty he urges to procreate. What then is the ratio between this inspiration and the master-mistress?

To answer this important question, let me observe that in round terms the poet's inspiration in the prefatory group is life itself and that the poet's activity is ancillary to the life process. Next, I would observe that in the main group of sonnets the poet's emotional activity is endlessly explored but that the master-mistress tends to remain the sketchily-defined recipient of the poet's exclamations. These point to the master-mistress as that superior muse around which or by means of which the poet orders his life. We can now answer our question. Very clearly, Shakespeare in the first nineteen sonnets thinks of poetry as subordinate to life but in the next 105 sonnets he thinks of poetry as ordering life.

One explanation why Shakespeare prefaces theory two with theory one is certainly very tempting, in view of studies like Mr. R. A. Foakes's, "The profession of playwright," in *Early Shakespeare*,

Stratford on Avon Studies No. 3, pp. 11–33. It is not implausible to suppose that the master-mistress of Shakespeare's passion, the tenth muse who replaces the muse of Sonnets 1/19, is in fact the muse of the poet-playwright, or even the theatre itself. But we must dismiss this idea. If Shakespeare were thinking out, while he was writing the sonnets, the distinction we would today make between poet, poet-playwright and playwright, his adoption of the convention of sonneteering, with its rigid image of the poet as Petrarchan or anti-Petrarchan lover, must have prevented him from expressing the distinction. Much of Shakespeare's thinking in the sonnets must have been triggered by his experiences as playwright. But the sonnet form kept the master-mistress vaguely defined, despite the woman's face painted by Nature, the male sense of order and man's ability to order, and the male sex, quite unnaturally donated by Nature herself, no doubt to exact her debt to be, the poet alleges, woman's pleasure.

The third group of sonnets concerns the Dark Lady. The first nineteen sonnets suppress the word "black," even where it might be expected to appear—thus Sonnet 12 speaks of "sable curls . . . silver'd o'er with white" and Sonnet 15 refers to "sullied night." The Dark Lady sonnets, 127/152, make good this suppression by developing a genetic paronomasia on the world "black."

This genetic wordplay progresses via *black* (Sonnet 127, "But now is black beauty's successive heir, / And beauty slandered with a bastard shame"), via *jacks, saucy jacks* (= black spinet keys = upstart jacks, Sonnet 128), via *lust* (Sonnet 129), *false compare* (Sonnet 130), *dear doting heart* (Sonnet 131, cf. also Sonnet 127, "Fairing the foul with art's false borrowed face"), towards *will* (Sonnet 134), *wish* (Sonnet 135), *blind soul* (Sonnet 136), *over-partial looks* (Sonnet 137), *false-speaking tongue* (Sonnet 138), *mad slanderers* (Sonnet 140), *base touches* (Sonnet 141), *false bonds* (Sonnet 142), etc., until we reach in this catenary listing of false things *conscience, flesh . . . proud* in the sense of illicit sexual excitation but yet, as the paronomasia pivots, still to be called a *poor drudge* (Sonnet 151), *oath's breach, oath's but to misuse,* which since they were sworn with respect to non-existent love, truth, and constancy, in effect gave, the sonneteer concludes, *eyes to blindness* (Sonnet 152).

From this genetic wordplay we can draw a number of conclusions. First, that the sonnets from 127/152 make up an integral structure. Second, that this group of sonnets is linked to the preceding two groups. Third, that the three genetic puns were conceived together or at least devised before the three groupings were finalized. And fourth, that the ratio of the Dark Lady to the three genetic puns which control the sonnets in their entirety must be dealt with before we can properly treat of her ratio to experience in general.

Let me deal with the first three conclusions first of all. As for the first point, we can note that the genetic pun on *black* deals with truth and convention, perception, will, the appetites, and the senses. The *will* sonnets, distinguished by a somewhat heavy-handed punning on *will*, are an integral part of both the formal structure and the meanings of the genetic wordplay being described. The second point has to do with group linkage. We may note that the Dark Lady group is linked to Group One through the genetic punword, *black*, Time's "antique pen" in Sonnet 19, "Time's pencil," the poet's "pupil pen" and "lines of life" in Sonnet 16, and "eternal lines" in Sonnet 18. There is linkage between *will, art, heart, art's false-borrowed face,* in the Dark Lady group, and the beauty-derived *art* of Sonnet 14; and, since Nature is contrasted with art, between the Dark Lady group and Nature in Sonnets 4, 11, and 20. There is another linkage between the "woman colour'd ill," "devil," "fiend," "angel in another's hell," "better angel," "man right fair," of Sonnet 144 and "fairest creatures" of Sonnet 1. The fact that these and other linkages occur makes the third point likely, since once a poem has been finalized it would seem difficult to intrude structural wordplay into its textures.

We may now proceed to relate the Dark Lady to the structures in which she exists. Let us consider her ratios to the "fairest creatures" of Sonnet 1, to the master-mistress, and to the poet himself, and let us examine these ratios at three points in the Dark Lady series, at the beginning, at the middle, and at the end of the series. *At the beginning,* her ratio to the fairest creatures of Sonnet 1 is that of *honest black* to *ideal beauty*; her ratio to the master-mistress is that of the *real object* to *organizing principle*; her ratio to the poet is expressed in Sonnet 130—she is no goddess, but she walks on the ground (that is, she is within his reach). *At the middle of the series,* the Dark Lady's ratio to the fairest creatures is that of *grief for the falsity of those who mimic ideal beauty*; her ratio to the master-mistress is this, *her black is being erected into a false beauty*; her ratio to the poet, *perplexity as to what fair beauty is. At the end of the series,* the Dark Lady's ratio to the fairest creatures is that of *falsest black* (as "black as hell," according to Sonnet 147) *to ideally fair*; her ratio to the master-mistress is that of *corrupter*; her ratio to the poet is that of *perjury*, for, as Sonnet 152, the last of the series, declares against her, "I have sworn thee fair; more perjured I, / To swear against the truth so foul a lie!"

Ironically, even her name is a misnomer. She is never referred to at all by Shakespeare as a lady. Only once—Shakespeare says she is "as dark as night" in Sonnet 147—does he use the term *dark* of her. It is much easier to describe her than it is to describe the master-mistress, however; because in the master-mistress sonnets the genetic wordplay isn't structured on the master-mistress, but on Shakespeare's passion for this muse of his. But the genetic wordplay in the Dark Lady section of the sonnets is structured upon the Dark Lady—upon the colour of her hair and eyes, her heart, her will, her wish, her bed-vows broken, etc. Though it is likely that the master-mistress is the muse of dramatic poetry for Shakespeare, what the master-mistress does is to awaken in the poet all that interior emotional life which is recorded in the middle group of sonnets. What the Dark Lady does, is to falsify every access to Shakespeare's soul. But she blocks the doorways from the outside. She makes the poet aware of these entrances—his senses, his appetites, his will, his rational soul—and she makes him aware of them in an outgoing way. Though she makes him despair of objective truth, she makes him frantically aware of the need for it.

Shakespeare calls her his mistress, and it is a pity that we have improved her into a lady, for the word mistress was as useful to Shakespeare as it was to John Donne, in Satyre III. John Donne asks, "Is not our Mistresse faire religion?" and he goes on to specify the various false emphases afflicting the religion of the day. Shakespeare's master-mistress is a major misemphasis. Had Shakespeare been unwilling to be a "false Hector, a false Andromache, a false Hercules," could he have been a "true tragedian"?[8] It is St. Augustine's question, and the saint seems to have thought there wasn't much sense to being false in order to be true. Shakespeare finds an answer to this question in the sonnets about the Dark Lady. What he loved her for first of all was her truthfulness. This is why he rages so, when he finds her out. This mistress proves to be a catastrophic misemphasis. He takes her to stand for life, but she doesn't; life is a confusion, even if a confusion of forms. Quite plainly she is life perverted by art, and this is perhaps why Shakespeare says in Sonnet 144, "I guess one angel in another's hell," and why he thinks it may help if his "bad angel fire" his "good one out." That is to say, if we could get rid of art, at least we'd know where we are at.[4] If in the master-mistress sonnets we have a sense of a problem unresolved, in the Dark Lady sonnets we sense (despite or rather because of their clamour against the intractability of the anti-poetic this new mistress provided him with) that Shakespeare has come to an important recognition. He has come to see the area which is his responsibility as a poet; poems are not made out of life, poems are not made out of other poems; they are made, if they are made at all, out of some ragged edge in between. If we like, we can call the Dark Lady Shakespeare's anti-poetic.

NOTES

1. The text used is that of *The London Shakespeare*, ed. John Munro (London: Eyre and Spottiswoode, 1958), vol. IV. I have, however, taken the liberty of retaining the Arabic numbering of the Thorpe Quarto.
2. For a brief discussion of "genetic" wordplay, see Wilfred Watson, "Interstructuralization in Drama and the Other Arts," *Thought from the Learned Societies of Canada, 1961* (Toronto: Gage, n.d.), pp. 18–19.
3. *Soliloquies*, bk. II, sect. 18, tr. C. C. Starbuck, *Basic Writings of Saint Augustine*, ed. Whitney J. Oates (New York: Random House, 1948), vol. I.
4. But see Leslie Fiedler, "Some Contexts of Shakespeare's Sonnets," *The Riddle of Shakespeare's Sonnets*, ed. Edward Hubler (London: Routledge & Kegan Paul, 1962), pp. 57–90; and especially: "If all the sonnets except 144 were to disappear tomorrow, we would be left in possession not only of the story Shakespeare tries to tell—the account of a poet who, seeking to divide his love in two, directing all that is ennobling in it toward one object, all that is vile toward another, ends by suspecting his two loved ones in each other's arms—but also of the moral significance that story is intended to convey. . . ." (pp. 60–61). This is to see Sonnet 144 as a key. I should prefer to see it as a piece of mosaic, contributing meaning to a total pattern, and deriving meaning from that total pattern.

PIERRE VAN RUTTEN

Oiseaux, ou l'esthétique de Saint-John Perse

Dans le recueil *Oiseaux*, peinture et poésie s'éclairent mutuellement; les deux arts convergent vers une même esthétique, vers une première transparence de l'Idée dans la matière. La recherche de l'art y est quête de l'esprit non au delà mais à l'intérieur des choses mêmes.

Oiseaux de Saint-John Perse se compose d'une suite de treize méditations poétiques dont la langue est si travaillée, si artistiquement modelée que d'elle-même, par une sorte de diaphanie, elle se métamorphose en poésie. Pourtant, éloignée ainsi du langage prosaïque, elle demeure adéquatement objective. Par le commentaire des eaux-fortes de Braque, l'auteur au prix Nobel, l'écrivain de « Poésie » nous expose sans mystère, en ces méditations, sa conception de l'art. Mais « commentaire » est un mot si peu opportun pour qualifier le texte de Saint-John Perse. Il s'agit d'un même thème, éclairé conjointement par deux matériaux différents — le dessin et la langue — dans une même perspective esthétique, dans une même participation au rythme universel rendue diversement consciente.

Les poètes avaient coutume de nous offrir des recueils de poèmes variés portant un titre qui n'était qu'un prétexte et dont l'unité thématique se fondait sur la personnalité de l'auteur. Saint-John Perse nous livre des œuvres qui constituent un tout homogène et dont les parties ne sont que les phases de développement et les faces complémentaires d'un sujet unique. Sa concision extrême, son étrange correction, l'exploitation des infimes vibrations de la langue, valorise chaque vocable, aggrave son texte et ses vastes poèmes ne sont ni diamants ni fleuves mais écoulements de reflets harmoniques. Dans *Oiseaux*

HAB vol. xv, no. 2, autumn 1964.

chaque méditation nous fait avancer d'un pas vers l'éclosion de la pensée; de l'oiseau décrit au premier chant dans l'objectivité ambigüe de son destin, on évolue vers un envol d'oiseau illuminé par l'art jusqu'à son essence même, annonciateur d'une aube révélatrice « du songe de la création ».

Plus tard, lorsque l'on aura découvert sa profondeur solitaire loin des querelles d'école contemporaines, on comprendra le renouvellement de la poésie opéré par Saint-John Perse. Les mondes du Symbolisme se superposaient, l'image était une ouverture sur l'au-delà, sorte de bond vers un monde second, éthéré, qui est refus de notre situation matérielle. Saint-John Perse ne repousse pas notre condition, il l'étreint dans ses forces premières et, par la jonction de son regard poétique et de son adhérence au réel, il en exprime — littéralement — les suc secret, saveur spirituelle. L'oiseau n'est pas symbole d'autre chose, il est lui-même objet de la compréhension poétique, lieu de l'unité de sa « double allégeance ». « Sa grâce est dans sa combustion. Rien là de symbolique : simple fait biologique. »

« Aile falquée du songe », « Maître du Songe, dis-nous le songe ... », « il navigait avant le songe », « quelque chose du songe de la création », voilà, parmi d'autres, quelques expressions où un mot-clé revient; souvent il est associé à la clarté ou à la vision créatrice du poète au-delà du raisonnement. On penserait volontiers au lieu de l'Azur de Mallarmé où vole l'oiseau qui mène le poète « ce soir, sur d'autres rives ». L'oiseau, objet de méditation, « par la transe et l'avant-création », illumine la nuit obscure de l'homme « où s'exerce la logique du songe », lieu de révélation dans les ténèbres de l'esprit. L'oiseau, inspirateur du poète, lui donne « une audace nouvelle incitant l'homme à l'imitation créatrice du vol ». Les paroles de Saint-John Perse répondent à une double vocation laissant sourdre, en les unissant, l'esprit de la matière.

L'ambivalence de notre univers, temporel et intemporel, matériel et immatériel, fusionne le direct et l'indirect, engendre une poésie de l'immédiat, de l'unité retrouvée après une tradition d'écartèlement. Dirais-je que cette poésie est dialectique, que les contraires sont abolis ? Pourtant les mots *synthèse* ou *synthétique* apparaissent à plusieurs endroits. On rencontre aussi un *dialectique* et un *aliénation* se glissant, bien à propos, dans les poèmes. Le sens du temps, de l'évolution, de l'historicité de la poésie, disons du devenir de la pensée, participe à la thématique fondamentale de Saint-John Perse.

Dans la poésie universelle de Perse, la dialectique de l'unité des deux faces de la réalité forme un point de rencontre de la pensée de l'Occident et de l'Orient. Au chant onzième, il cite le Ying et le Yang, les principes actif et passif, mâle et femelle, du Taoïsme. Après le monde de la mer, l'Orient fournit au poète une affluence d'idées et d'images.

Par sa configuration géminée et son mouvement, l'oiseau symbolise l'ambivalence du langage poétique. « Au fléau de son aile, l'immense libration d'une double saison », « l'alternance est sa loi, l'ambiguïté son règne » sont des expressions signifiant sa « double allégeance, aérienne et terrestre ». Et ici un mot abstrait comme « allégeance » peut être pris dans un sens très concret, il démystifie ce faux intellectualisme qui façonne constamment notre langage contemporain et a tant contribué à nous éloigner d'un proche contact des réalités.

L'Oiseau « thème et propos » du livre devient un microcosme, « une parcelle infime du territoire terrestre », « un satellite infime de notre orbite planétaire », en lui, il concentre dans son point d'espace une conception du monde et l'on pourrait parler longtemps de toutes les implications de la vision poétique de Saint-John Perse. Le corps de l'oiseau devient l'encagement de « cette force secrète », une précise science cosmique l'a construit avec une telle perfection qu'il « défiait toutes notions acquises en aérodynamique ».

« L'avidité d'être » sa « fièvre de sang » doucement mueront l'oiseau en art. La description précise et objective du début glissera vers la transfiguration, l'appréhension esthétique. Dans la révélation du mystère, à la « conjuration du peintre et de l'oiseau » s'ajoutera celle du poète. « Par son rapt » l'artiste s'empare de l'oiseau comme thème de l'œuvre et

> l'oiseau hors de sa migration ... a commencé à vivre le cycle de ses mutations. Il habite la métamorphose. Suite sérielle et dialectique. C'est une succession d'épreuves et d'états en voie toujours de progression vers une confession plénière, d'où monte dans la clarté, la nudité d'une évidence, d'un mystère d'identité : unité dans la diversité.

Suivons ce cheminement de l'oiseau vers sa « confession plénière » par l'art, vers son dévoilement « chargé d'histoire ». Nous voilà de nouveau face au temps que la poésie traditionelle affectionne éliminé au profit d'une contemplation statique. Pour Saint-John Perse, la révélation est émergence du temps, progression de l'Idée à travers l'Histoire. « C'est une connaissance poursuivie comme une recherche d'âme et la nature enfin rejointe par l'esprit, après qu'elle lui a tout cédé ».

L'oiseau « sur l'aplat de la toile » devient « la somme vraie d'une mince tache de couleur » mutation initiale « de ce fragment d'espace fait matière ... soustrait à sa troisième dimension ». La catharsis de Saint-John Perse réside dans la réduction de l'objet à l'essentiel. Le texte est parsemé d'expressions traduisant ce dépouillement de l'accessoire dans l'oiseau, du superflu dans le texte : « l'arrachement », « la concision », « le laconisme », mots concernant autant les poèmes que les dessins. Le mystère n'apparaît que dans le renoncement à l'accidentel qui le cache, position que rejoint la plus pure tradition greque. « De tout ce qu'élude, sciemment ou non, l'oeuil électif du peintre, la connaissance intime lui demeure », nous affirme l'auteur. Alors, cet oiseau « succint » prend vie et devient énergie lumineuse, pureté, et, par « l'abréviation » même de son objet, l'homme atteint « la clarté de l'épée », la vision pénétrante des choses.

Peinture et poésie fusionnent : « Les oiseaux sur le papier ont muri comme des mots ». Mais le poète connaît le dynamisme du verbe. « Et bien sont-ils comme des mots sous leur charge magique: noyaux de force et d'action, figures d'éclairs et d'émissions portant au loin initiative et prémonition ». Le mot ainsi recréé par son usage exact et inattendu, est rayonnement de messages dont les sens se répercutent entre eux comme des échos. Alors le texte (comme les dessins Georges Braque et j'inverse la comparaison de l'auteur) devient incantation, magie divinatoire mais qui sublime le sens.

Force secrète de l'oiseau, force des mots, manifestent, en mouvement, le rythme, pulsation du monde. Rythme du langage et du vol n'est que participation à la respiration universelle, et les oiseaux dans les airs sont « la plus large strophe errante que l'on ait vue jamais se dérouler dans le monde ». » La délectation et le loisir de vol lent et majestueux » se réfléchissent dans le poème et les oiseaux, s'élevant de la terre au ciel, sont des médiateurs qui, comme le poète, transportent nos regards des apparences opaques aux espaces transparents.

Après avoir comparé l'oiseau à des graines ailées Saint-John Perse s'écrie : « Braque, vous ensemensez d'espèces saintes l'espace occidental ». Mais ces oiseaux sont « plus près du genre que de l'espèce, plus près de l'ordre que du genre ». La mission de l'artiste sera donc de manifester l'Ordre, c'est-à-dire l'archétype, l'idée que préside à l'agencement du monde, pour lequel les Grecs avaient le mot *cosmos* qui désignait aussi bien l'univers que l'ordonnance et dont Aristote se servait pour définir le beau.

A travers une langue spirituellement diaphane, la description de Saint-John Perse est objective, immédiate. Les mots abstraits doivent être compris dans le sens concret qu'ils avaient à l'origine. L'artificiel horrifie le poète en quête d'authenticité, aussi sa sévérité pour la culture morte dont on intoxique les lettres ne désarme pas. En sa douzième méditation, il stigmatise les érudits qui utilisent la colombe de Noé, le vautour de Prométhée. Ainsi conclut-il à propos des eaux-fortes de Braque : « ... les oiseaux sont de faune vraie ... Leur loyauté, sous maints profils, fut d'incarner une constance d'oiseau ». Après avoir mentionné les grands oiseaux des grands auteurs, il affirme que ceux de Braque « n'en tirent point littérature ». Peut-être ?

Ce poète à la réputation d'hermétisme est un grand réaliste, un homme qui ne veut se laisser un instant distraire de cette adhésion profonde aux choses. Son vocabulaire même, qui demande si souvent un effort est précis, parfois savant et technique. Sur le point de quitter les oiseaux de Braque, le poète les confie, comme ses écrits, « à leur destin d'êtres créés » où va le mouvement des réalités. Ils révéleront l'aurore de l'esprit, la libération de l'obscurité étouffante que le poète laisse deviner.

Que nous sommes loin de la poésie traditionnelle ! Il n'y a plus un monde ordinaire *et* un monde poétique l'un étant soit la projection soit l'évasion de l'autre, mais transfiguration par l'art de notre monde qui en devient intelligible. Voilà l'office du poète, médiateur comme l'oiseau qui nous élève dans l'espace poétisé et nous place « entre un aval et amont d'éternité ».

Saint-John Perse arrive à la transparence spirituelle de l'objet par des voies inverses aux procédés habituels, qui utilisent le mot concret — qui fait image — pour inviter l'esprit, par un jeu de correspondances, à percevoir une structure de relations secrètes. Perse, au contraire, emploie le mot abstrait dans un sens très concret, souvent effacé par le temps, intellectualisant ainsi la réalité même, dépouillant le langage de son abstraction qui éloigne du monde et crée un univers imaginaire.

Toutes les ressources sensibles de la langue sont exploitées; les assonances sont significatives, elles contraignent les mots à un face à face d'où jaillissent des sens, éclairant comme des étincelles. Les renforcements et mises en relief d'idées proviennent de redondances sémantiques, de doublets où des mots de même racine et consonance se suivent : « Ils sont pèlerins de même pérégrination »; « Dans la maturité d'un texte immense en voie toujours de formation, ils ont muri comme des fruits ou mieux comme des mots ». Cette langue s'adressant intensément aux sens pour atteindre l'esprit, selon les lois de la nature, en reçoit une densité accrue. D'ailleurs, aucun mot n'est gratuit dans ces phrases si harmonieuses. Qu'on supprime ou déplace un mot, qu'on modifie un son ou un rythme, et le texte en perd de sa richesse. Tout fait pression sur la pensée par la concentration sans faille des moyens; le sens atteint la consistance des classiques, le mot, revigoré par un emploi rare et par son contexte, lourd de sa valeur plénière, informe un texte robuste, puissant, éloigné d'un vain rêve.

Oiseaux tiendra une place particulière dans l'œuvre de Saint-John Perse et que ceux qui désirent aborder cet auteur difficile commencent, après avoir lu le discours de Stockholm, par ce dernier ouvrage qui éclaire toute la poésie d'*Eloges* à *Chronique*. On y découvre toute une esthétique qui fécondera un courant nouveau de la littérature, dont la mission actuelle est d'exprimer par l'art des Belles-Lettres la nouvelle vision du réel qui s'élabore dans les recherches contemporaines et d'y proclamer la place singulière de l'humain dans son intégration au monde.

A. P. CAMPBELL

Chaucer's "Retraction": Who Retracted What?

Settling the problems arising from the words of retraction found at the end of Chaucer's *Parson's Tale* is not, perhaps, the most important assignment in Chaucerian studies: you can still love and enjoy the great poet without giving serious attention to this problem. Yet it is important and enlightening to discuss this apparent about-face of Chaucer's that has caused in some hearts great dismay. In my view, the solution is found in the remarkable subtlety of Chaucer's artistic technique. A very useful survey of opinions on the *Retraction* appeared recently from the pen of James D. Gordon;[1] a careful study of the previous solutions has convinced me that there is still need for clarification, however.

First, let us take a look at the famous words of retraction. At the conclusion of the *Parson's Tale*, varying somewhat in different manuscripts, but substantially the same, appears this message from Chaucer:

> Heere taketh the makere of this book his leve.
>
> Now preye I to hem that herkne this litel tretys or rede, that if there be any thing in it that liketh hem, that thereof they thanken oure Lord Jhesu Crist, of whom procedeth al wit and al goodnesse./ And if ther be any thyng that displese hem, I preye hem also that they arrette it to the defaute of myn unkonnynge, and not to my wyl, that wolde ful fayn have seyd bettre if I hadde had konnynge./ For oure book seith, "All that is writen is writen for our doctrine" and that is myn entente./ Wherefore I biseke you mekely,

HAB vol. xvi, no. 1, spring 1965. From an address to the annual meeting of the Association of Canadian University Teachers of English, 1964; first printed in *La Revue de l'Université d'Ottawa* (January–March 1965). The first paragraph has been omitted in this reprinting.

for the mercy of God, that ye preye for me that Crist have mercy on me and foryeve me my giltes;/and namely of my translacions and enditynges of wordly vanitees, the which I revoke in my retracciouns:/ as is the book of Troilus; the book also of Fame; the book of the .xix. Ladies; the book of the Duchesse; the book of Seint Valentynes day of the Parlement of Briddes; the Tales of Caunterbury, thilke that sownen into synne;/ the book of the Leoun; and many another book, if they were in my remembrance, and many a song and many a leccherous lay; that Crist for his grete mercy foryeve me the synne./ But of the translacion of Boece de Consolatione, and othere bookes of legendes of seintes, and omelies, and moralitee, and devocioun,/ that thanke I oure Lord Jhesu Crist and his blisful Mooder, and all the seintes of hevene,/ bisekynge hem that they from hennes forth unto my lyves ende sende me grace to biwayle my giltes, and to study to the salvacioun of my soule, and graunte me grace of verray penitence, confessioun and satisfactioun to doon in this present lyf,/thurgh the benigne grace of hym that is king of kynges and preest over alle preestes, that boghte us with the precious blood of his herte;/ so that I may been oon of hem at the day of doom that shulle be saved. *Qui cum patre et Spiritu Sancto vivit et regnat Deus per omnia secula. Amen.*[2]

We notice that Chaucer attributes any faults in the works to his ignorance rather than wilful intention; we mark for future reference his quotation from Paul *To the Romans* that "All that is written is written for our doctrine." It is not difficult to pinpoint most of the works he does not mention by name. His translations of "worldly vanities" would be *The Romance of the Rose,* the courtly love book par excellence, translated from the French. He retracted his *Troilus and Criseyde, The House of Fame, The Legend of Good Women, The Book of the Duchess, The Parliament of Fowls,* and those Canterbury Tales that "sounen into sin"—that tend toward or "smack of" sin: the *Miller's Tale, The Reeve's Tale, The Merchant's Tale,* etc. We do not know what the Book of the Lion was; there are theories on this point, if one wishes to follow them up, but the work, as far as we know, is not extant. He thanked God for his work on Boetius, his sermons, saints' lives and other works of devotion.

Needless to say, the reactions to this curious statement have been varied over the years. Some critics at once said it was spurious, an interpolation by Chaucer's literary executor. Gascoigne said Chaucer had bitterly repented of many of his works; Robinson says that in the fifteenth century the story of Chaucer's deathbed repentance was believed. Many, such as Manly, believed the document genuine, but inspired by the "brainwashing" of the monks, under whose influence Chaucer had spent his last days.[3] It is rather typical of the nineteenth century critics that they looked especially for monkish interpolation. One wonders how this great activity on the part of the monks (who had also interpolated the Christian elements of *Beowulf*) squares with the then popular picture of the fat and lazy monks. Although varying in their explanation of the meaning of the lines, most critics today accept their authenticity; without adducing argument on this point, as time is short, I ask your indulgence and proceed upon the premise that the work is genuine.

Accepted as genuine, what does this retraction mean? Again, as we have indicated, there are many opinions. Pollard accepted the retraction as "really the work of Chaucer's old age"; Skeat says the retraction is a disclaimer on Chaucer's part of all that did not lead toward the salvation of his soul. Skeat goes a bit further than this, however, and says, "It is only fair to add that the poet had good cause to regret such tales as those of the Miller, the Reeve and the Merchant."[4] Tatlock views this retraction as part of the tradition flowing from Augustine to Boccacio.[5] He says that Chaucer's disclaimer seems to surpass the others in solemnity, and that Chaucer was no longer himself if he seriously would like to blot out on religious grounds the works indicated. "With Chaucer there is to be considered the enormously strong pull of the whole spiritual teaching of the Middle Ages toward the ascetic attitude to worldly pleasure, which often has become stronger on a man as he has aged." (p. 528) Root says, rather savagely, "The poet's conscience was seized by the tenets of a narrow creed, which in the days of his strength he had known how to transmute into something better."[6] Lounsbury says, "The genuineness of the retraction can only be conceded on the assumption that the poet, at a period of life when physical and intellectual strength were failing, had fallen under the influence of men of very earnest convictions and very limited ideas."[7] The conviction that this tale and retraction belonged to Chaucer's latter end, and are to be attributed to fear of death, or to the awakening of a Catholic conscience, has continued down through Brewer,[8] Chute, Sister Madeleva,[9] Canon Looten[10] and others. Sister Madeleva and Father Thurston find that Chaucer's *fabliaux* and love stories were scandalous and needed to be retracted. Father Thurston writes at one point:

Boccaccio, Chaucer, and their emulators knew quite well that they were at heart insincere, that a good deal of what they wrote, by proclaiming the divinity of the goddess Venus and by satirising with grievous exaggeration the moral transgressions and cupidity of the clergy, were doing the devil's work.[11]

One wonders whether Father Thurston would include *Piers Plowman* among the works scandalous for attacks upon the clergy. Certainly Langland was more severe than Chaucer in this respect. The will of Sir Lewis Clifford, a pretty grim document full of repentance for sin, is cited by many, notably Chute[12] and Thurston,[13] as a parallel to Chaucer's retraction. But these critics have not well considered the difference between these two situations: Clifford's repentance is for *heresy* in an age when a lapse from orthodoxy might lead to the stake; it surely is no parallel to Chaucer's rejection of certain of his tales and translations. What is true, we might suggest, is that rather notorious cases such as Clifford's and a rather common habit of penitential statements gave Chaucer a model and a precedent for a retraction, serious or otherwise. Although recent criticism has other views, Chaucer's courtly love poems were for some time considered sinful by strict critics. William Madden, for example, in 1955, says that Chaucer's ending of the *Troilus* (the so-called *palinode*) is a forecast of his final retraction at the end of the *Canterbury Tales*:

Thus the so-called "retraction" of *Troilus* is an obviously sincere statement of Chaucer's final view of such "wordly vanities" and confirms by anticipation the more sweeping and genuine Retraction of all his works in the courtly-love tradition at the end of the *Canterbury Tales*.[14]

Against this statement place one or two of the most recent opinions. Father Dunning says, "The ending of the Troilus and Criseyde is the culmination of a study of human love in the perspective of Divine Providence . . . ."[15] Donaldson, similarly, takes a different view of the *Troilus* ending: "For the morality of Troilus and Criseide (and by morality I do not mean 'ultimate meaning') is simply this: that human love, and by a sad corollary, everything human, is unstable and illusory."[16]

Without at this point attempting a detailed answer to any of the theories that seek an explanation on the assumption that Chaucer found a conscience or that "the fear of death . . . suddenly closed down upon him," we must say that there is no certainty that the *Parson's Tale* or the retraction did belong to his old age; some critics say the tale was translated quite early, and the retraction, according to Hammond, to cite one critic, was planned and written early in his life.[17] The assumption that statements about the lack of human stability and the fickleness of fortune are the exclusive products of Chaucer's last years seems to be basic with a certain class of critics. Brewer, for example, cites such poems as *Lack of Stedfastnesse, Truth, The Former Age,* and *Fortune* as poems related in spirit to the *Parson's Tale*; these works, he says, "may belong here."[18] That is, at the end of his life, when it is assumed the Tale was written. It is a bit more than ridiculous to argue in this vein, for such poems are very probably all very early: if Chaucer needed a source, he found them all in the *Romance of the Rose.* It might be observed that poems on the instability of love and human things generally come more frequently from the young than from the old.

A somewhat more recent approach is through the consideration of the concept of a pilgrimage, and the propriety of putting aside all vanity at the end of such a journey. As life is a pilgrimage, it is argued, one rejects all vanity at the latter end of life. But to carry this over into a literary work is another matter. Donaldson (whose ideas on Chaucer are very various) manages to combine this explanation with the fear of death theory:

> . . . it is convenient to believe that . . . the poet passed the last months of his life close to the monks of Westminster. If this is true, then it is almost necessary to suppose that the *Introduction to the Parson's Tale* and *Chaucer's Retraction*—though not the *Parson's Tale* itself—were composed within the same period.[19]

This is some of the most cautious supposing that was ever supposed. He continues into the pilgrimage motif:

> To some of Chaucer's contemporaries his avoidance throughout most of the *Canterbury Tales* of the expected implications of the pilgrimage must have come as a surprise. It is not until they read the Parson's introduction that they would have found the journey taking on the metaphorical connotations that were hitherto lacking. Gone is the illusion of everyday reality that we have been accustomed to. . . . The pilgrimage is hastening to an

end and the poet's spirit—doubtless guided by the monks of Westminster, is concerned more urgently with the Celestial City.

There is hardly time for the telling of one more tale. . . . The Host speaks to the Parson as if he had never seen him before. (p. 148)

He sums up as follows: "The retraction must be taken as heartfelt. The poet was to die and he feared for his soul." (p. 149)

Baldwin in his essay on *The Unity of the Canterbury Tales* pursues the pilgrimage concept to the point where each of the tales represents one of the deadly sins to be encountered in life and condemned in the Parson's tale. "The Parson's tale" he says "marks the culmination of the Pilgrimage and Chaucer's immediate recantation is the denouement of the pilgrim-drama."[20] Gordon remarks justly about this theory:

What is necessary to the dramatic representation of man in his earthly pilgrimage to the New Jerusalem, including the role of sin and penance in such a drama, need not be cancelled. The moral and artistic purpose of such material should be sufficient guarantee of innocence.[21]

Baldwin's cannibalistic view of unity reminds one of the old jingle:

There was a young lady of Niger
Who smiled as she rode on a tiger;
They came back from the ride
With the lady inside
And the smile on the face of the tiger.

The only difference is that there is a frown on the face of the parson.

To accept Baldwin's view is to assume that the framework of the *Tales,* for one thing, is theological rather than literary. Such an estimate is entirely wrong; Chaucer, indeed, seems to have most pointedly indicated the literary context of his tales by giving us a sample of almost every genre of tale known to mediaeval man: romance, *fabliau,* saint's life, allegory, mock-heroic animal fable, and prose treatise.[22]

It is interesting—and to me, at least, amusing—that Gordon after running through the various opinions on the *Retraction,* attributes Chaucer's doubts to a "lack of theory to sustain him." He says:

We may surmise from the attitude of Gower and the substance of Gascoigne's report that Chaucer's doubts as to the propriety of his work were first awakened by unfriendly criticism of his vivid, realistic and sometimes coarse presentation of the physical aspects of love, to which the English public was perhaps especially sensitive; and that these doubts, once aroused, suggested a total reappraisal of his work and led at last to the renunciation of all his wordly achievements. Despite this reversal of values, the fact remains that part of the genius of Chaucer was his farsighted intimation of new and greatly enlarged possibilities for the literary artist. What he lacked was a theory to sustain him.[23]

It is rather that we lack perception of his subtle artistry than that he lacked method. Gower keeps popping into Chaucerian criticism like the head of King Charles.

What is my position, you ask, now that I have rejected deathbed repentance, awakened conscience, interpolation by the monks, or the necessity of retraction in the pilgrimage framework? The answer, as I see it, is quite simple; it is found in the subtlety of Chaucer's ironical humour, hinged upon the Parson's *Prologue*.

In order better to present my view, I should like to run through some of the chief features of Chaucer's narrative and poetic technique, especially as used in the *Canterbury Tales*. One of Chaucer's most persistent habits is a pretense of ignorance and ineptness: he can't succeed in love; he can't write; he knows very little of poetry and rhyme. In the prologue to the *Man of Law's Tale* we hear:

> I kan right now no thrifty tale seyn
> That Chaucer, thogh he kan but lewedly
> Of metres and on ryming craftily,
> Hath seyd hem in swich Englissh as he kan. (46–49)

If one is not wary, he may be taken in by Chaucer. At the end of the *Troilus* he appealed to Gower to correct what was wrong in the poem:

> O moral Gower, this book I directe
> To the and to the, philosophical Strode,
> To vouchen sauf, ther nede is, to correcte,
> Of your benignites and zeles goode. (v, 1856–1859)

I can only feel that this was a little joke he could not resist, either because Gower was too serious or because they were good friends. Certainly, the relationship between Chaucer and Gower, though often referred to, has not been properly explored.

Throughout the *Canterbury Tales* he carries on intermittent master-of-ceremonies patter, excusing the rough language of the low characters, explaining that after all there is not much he can do, if we are to hear the stories, but let them tell them in their own way: "The word must be cousin to the deed." About the miller he says:

> M'athynketh [I regret] that I shall reherce it heere,
> And therefor every gentil wight I preye,
> For Godes love, demeth not that I seye
> Of yvel entente, but for I moot reherce
> Hir tales alle, be they bettre or werse,
> Or elles falsen som of my mateere. (Prologue, 3170–3175)

If anyone has very delicate ears, let him read another tale, for there is sufficient variety to please them all:

> And, therefore, whoso list it not yheere,
> Turne over the leef and chese another tale:
> For he shal fynde ynowe, grete and smale,
> Of storial thyng that toucheth gentilesse,
> And eek moralitee and holynesse. (3176–3180)

Failure to catch the true note of Chaucer has led many to take such sections as an indication that Chaucer was worried over the propriety of his *fabliaux.* Madden, for instance, says:

> . . . he is clearly uneasy, and it may not be an accident that the series suddenly breaks off. For, like the courtly-love literature, the *fabliaux* genre to which the Miller's Tale and its two successors belong threatened moral and social consequences of which Chaucer could not be unaware.[24]

The series does *not* suddenly break off; it is in the very nature of the *Canterbury Tales* framework to give us a varied assortment of stories. Perhaps Madden did not catch what Chaucer said in the following lines: "eek men shal not maken ernest of game." In other words, don't take a bit of fun too seriously.

Part of this same pose is a hasty passing of the blame to someone else when he has been rather roguish, or as the English say, "saucy." Take, for example, these deliciously solemn lines from the *Nun's Priest's Tale*:

> Wommenes conseils been ful ofte colde;
> Wommenes conseil brought us first to wo
> And made Adam fro Paradys to go,
> Theras he was ful myrie and wel at ese. (3256–3259)

Chaucer says, I didn't say this—the rooster did. *I* don't see anything wrong with women:

> Thise been the cokkes wordes, and nat myne;
> I kan noon harm of no womman divyne. (3265–3266)

In the *Prologue* to the *Man of Law's Tale*—already referred to—after he has gabbled off the list of stories written by Chaucer (some of which were Gower's and not his) we read that Chaucer never wrote such nasty tales as *Appolonie of Tyre* (written by Gower); "of swich cursed stories I sey fy!" This might be all right for Gower, but not for Chaucer. This sounds a bit like the exchanges between Bob Hope and Bing Crosby when they were making films together. By using this great pretense of delicacy, Chaucer has picked up more sly laughs and ironic chuckles in a year than the Pardoner did marks with his highly developed craft.

No English writer ever knew or used to better advantage than Chaucer the technique of contrast: the sudden change of pace, the lightning shift from serious to comic, the juxtaposition of contrary characters, the single sudden flash of grave or comic from a whole field of its opposite—the Wife of Bath's sudden cry, "Alas, alas, that ever love was sinne." In all places at all times, Chaucer has a perfect sense of timing. At one point in the *Nun's Priest's Tale*, after getting himself involved in a long, technical, and rather headlong discussion of free will and God's foreknowledge, he suddenly breaks off with a shrug of his shoulders and a grin and says: "Let's leave this to St. Augustine and Bishop Bradwardine. *My* story is about a cock who got into trouble because he took his wife's advice."

Due in part to the dramatic quality of the *Canterbury Tales* (to be discussed in a moment), and in part to the fact that he never could resist flipping the coin over, Chaucer used the contrast principle to great advantage at the end of individual tales, where we find many a pretended or real about-face. Perhaps the best example of this little trick is what happens at the end of the touching and deeply moral tale of "vertuous souffrance," the clerk's story of patient Griselda. After explaining that this tale is to be understood in a rather allegorical and not realistic way, Chaucer tosses you into the air with a song in praise of the Arch-wife, the Wife of Bath:

For the wyves love of Bathe—
Whos lyf and al hire secte God mayntene
In heigh maistrie, and elles were it scathe—
I wol with lusty herte, fressh and grene,
Seyn you a song to glade you, I wene; (1170–1174)

The song is ironical advice to women not to be like Griselda. This is in no way intended to detract from the serious nature of the tale, for

Chaucer leads into the song with the words "Let us stynte of ernestful matere." Let us have a little break from seriousness. It is like the appearance of Falstaff upon the battlefield. This same technique is used in the opposite direction to have some extra bit of fun at the end of a not too serious tale. For instance, in closing his delightful mock heroic *Nun's Priest's Tale,* Chaucer says, pulling a serious face: Don't think this is just fun; it is a serious story with a moral in it—so just take the moral and never mind the rest:

But ye that holden this tale a folye,
As of a fox or of a cok and a hen,
Taketh the moralite, goode men.
For Seint Paul seith that al that write is,
To our doctrine it is ywrite, ywis;
Taketh the fruyt, and lat the chaf be stille. (3488 ff.)

The words of St. Paul from *Romans* had a somewhat different context! Chaucer takes advantage of the authority of the written word in his day, and builds up a syllogism on Paul: "This is written down; therefore, it is for your profit."

While we are denied the supreme delight of hearing Chaucer read these priceless lines, we do have some compensation in the sight of the many serious, gnomish (*Rape of the Lock!*) critics who seize upon this and other parts of the tale to knit up a whole sleeve of *sententia,* catch flashes of the true mediaeval Chaucer and start watching for him to hatch out more retractions for his (or your) flippancy. In the first rank of these stands David Holbrook, who can suck morality out of a mock heroic faster than a weasel can suck eggs. "For all the wit and comedy, the interest in Chanticleer is serious."[25] The poem is a rejection of courtly love, for "The courtesy of the yard [O Chanticleer!] is revealed as surface deception, and so the rest of the story concerns the consequences of Chanticleer's self-deception." (p. 121) Those heavy hearted critics deserve their own blindness. For example, when Chanticleer, in his superior, masculine, and Latin-quoting way, pulls off a bit of delightful wife-hoaxing such as this:

For al so as *in principio*
Mulier est hominis confusio,
Madame, the sentence of this Latin is
Woman is mannes joye and al his blis,

Holbrook calls it culpable mistranslation, Chanticleer's abuse of his intellect. (p. 124) Of what use to some men are Shakespeare, Shaw, or Christopher Fry?

This fisty pouncing upon his mock heroic poetry has been a great barrier to the full comprehension of Chaucer. Baldwin, referring to the final lines of the *Nun's Priest's Tale*, says, "The moral, didactic, and even allegorical intentions here are made quite clear";[26] and so we see that when Chaucer said "taketh the fruyt and lat the chaffe be stille," he gave too many critics a chance to expatiate on the seriousness of the mediaeval mind (even in the middle of a joke) and offered to that new Amos and Andy of sententious appreciation, Robertson and Huppé, the title and content of a new book. I do not mean to say that Chaucer is never serious: *Troilus* is serious; so is the *Knight's Tale*, so is Griselda. But Chaucer always knew when he was serious, and this moral squeezing of his lighter verses leads critics inevitably to hanker for some kind of deeper, fun-retracting seriousness: and when they seem to find it, "Ah ha!" they say "we knew where he was heading all the time."

There is another very carefully developed and highly significant technique which Chaucer shares with Shakespeare and Milton: a quiet and sly planting of a word or phrase or *sententia* in a perfectly plain and straightforward manner; then letting this spring up at you later like a jack-in-the-box. Something, I mean, like "honest, honest Iago," which is innocent enough in Act I, but by the end of *Othello* has climbed to a screaming note. For instance, in the *Knight's Tale*, the beautiful courtly heroine, Emelie, after many months finally gives her love to the worthy and patient suitor, for "Pitee renneth soone in gentil herte." (1761) We remember this consoling act and doctrine; but in the *Merchant's Tale* this same sentence pops up when we hear that the young wife of January after two or three days of marriage takes her husband's squire as her lover, for "pitee renneth soone in gentil herte." (1986) We need no further comment upon her character or upon the deed. In this same tale old January speaks of the earthly paradise, the garden of pleasure, that a wife will be; and that he wants a young wife, for she can be moulded to his tastes as a man moulds wax in his warm hands. This very expectation is ironical, but it becomes razor sharp when January is cuckolded in the garden he has built for their love, and the only moulding of wax is that employed by the squire to make a secret key to slip into the garden and hide under a bush. (2117)

To convince you that this really is a regular technique of his, I will cite two other such examples from Chaucer. At the beginning of the *Summoner's Tale*, the money-grubbing friar denounces the careless secular priest to the sick man he visits:

> Thise curatz been full necligent and slowe
> To grope tendrely a conscience
> In shrift. (1816–1818)

He proceeds to grope the conscience of the sick man, looking for profit; finally he is told that there *is* something reserved for him and his community:

> . . . grope wel bihynde
> Bynethe my buttock there shaltow fynde
> A thyng that I have hyd in pryvetee. (2141–2143)

What the friar receives is a just reward for his greedy groping and a good commentary upon the worth of his ministry.

Very often there is something in the prologue to a tale that is striking enough to stand out in the reader's memory and re-echo strongly when it arises in the tale itself. One example comes to mind: the miller, who is a jealous and perilous man, says:

> An housbonde shal not been inquisitif
> Of Goddes privetee, nor of his wyf. (3163–3164)

This statement is wonderful in the mouth of the miller; but it is pure gold when it flows—in part at least—from the mouth of the duped reeve, who is trying to shake out of his pretended ecstasy "hende" Nicholas, who is on the way to cuckolding him: "Men sholde not knowe of Godes pryvetee." (3454) We hear the first part of the miller's statement but remember the second part; and, as "privetee" had two meanings, we are ready to laugh at the reeve, who was not able to guard his wife's pryvetee!

There are many more examples of this drop-the-handkerchief technique; suffice it to say that the reader of Chaucer does finally begin to catch the true tone and anticipate the fun of the ironical laughter of the pick-up. This careful exposition of the technique is for the sake of showing that it operates strongly in the *Parson's Prologue and Tale.*

As we have already said, and as is to be inferred from what we have noticed about the interplay of the prologues and tales, there is a strongly dramatic character to the *Canterbury Tales.* The character of the parson has not been considered very much by critics in the totality of the Tales, but he is one of the actors in the drama from beginning to end, as we see. And along with him, very significantly for the problem we have in hand, is Chaucer the pilgrim. Without digressing too far from the path, let us for a moment look at what one of two critics have said about the dramatic interplay of the persons in the pilgrim-troupe. Kittredge, of course, has the classical statement of the dramatic quality of the great work:

> The Canterbury pilgrimage is, whether Dryden meant it or not, a Human Comedy, and the Knight and the Miller and the Pardoner and the Wife of Bath and the rest are the *dramatis personae*. The prologue itself is not merely a prologue: it is the first act, which sets the personages in motion. Thereafter, they move by virtue of their inherent vitality, not as tale-telling puppets, but as men and women. From this point of view, which surely accords with Chaucer's intention, the pilgrims do not exist for the sake of the stories, but *vice versa*.[27]

Note that he says *from this point of view*, the stories exist for the personages. He continues: "The action of the plot, however simple, involves a great variety of realities among the pilgrims . . . things happen to them. . . . Their personalities act and react." (pp. 155–156) Every reader knows, without being told by Kittredge, that a great deal of the vitality of the work of art known as the *Canterbury Tales* comes from the dialogue flashes and interchanges between the tales. Perhaps not everybody, however, has noted the simple fact that Chaucer the pilgrim is there. Donaldson says:

> Perhaps first among these elements is the fictional reporter, Chaucer the pilgrim and the role he plays in the *Prologue to the Canterbury Tales* and in the links between them. He is not really Chaucer the poet. . . .
> He is the chief agent by which the poet achieves his wonderfully complex, ironic, comic, serious vision of a world which is but a devious and confused, infinitely varied pilgrimage to a certain shrine.[28]

It is this pilgrim Chaucer, wide-eyed and simple, who admires the monk and thinks he should be an abbot; it is he who babbles the delightful doggerel parody upon upper class tales of knight errantry in his *Sir Thopas*, "with sides smale." It is he who sees all, reacts to all and may be expected to have something final to say, thrilled and happy always to be "one of the gang."

We are beginning to sound like Sir Thopas, who never did get to the action of his story; but with those various techniques in our eye, we are now ready to look at the parson, his prologue and his tale, and the *Retraction*—for they are all united.

First the parson as a member of the cast. As a general rule, the characters of the Prologue do not develop or change with the progress of the pilgrimage; but the parson does show sides to his nature not manifest in the idealized portrait of the *General Prologue*. There has been much discussion among critics over the question whether Chaucer left the *Canterbury Tales* unfinished—for he had promised two tales from each pilgrim and each had delivered only one. Kemp Malone very sensibly remarks that one should not worry too much over such seeming inconsistency: "In creative writing," he says "the important thing is to get started."[29] And Chaucer started with a noble portrait of a perfect country priest. Gentle, but firm; no man ever spoke an out-of-the-way word in his presence, for he commanded too much respect. Now we find that, for the sake of an extra bit of irony, Chaucer changed the character a bit to suit the needs of his over-all pattern. He allows the host to bait the parson by swearing. When the host swears "by Goddes bones," and the parson checks him up at once, instead of subsiding, the host begins to jibe at him saucily: "O, Jankyn be ye there? I smell a Lollere in the wynd."[30] Jankyn, Skeat says, is diminutive for John, a derisive word for a priest.[31] Chaucer continues:

> "Now! goode men," quod oure Hoste, "herkneth me;
> Abydeth, for Goddes digne passioun,
> For we schal han a predicacioun;
> This Lollere heer wil prechen us somwhat." (1172 ff.)

The shipman objects to Lollardish preaching, which will sow tares in the pure wheat, "He shal no gospel glosen here ne teche." The word *glosen* has a number of meanings and Chaucer exploits all of them masterfully. The friar has said the "glosynge is a wondrous thing certayn"; by this he means expounding your meaning in scripture. The shipman simply means that the parson will falsify the meaning of the text. Kittredge said that the shipman was not worried about heresy, but rather feared a tedious sermon. And yet they all suffered cheerfully through Melibee without a word.

It has often been suggested that the host and the shipman are only joking with the parson; but they do continue to swear, and it is quite clearly scornful baiting, deliberately prodding the anger of an arch puritan. There is little doubt that the tale of the parson is orthodox enough (although hardly liberal!) for Chaucer was certainly orthodox in every particular;[32] might it not be one last bit of superb irony to have a Lollardish parson tell an orthodox tale? Lollard or not, the parson is a puritan, and the ground has been carefully prepared for the scene in which he will dramatically *denounce all frills and all fables*. When it is time for the last tale, the host turns to the parson with a certain amount of courtesy (but with two oaths *by thy fey*, and *for cokkes bones*) and asks for a *fable*:

"Sire preest," quod he "artow a vicary?
Or arte a person? sey sooth by thy fey!
Be what thou be, ne breke thou not our pley;
For every man, save thou, hath toold his tale.
Unbokele and shewe us what is in thy male;
For, trewely, me thynketh by thy cheere
Thou sholdest knytte up wel a greet mateere.
Telle us a fable anon, for cokkes bones!"[33]

This speech was seemingly rather innocent, but it was loaded against the parson; and he was not slow to react:

This Persoun answerde, al atones,
"Thou getest fable noon ytold for me;
For Paul that writeth unto Thymothee,
Repreveth hem that weyven soothfastnesse,
And tellen fables and swich wrecchednesse.
Why sholde I sowen draf out of my fest,
Whan I may sewen whete, if that me lest?
For which I seye, if that yow list to heere
Moralitee and vertuous mateere,
And thanne that ye wol yeve me audience
I wol ful fayn, at Cristes reverence,
Do yow plesaunce leefful, as I kan." (30–41)

The parson quotes a pretty strong text here, for St. Paul places fables opposite to truth.[34] The parson is ready to tell a tale that is properly "vertuous," with no frills. He will not "glose," the meaning here being that he will not soft-pedal the plain truth:

But trusteth wel, I am a Southren man,
I kan not geeste "rum, ram, raf" by lettre,
Ne, God woot, rym holde I but litel bettre,
And therefore, if you list—I wol nat glose—
I wol yow telle a myrie tale in prose
To knytte up al this feeste, and make an ende. (42–47)

Some have thought that this passage shows a sense of humour in the parson. *He* is deadly serious, but Chaucer is having fun. The "rum," "raf" business is no doubt a good natured dig at the popularity of the alliterative religious poetry, notably *Piers Plowman*. You could hardly use a better example to show the aversion the parson had to poetry and frills of any kind when he objects to such a moral work as *Piers Plowman*.

This very severe attitude was not, as some claim, a common attitude on the part of the clergy; many were very frank and easy-going in this respect, as we see by examining mediaeval writing generally. A good example would be the mediaeval mystery cycles in England. These are full of rough humour as well as much holiness; they were written by the clergy, acted by monks and later by friars, undoubtedly, before they were taken over entirely by the guilds. It is amusing to look at our nineteenth-century editors of mediaeval drama and see how many blanks they left, indicating something unfit for delicate ears. Lounsbury, in a passage worth quoting, indicates that it was the puritans only who objected to the realistic side of Chaucer's writings; the parson I feel, represents this attitude:

> There is evidence, indeed, that Chaucer's writings were looked upon coldly by men of that class to whom all efforts of the creative imagination lack what they are pleased to call truth. So wide was his popularity, so universal was the acquaintance with his writings that his greatest work came early to be almost a synonym for fictitious narrative of any sort. As such it would naturally fall under the ban of that somewhat dreary body of men, in whom the Anglo-Saxon race has always abounded, who look askance upon all literature which deals with matters outside of the region of figures and facts. This class, often composed of good men, invariably of prosaic men, did not escape the observation of Chaucer. He represents as belonging to it his parsoun, a man morally of a lofty type of character, but plainly marked in certain respects by intellectual narrowness.[35]

That this class did exist and had a voice may be borne out by a glance at the complaints against the miracle plays. We do hear that ever and anon there were rumblings and objections to these plays, even in England, where they were relatively innocent. One of the most famous of the documents aimed at the miracle play is one called *A Treatise of Miraclis Pleyinge*. Craig calls this a Wycliffite tract.[36] The interesting point is this: the strongest objection to the plays is that they are not all *literally* true; in this work you find the phrase "turn your eyes away from beholding vanities."[37] To dip into it is to find matter that sounds like the *Retraction* of Chaucer: "Goode men, therefore, seeing their time too short to occupy them in good ernest works, and seeing the day of their reckoning draw quickly near, and not knowing when they must go hence, flee such idleness."[38] The parson asks God to give him the power to preach a sermon that will take them to the glorious celestial pilgrimage.

Perhaps it has not been generally noticed that Chaucer has a conventional—with variations—manner of ending all his tales. The formula is that of the oral tale, which ended with a compliment or a prayer. If you read through collections of such folk tales as those collected in Ireland, for instance, you will often find a prayer ending a tale that is in no way pious. This is what you have in Chaucer, although the genius of Chaucer adapts this, as all things, to special meaning when it is convenient. Even the *fabliaux* end with a prayer or a blessing, which serves to bring us back to the reality of the pilgrims and their voyage, and the fact of the merry tales told for entertainment along the way. By actual count, fifteen tales (including the Pardoner's—and the blessing has nothing to do with the Pardoner's spiritual state) end with a prayer; three end with moral *sententia*, advice; the "Wife of Bath" ends with a prayer that delightfully combines a blessing on tractable husbands and a curse on those who will not be governed by their wives.

As it was the end of the *Canterbury Tales*, we naturally expect the conclusion of the *Parson's Tale* to be followed by a prayer of some sort, either a simple conventional one, or a more lengthy prayer for the soul of the writer. Chaucer did give us this, but he could not resist giving us more. Wit, like murder, will out. What he does is switch us back to Chaucer the pilgrim, who has listened with his usual enthusiasm and commitment, to the Parson's sermon on rejection of worldliness and the necessity of repentance. A perfect foil for Chaucer's sly wit and bearing the cloak, as it were, of the poet Chaucer, our pilgrim rises to final grandeur: he springs up and, ringing the parson's bell, proceeds to denounce all *fables*—all works of the imagination—found in Chaucer's writings to date. This is the explanation to the rejection of such innocent works as *The Parliament of Fowls* and the *Book of the Duchess*. They are made up, not true.

And thus Chaucer, in the manner he has followed throughout the

Tales, has with a flip of the wrist, restored the balance of good humour and, while not detracting from the worth of the sermon, places it within the context of optimistic humanity.

Perhaps he still leaves us wondering what *he* means by quoting St. Paul's "all that is written is for your doctrine." Perhaps he means to hint that there are different ways of seeing truth and doctrine. Certainly Chaucer could never let you go without one last quip to keep you pondering.

Now that I have come to the end of my rambles, I am ready to answer in one sentence my own question, "Who retracted what?"

Chaucer the Pilgrim retracted *fables.*

NOTES

1. James D. Gordon, "Chaucer's Retraction: A Review of Opinion," in *Studies in Medieval Literature in Honor of Albert Croll Baugh,* ed. MacEdward Leach (Philadelphia, 1961), pp. 81–96.
2. *The Complete Works of Geoffrey Chaucer,* ed. F. N. Robinson (Cambridge, Mass., 1933), p. 314. All quotations are from this edition.
3. Gordon, pp. 82 ff.
4. W. W. Skeat, *The Works of Geoffrey Chaucer* (Oxford, 1952), III, 503–4.
5. J. S. P. Tatlock, "Chaucer's Retractions," *PMLA,* XXVIII (1913), 521–29.
6. R. K. Root, *The Poetry of Chaucer* (Boston, 1906), p. 288.
7. T. R. Lounsbury, *Studies in Chaucer* (New York, 1962), III, 40.
8. D. S. Brewer, *Chaucer* (London, 1961), "The Last Years," pp. 179 ff.
9. Sister Madeleva, *A Lost Language* (New York, 1951), pp. 108–10.
10. Chanoine Looten, *Chaucer, ses modèles, ses sources, sa religion* (Lille, 1931), p. 243.
11. Herbert Thurston, S.J., "The Conversion of Boccacio and Chaucer," in *Studies,* XXV (1936), 220.
12. Marchette Chute, *Geoffrey Chaucer of England* (London, 1946), pp. 311 ff.
13. Thurston, p. 225.
14. William Madden, "Chaucer's Retraction and Mediaeval Canons of Seemliness," *Med. Studies,* XVII (1955), 182.
15. T. P. Dunning, "God and Man in *Troilus and Criseyde,*" *English and Medieval Studies Presented to J. R. R. Tolkien,* ed. N. Davis and C. L. Wrenn (London, 1962), p. 164.
16. E. Talbot Donaldson, "The Ending of Chaucer's *Troilus,*" *Early English and Norse Studies Presented to Hugh Smith,* ed. Brown and Foote (London, 1963), p. 35.
17. E. P. Hammond, "The Book of the Twenty-five Ladies," *MLN,* XLVIII (1933), 514–16.
18. Brewer, p. 183.
19. E. Talbot Donaldson, *Chaucer's Poetry* (New York, 1958), p. 147.
20. Baldwin, in *Chaucer Criticism: The Canterbury Tales,* ed. Schoeck and Taylor (Notre Dame, 1960), p. 40.
21. Gordon, pp. 87–88.
22. One of the best studies of Chaucer's literary background is Charles Muscatine's *Chaucer and the French Tradition* (Univ. of California Press, 1957).

23. Gordon, p. 93.
24. Madden, *op. cit.* (above, note 14), p. 181.
25. David Holbrook, "The None Preestes Tales," *The Age of Chaucer*, Pelican Guide to English Literature (London, 1959), I, 121.
26. Baldwin, p. 32.
27. G. L. Kittredge, *Chaucer and His Poetry* (Cambridge, Mass., 1939), pp. 154–55.
28. Donaldson, "Chaucer the Pilgrim," *Chaucer Criticism*, ed. Schoeck and Taylor, I, 1–3.
29. Kemp Malone, *Chapters on Chaucer* (Baltimore, 1951).
30. Epilogue, "The Man of Law's Tale," 1172.
31. Skeat, *Works of Chaucer*, V, 166.
32. This in spite of a rather ridiculous article by R. S. Loomis, "Was Chaucer a Free-thinker?" *Studies in Honor of A. C. Baugh*, pp. 21–42.
33. Prologue, "The Parson's Tale," 22–29.
34. See I Tim. 1:4; 4:4.
35. Lounsbury, *Studies in Chaucer*, III, 39–40.
36. Hardin Craig, *Religious Drama in England* (Oxford, 1955), p. 92.
37. *Medieval English Verse and Prose*, ed. R. S. Loomis (New York, 1948), p. 291.
38. *Ibid.*, p. 292.

GERALD McCAUGHEY

An Approach to *Wuthering Heights*

Faced with the problem of analysing as complex a work as *Wuthering Heights*, the critic must instantly be aware of his own limitations and beware of any glib, facile interpretations that can only serve to demonstrate a superficial acquaintanceship with the intricate web that constitutes that novel.

Nonetheless, while recognizing the obvious shortcomings and one-sidedness of attempting to construe a specific meaning out of the novel, I feel that some slight justification of the "specific" might be found in terms of the "meaning" of the whole shape and form of that work of art that is *Wuthering Heights*. And if the anagogical exegesis which follows appears to slight completely other very important aspects of the technique of *Wuthering Heights* (such as the role of the narrators, which has received considerable attention recently[1])—then I can only answer that this is a measure of the genius of Emily Brontë, that her work cannot be finally pinned to one definitive meaning, certainly not by one as newly awakened to the intricacies of that work as myself.

Seen from one narrow viewpoint, then, *Wuthering Heights* can be a tale of trial, specifically the trial of the Earnshaw family. And what is most important to the whole story is the resurrection and the tempering by fire of this old Yorkshire family, fallen into moral disrepute.

Now this, of course, is rather in defiance of the age-old concept of the "great love" story. And while *that* is something one should certainly face up to eventually, I feel it has been perhaps overemphasized at the cost of the other unifying concepts of the story. When we con-

HAB vol. xv, no. 2, autumn 1964. From an address to the annual meeting of the Association of Canadian University Teachers of English, 1964.

sider that forty-five percent of the novel concerns itself with the younger generation of Catherine Linton, Linton Heathcliff, and Hareton Earnshaw, one is surely justified in questioning any interpretation that wishes to dismiss the ultimate coming together of Catherine junior and Hareton as merely a happy culmination—or even worse, a Heathcliff-Catherine senior romance in a more propitious circumstance! Having delivered this much *apologia,* I feel obliged now to strike out bravely on my own path across the moor, head high in the fog of critical ignorance. To reach (I hope) Wuthering Heights.

What I would see in this story, then, is the tale of an old Yorkshire family, one of some historical significance (see Nelly's comments to Lockwood: "Very old, Sir!"); but one that, at the beginning of Nelly Dean's revelations, has lost its hard strength of character; and, as a result, is unable to cope with the realities of life in a harsh, cruel world. For it is no secret that Yorkshiremen, particularly of the North and West Ridings, are shaped by nature, so to speak, to a rugged stubbornness of character that one must have to survive the realities of their life.[7] The Earnshaws, then, have lost some of their necessary moral fibre, are a family turned sour. By this same token, the Lintons should represent a civilizing force upon the rugged moor-dwellers, yet these too are soft and yielding as perhaps they must be for the purposes of the story. More important than these, however, is the problem of Heathcliff. By this interpretation I would see Heathcliff as a force, a sort of purgatorial fire acting upon the Earnshaw family. He is the necessary challenge to split out the weaknesses of the Earnshaw character. And when he has successfully performed his function, the Earnshaws remain, still in control of their lands, yet certainly shed of the fatal weaknesses that had destroyed both Hindley and Catherine senior. And it is really because of Heathcliff rather than in spite of him that Hareton and Catherine junior can take their places in the world of harsh reality with the reader completely satisfied that they will survive, perfectly able to cope with any situation, and obviously meant for each other (again thanks to Heathcliff's machinations).

Now this, of course, does not in any way come to grips with the problem of the mysterious Lockwood, and his own rather distasteful character. Yet, as I have said already, the many-sided qualities of the story cannot all be successfully dealt with, and I am forced to ignore all others in the attempt to justify my own approach, hoping only that no too great distortion has taken place in the process. Let us, then, look for the evidence to support the theory advanced.[3]

In the very first chapter, before Lockwood even crosses the threshold, he reports a significant thing:

> I paused to admire a quantity of grotesque carving lavished over the front, and especially about the principal door; above which, among a wilderness of crumbling griffins and shameless little boys, I detected the date "1500" and the name "Hareton Earnshaw." (p. 5)

Now this tells us two important things about the family in general and the story in particular. First, that the family of Earnshaw has been established on this site for at least three hundred years, and second, in terms of the story, the uniqueness of the name being the same as that of Hindley's son who in the end will become the master of Earnshaws. At the very least, then, the author has cunningly bracketed the story by the use of this name. And again by virtue of the clever narrative technique, we are early introduced to those two who will ultimately run the estate, Hareton and Catherine junior, in spite of the little apparent likelihood of that end being exhibited at this juncture.

But are the Earnshaws really fallen into evil ways before the advent of a "revenge-seeking" Heathcliff (that is, Heathcliff as he returns a man)? Well, let us just look at them. The first indications we have are in the writings of Catherine senior that Lockwood takes up on that early night when he is forced to remain at the Heights. Here we see Catherine and Heathcliff being bullied by Hindley, Frances, and Joseph alternately: three hours mounted on a corn sack listening to Joseph with Hindley's tart: "What, done already?" as their only recompense; or "Frances, darling, pull his hair as you go by, I heard him snap his fingers!"; or Joseph tearing down Catherine's curtain and boxing her ears. (pp. 24–25) I needn't dwell on the wonderful irony of Joseph's cry of horror: "Miss Cathy's riven the back off the *Helmet of Salvation* and Heathcliff pawsed his fit into t' first part o' t' *Broad Way of Destruction.*" (Heathcliff certainly had—and "pawsed" more than just his "fit"!)

Hindley hardly demonstrates the qualities necessary to a mature acceptance of the role of master of the Heights—bullying the younger ones and "like two babies, kissing and talking nonsense by the hour" (p. 24) with his wife. Then as Nelly commences her chronological tale of the past events, we are given a good opportunity to see just what is wrong with the Earnshaws. For Mr. Earnshaw surely performs a Christian act in bringing home the foundling Heathcliff, yet neither Catherine nor Hindley respond in any Christian fashion, she even "spitting at the stupid little thing" (p. 43), and Nelly putting *it* out on the landing for which uncharitable act she is banished. Heathcliff, in fact, is sore put upon what with Hindley's "blows" and Nelly's "pinches." (p. 44)

Old Mr. Earnshaw is not exempt from criticism either, for instead of preparing his son Hindley for the realities of life, he spends his latter years exhibiting obvious favouritism for Heathcliff and thereby creates strife and jealousy in the children's world, heinous that an adult should so cause this![4]

Hindley starts off lording it over all immediately on his father's death, ordering the servants into the back kitchen, and driving Heathcliff out to labourer status. After the subsequent death of his wife, he rushes headlong into a destruction that Heathcliff is certainly not responsible for. And far from merely bullying Heathcliff, Hindley actually abuses his own son in worse fashion than ever Heathcliff does when he is in control: "Kiss me, Hareton! Damn thee, kiss me! By God, as if I would rear such a monster! As sure as I'm living, I'll break the brat's neck." (p. 87) It is at this point that he drops the child over the stairs and Heathcliff is the instrument of its salvation. While Nelly records this act as though Heathcliff regretted it, we cannot escape the obvious significance in Heathcliff being cast in this role of Savior in view of Hareton's ultimate position in the story. And in case we wish to blame Heathcliff for Hindley's utter degradation, Nelly spells out for us Hindley's own complete responsiblity: "They all hate you—that's the truth! A happy family you have and a pretty state you've come to!" (p. 89) While critics are prone to stress Heathcliff's brutality to others, how many have noted Hindley's "Damm it, I don't want to be troubled with more sickness here" (p. 102), or his bullying of even his sister, "I shall only have the more humour for you" (p. 103), with Heathcliff gone!

On Heathcliff's return, while it may be helpful to his desire for revenge, we cannot escape the truth that Hindley is utterly degenerate by this time. Even his motives in inviting Heathcliff to stay are bad, remembering he is anxious to both recoup what amounts to a fairly limited gambling loss at this time, and to grasp a thoroughly unnecessary rent; whilst Heathcliff appears to have a fairly honest "wish to install himself in quarters at walking distance from the Grange." (p. 116) Even young Hareton finds Heathcliff an ally against the bullying of his own father, "he pays Dad back what he gives to me." (p. 129) That Hindley is a cowardly bully is spelt out for us in his inability to take forceful action against the interloper, the bungling mess he makes of his one attempt to deal with Heathcliff, and his pitifully inadequate mouthings of dreams of revenge. "Oh if God would but give me strength to strangle him in my last agony." (p. 212) Yet Heathcliff's ability to act without consequence of the norms of law and order makes us surely question Hindley's inability to do something direct about his enemy, and conclude that the reason lies in just that weakness of character that is part of Hindley's make-up. Nor can we avoid the obvious fact that he would have drunk and gambled away his estates, Heathcliff notwithstanding. As a result, it is because of Heathcliff's plottings that Hareton will ultimately enjoy ownership!

Catherine senior is also lacking in qualities of a true Earnshaw, and whilst she has far more spunk than brother Hindley, she is too easily seduced from true love to the civilized graces of the Linton family. Yet it is probably essential to the plot, for Heathcliff to be the purgatory of the Earnshaws and for the Lintons to present at least some of the redeeming civilizing features to the tempered, purified Earnshaws. For we must remember that in the end it is Catherine junior and Hareton who inherit—both Earnshaws, one with some of the good Linton qualities, and nary a touch of Heathcliff left.

Catherine senior tries to remain true to Heathcliff but as Hindley weakens over liquor, she weakens over the effete civilized qualities of the Lintons; yet in one of her fits of violent temper, shows even Edgar her ability to lie and bully (notice the scene early on when she attempts to get rid of Nelly and leaves Edgar "greatly shocked at the double fault of falsehood and violence which his idol had committed" [p. 83]), after which she really bamboozles him into his proposal and accepts knowing full well she is not in love with him. Yet the curse of pride and her philosophy of pragmatism, "I have only to do with the present" (p. 93), drive her into this position, "It would degrade me to marry Heathcliff now." (p. 95) She attempts to rationalize away her reasons for marrying Edgar, saying she will not "consent to forsake Heathcliff" and "if I marry Linton, I can aid Heathcliff to rise." (p. 96) Yet she quite rightly recognizes that marriage to Heathcliff would bring impoverishment, and for our purposes would be disastrous in terms of the resurrection of the Earnshaw clan. It is significant, too, that she, carrying the "curse" of Earnshaws, is instrumental in causing the deaths of both Linton parents when they take her fever, after bringing her in to care for her.

Catherine shows up well against the background of her cowardly, snobbish husband, and weak, foolish sister-in-law, for she has learned the bitterness of a loveless marriage, and comes to despise her husband. Yet she too has traits of character that are anything but admirable. For we notice how she is instrumental in promoting Isabella's infatuation for Heathcliff, first taking Isabella to Wuthering Heights (p. 117), even though she does decry Heathcliff's character to the former. And when Edgar attempts to have Heathcliff ejected bodily from the Grange, Catherine perversely sides against her husband, presumably disgusted with Edgar's lack of physical courage, yet failing to see the anomalous position Edgar is in with her constant entertaining of Heathcliff. After having made the wrong decision to marry Edgar, Catherine has not the character to renounce either husband or lover, but must retreat into a state of physical morbidity that results ultimately in her thoroughly unnecessary death (as Kenneth puts it, "A stout hearty lass like Catherine does not fall ill for a trifle" [p. 153]), fortunately only after she has given birth to a Catherine Earnshaw of more stability and resilience, one who can stand the hot fire of the Heathcliff purgatory.

Of the Lintons little need be said. Edgar is obviously weak, despicably unable to act the man's role even though he has the backing of constituted authority (as local magistrate). He cannot cope with Catherine. Even when it comes to a showdown over Heathcliff, he is unable to more than *ask* her to choose between them, "Will you give up Heathcliff hereafter, or will you give up me?" (p. 139) As her husband he should have the courage to *tell* her, but as Heathcliff has put it, he is "a milk-blooded coward" (p. 136) which Catherine should have been able to appreciate from his first courting of her, when he was too timid even to risk encounter with the loud-mouthed bully, Hindley. In passion even his "veins are full of ice water" as Catherine puts it (p. 139), and when faced with the difficult problem of his sister's having run off with the villain, Edgar can only react with passive acquiescence, not even disowning her but saying only "she has disowned me" and taking no steps whatever to protect her or the family property which will ultimately pass on to her and not to his own daughter. (p. 193) Even Isabella is astounded at her brother's passivity over Heathcliff's interference with the ailing Catherine, "I wonder Edgar did not send for a constable and give him into custody." (p. 204) But in spite of Nelly's seeing Edgar as remaining at the helm of the family ship (p. 126), one must surely wonder at his retirement from life, his refusal to take any action whatever, and his cowardly willingness to turn over Linton Heathcliff to the enemy in spite of Isabella's last wishes, even to the extent of sending him out at the break of day to avoid an encounter with Heathcliff:

> "Varrah Weell!" shouted Joseph, as he slowly drew off. "To-morn, he's come hisseln and *thrust* him out, if you dare!" To obviate the danger of this threat being fulfilled, Mr. Linton commissioned me to take the boy home early [aroused from his bed at five o'clock]. (p. 240)

Isabella is no better than her brother. Infatuated with Heathcliff, she throws herself at him in spite of his obvious warnings of what she can expect as his wife; and, having no courage to sustain her, perishes in the hot fire of his chastisement, losing all spirit so rapidly that Nelly, on visiting the Heights, remarks: "so much had circumstances altered their positions that he would certainly have struck a stranger as a born and bred gentleman, and his wife as a thorough little slattern!" (p. 172)

With the younger generation, we see the obvious contrasts. Hareton, cheated out of his inheritance, brought up as a rustic, has the stamina to survive that his father lacked. While he exhibts many Heathcliffian traits, i.e. hanging puppies, etc., he is essentially a good person (p. 249), one whose Earnshaw character has hardened into strong moral fibre under the baptism of Heathcliff's fire. For when all is said and done, Heathcliff really admires him, especially in contrast to the puling ninny that is ironically his own son. And when it becomes necessary for Hareton to stand up to Heathcliff on Catherine junior's behalf, he will do even that, much as he loves the so-called villain of the piece. Yet he is sufficiently strong of character to refuse to hear tales against Heathcliff—"He said he wouldn't suffer a word to be uttered in his disparagement!" (p. 380)—be they true or false. In other words, he has the nobility that is presumably necessary for the continuance of the family of Earnshaw in the hard world of reality.

Catherine too, is of better stuff than her mother. For while she appears spoiled, and subject to the same foolish seduction by weakness in the shape of Linton, she learns better and survives the brutalities Heathcliff puts upon her, "bloody but unbowed" so to speak. She acknowledges his physical mastery, but refuses to yield in spirit: "I'll put my trash away, because you can make me, if I refuse. . . . But I'll not do anything, though you should swear your tongue out, except what I please." (p. 35) Young Catherine is foolish in her attachment to Linton, and cruel in her mocking of Hareton, and refusal to aid him in his attempts to better himself. But after she has suffered the dominance of Heathcliff, she appears to have been purged of all these qualities; and, with spirit intact, can go forward to happiness with Hareton, Earnshaw with Earnshaw, the family restored and certainly purged of the fatal weaknesses of the older generation.

And what of Heathcliff? Well, by this interpretation he represents mainly a force of power, a catalyst in operation, something the Earnshaws badly needed. In his machinations against the family, he has won control of Wuthering Heights, and by his marriage to Isabella he has Thrushcross Grange. Yet it is thanks to Heathcliff's forceful actions that the Earnshaw lands are not lost to some other gambling companion of Hindley's and by reason of his brutal insistance on the Catherine-Linton marriage, that Catherine is able to control her father's land, which would have otherwise been lost to her. Thanks also to that same marriage that Catherine is placed in Hareton's company, and that love should bloom between them so that he too will obtain his just inheritance through marriage with Catherine. Heathcliff, then, has hardly had "revenge," he has really saved the family, in fact both families if we can only take the long view of things, if we can only adopt the casual phlegmatism of the Yorkshireman on top of Mount Ararat with water up to his chin remarking to the passing Noah, "It's boon to tak' oop!" And if Heathcliff's methods have appeared to be brutal and callous and causing of destruction, then let us remember that the destruction was inherent in those destroyed and he merely served as the agent. But when he met with two who could withstand his buffets and blows, he became merely a purgative of a curse of weakness. And once more a Hareton Earnshaw is master of Wuthering Heights.

NOTES

1. See James Hafley, "The Villain in *Wuthering Heights*," *NCF*, XIII (December, 1958), 199–215.
2. V. S. Pritchett made much of this point in his article, "Implacable, Belligerent People of Emily Brontë's Novel *Wuthering Heights*," *New Statesman and Nation* (June 22, 1946), p. 453.
3. All page references are to the Modern Library College Edition.
4. Eric Solomon has suggested the possibility of Heathcliff's being in fact a by-blow of father Earnshaw. An interesting possibility. Certainly I have often wondered about that three-day hike of 120 miles that he made to Liverpool, the return half carrying the child. This perambulatory feat certainly puts Earnshaw ahead of the participants of the Nijmegen Marches, organized by the Dutch League of Physical Culture, where they manage 140 miles in four days, and consider that a feat of no little magnitude. However, I shall leave you to speculate for yourselves on the possibilities of where he might actually have gone. See Solomon, "The Incest Theme in *Wuthering Heights*," *NCF*, XIV (June, 1959), 80–83.

MAURICE LEGRIS

Structure and Allegory in Tennyson's *Idylls of the King*

Two of the most important points about Tennyson's *Idylls of the King* are its events structure and its allegorical structure. Talking about criticism which had appeared in the *Contemporary Review* and the *Spectator*, Tennyson said: "They have taken my hobby, and ridden it too hard, and have explained some things too allegorically, although there is an allegorical or perhaps rather a parabolic drift in the poem."[1] A close reading of the *Idylls* shows us that this parabolic "drift" has quite a strong current to it, in fact to such an extent that the poem can profitably be discussed from the point of view of its structure of events—much as any novel or play can be discussed—without having to force the poem to fit the events-structure formula. For my purpose this well-known "formula" comprises four steps: the first is the Introduction of the characters and situation and the Definition of the issue involved; the second is the Complication, as the characters become further involved in the issue, which becomes itself more clearly confirmed; the third is the Climax, or Culmination, in which the opposing forces come to grips; and the last is the Conclusion, in which the whole issue is finally resolved. Of course, a certain latitude of definition is necessary, especially with regard to the Introduction, some of the main characters not being introduced till quite late in the poem; and also because an attempt is not being made to treat the *Idylls* as a play, but rather to treat it as a collection of individual poems which has a definite dramatic effect.

With regard to allegory, in the short poem "To The Queen," offering his Idylls to Queen Victoria, Tennyson referred to "This old imperfect tale/ . . . shadowing Sense at war with Soul." He had also

HAB vol. XVI, no. 2, fall 1965.

spoken more specifically about allegory in this work: "Of course Camelot for instance, a city of shadowy palaces, is everywhere symbolic of the gradual growth of human beliefs and institutions, and of the spiritual development of man. Yet there is no single fact or incident in the 'Idylls,' however seemingly mystical, which cannot be explained as without any mystery or allegory whatever."[2]

Also to be kept in mind while discussing this poem is a point somewhat less important than the previous two, that is, the remarkable frequency of utterances or thoughts which all portend the eventual tragic outcome of the story; we find many such "tollings of doom," even in some of the earliest idylls.

As a last point before passing to the poem itself we should perhaps keep in mind a word of warning Tennyson had for his readers: "As for the many meanings of the poem my father would affirm, 'Poetry is like shotsilk with many glancing colours. Every reader must find his own interpretation according to his ability, and according to his sympathy with the poet.' " (p. 127)

The three principal characters of the poem are introduced in "The Coming of Arthur." At the very beginning of the poem Arthur confronts the same sort of problem which will beset him throughout his reign, whether or not he is conscious of it. He must defeat the rebellious kings who refuse to accept him as their monarch because of his doubtful ancestry, and even then he is accepted as king by warriors "few, but all brave." Great help is given him by Lancelot, he whom he loves most, and Arthur addresses him in these words: "Man's word is God in man:/Let chance what will, I trust thee to the death." (289, b)[3] Arthur does trust him to the death, his own and that of the Round Table. Then again, having once set eyes on the fair Guinevere, Arthur can do nothing:

> For saving I be join'd
> To her that is the fairest under heaven,
> I seem as nothing in the mighty world,
> And cannot will my will, nor work my work
> Wholly, nor make myself in mine own realm
> Victor and Lord. But were I join'd with her,
> Then might we live together as one life,
> And reigning with one will in everything
> Have power on this dark land to lighten it,
> And power on this dead world to make it live. (289, a)

Arthur, the Will of the Round Table, is powerless until he is joined with her who eventually will be the primary cause of his destruction; at their marriage he says: "I love thee to the death."

Having bound himself on the one hand with Guinevere and Lancelot, he now binds himself on the other hand with his knights, as he has them swear "so strait vows to his own self." The presence on this occasion of the Lady of the Lake and of the three queens bathed in mysterious rays of light gives to Arthur a sort of divine or religious aspect. The Will of the Round Table can also be considered now its Soul. Bellicent says that when Arthur spoke to his knights, she "beheld/From eye to eye thro' all their Order flash/A momentary likeness of the King." And after Arthur had finished knighting them:

> That when they rose, knighted from kneeling, some
> Were pale as at the passing of a ghost,
> Some flush'd, and others dazed, as one who wakes
> Half-blinded at the coming of a light. (291, b)

Later, in their rejoicing the knights sing a song in praise of Arthur, some lines of which further insist on their belief in the divine aspect of Arthur's mission: "Strike for the King and live! his knights have heard/That God hath told the King a secret word." (295, a) The purpose of the Round Table, its very *raison d'être*—to drive out the heathens and to do right and shun evil—is further illustrated by these two lines: "The King will follow Christ, and we the King/In whom high God hath breathed a secret thing." (295, b)

Two minor points in this idyll remain to be noted. As Leodogran confers with Bellicent about the advisability of marriage between his daughter and Arthur, Modred is eavesdropping. He is to do the same thing again several times later on, eventually being able to publicly disclose the alliance between Guinevere and Lancelot, this being one of the immediate causes of the break-up of the Round Table. Also, very little is made of Lancelot's journey to bring Guinevere to Arthur for the marriage, but much later, in the "Guinevere" idyll, as the Queen waits sorrowfully in the nunnery for whatever will befall her, she thinks back to the journey she had made under Lancelot's protection; in comparing Lancelot to her husband-to-be, Lancelot had even then been preferred.

Thus at the end of this idyll, Arthur, Soul and Will of the Round

Table, has bound to him by inviolable oaths Guinevere, Lancelot, and his knights. He has now "made a realm and reign'd." There are minor discordant elements, to be sure, but the Introduction to the poem emphasizes the strength and divine mission of the King and his Round Table.

As the second idyll begins, the situation of the Round Table is quite clear: Arthur has a divine mission to accomplish, and to aid him in its accomplishment he has bound to himself by inviolable vows both the knights and his wife; hence the principal characters and one of the two main aspects of the plot have been defined. Subordinate characters will continue to be introduced up to and including the ninth idyll. The other main aspect of the plot (besides the divine mission) is the gradual emergence of sin in the Round Table, but for these first few idylls it is but a minor consideration.

Gareth is the perfect example of the familiar knight in shining armor. Young, handsome, strong, and virtuous, he wishes to "follow the Christ, the King,/Live pure, speak true, right wrong, follow the King." (297, b) He is virtue personified, and consequently, by allying perseverance to virtue, he finally defeats the four evil knights who had been troubling Lyonors. The allegory here is obvious. With regard to events-structure, this is the story of a knight who goes, at the bidding of Arthur, to redress a wrong. It is the first such story in the poem, and because of its inherent simplicity and freedom from the complicating effects of sin as seen in the later idylls, it can well serve as a model for this type of story. There are several other points, all minor, but worthy of notice: Gareth intends to lie to Arthur in order to be admitted to the castle, but he does not after an old seer tells him Arthur abhors lies; Kay gives a rather sinister warning to Lancelot: "See thou to it/That thine own fineness, Lancelot, some fine day/Undo thee not." (303, a); Lynette, angry because Arthur had given her Gareth for this adventure instead of Lancelot, as she had asked, calls the King mad; Lynette is irritated that Gareth had not told her he was a noble, and had deceived her. "Where," she asks, "should be truth if not in Arthur's hall,/In Arthur's presence?" (315, a)

In the two idylls concerning Geraint and Enid there is a minor, but definite, advance towards the Climax. Geraint encounters evil in an unfaithful wife, although we know that he is actually mistaken; Enid encounters cruelty and injustice in her husband. Almost from the beginning of the "Marriage of Geraint" idyll to the end of "Geraint and Enid," Geraint is the picture of the virtuous knight horror-stricken not only because he has encountered evil, but because he has encountered it in one so dear to him. The same sort of profound shock is to be experienced later on by Balin, Pelleas, and Arthur. Geraint is so shocked at his discovery that he sets out on a long, rambling, pointless journey. His treatment of Enid during this time is cruel, especially when one realizes that he does not even bother to question Enid about the ambiguous "fragments of her later words" he had heard her say to herself. But Enid's conduct throughout the nightmarish ride is exemplary: she submits uncomplainingly to his every wish, and breaks his command not to speak to him only in order to warn him of great danger; later on she even resorts to simply pointing to the evil knights coming to slay him. She is the perfect Arthurian wife.

In these two idylls as in the previous two there is an undercurrent of wrongdoing. Geraint had originally taken temporary leave of the court with his wife because he did not wish her to become involved in a rumor concerning the guilty love of the Queen for Lancelot. Then in asking Arthur's permission to leave he had lied in giving a reason necessitating his departure. The reason he had given was that he had promised to chase bandits out of his princedom, a promise he never kept.

Both these idylls comprise essentially the story of a Good Knight with his Good Lady, but the story borders the tragic throughout: primarily it is the Good at odds with the Good because of a simple misunderstanding about Evil.

This treatment of good and evil in the fourth idyll serves as the transition between the first four idylls, concerned primarily with the triumph of good over evil, and the next three, in which evil and its effects assume the dominant role. Up to this point in Tennyson's work, the Complication of the issue introduced in the first idyll has gone on slowly but steadily. In its major emphasis this first part of the work has concerned itself with the triumph of Right over Wrong, in full accord with the vows to which Arthur's knights had faithfully the midst of Arthur's court, but this is still only a rumor and con- pledged. In its minor emphasis the work has hinted at serious evil in sequently has had little effect on the Round Table.

In "Balin and Balan" Tennyson plays a theme on the principal idea of the Geraint-Enid stories, with the tragic ending here being the main difference. With, of course, the exception of Arthur, Balin is in reality as good a knight as we find in the *Idylls*, but his character is seriously affected by a strange sort of inferiority complex. He tries hard to act correctly and to learn courtly manners by observing, ironically enough, Lancelot's gracious attitude to the Queen. But he unfortunately overhears Lancelot and Guinevere talking, and, not daring to believe what he has heard, leaves the court.

All the misfortunes that now befall him are a result of the stories being circulated about the illicit love of Lancelot and Guinevere. When the knights at Sir Pellam's castle taunt him about his refusal to believe the stories, he is extremely worried, and then he eventually kills one of them for the same taunts and must flee. He encounters Vivien, who tells him more things about Guinevere in the same vein. Consequently he tramples the Queen's crown on his shield, and is seen doing so by his brother. Because they are both armored they fight unrecognized, and both die. But before they die Balan tells Balin that Vivien is nothing but a harlot and had lied to him. They die, believing "pure as our own true Mother is our Queen." (353, a)

We have in this idyll what could perhaps be called ironic tragedy. Balan dies because he attacks someone defiling Guinevere's crown; Balin defiles the crown because of his extreme shock on learning of Guinevere's sin. They both die glorifying the pure Queen. We have a misunderstanding here as we had in the Geraint-Enid idylls, but it is caused by lies, and hence the ending is a tragic, not a happy one. And the tragedy is heightened in that the reader knows both knights actually are mistaken in their belief of Guinevere's purity.

This idyll marks a definite acceleration towards the Climax: there is less emphasis than before on the "quest for good," and, according to Sir Pellam's knights, the Queen's sin has now become public knowledge. It also marks the emergence of Evil triumphant over Good, the dominant theme of the entire work.

The significance of Evil as a principal element underlying the events-structure of the *Idylls* is forcibly brought out in "Merlin and Vivien" under two guises. The first is Vivien herself, who is inherently evil and glories in it: "There is no being pure," she says before she promises to Mark that she will corrupt all who are of the

Round Table. The second is simply numerical: as the poem approaches its climax more and more people are being surrounded by a net of evil which encompasses both major and minor wrongs alike.

Merlin is the magician of the Round Table, the great Seer. It was he who had protected Arthur during his youth, and had built the great castle for the Round Table. Besides the part he had played in Arthur's birth and youth, he has not figured prominently up till now; but whenever anyone has spoken of him it has always been with the utmost awe and respect for his great learning and wisdom. He is almost a personification of intellect, or science, or better still, of wisdom. Hence in the intellectual-emotional combat Vivien wages with him to get the power of his charm, what we really have is the war of Evil against Wisdom. Evil wins, just as it had in the previous idyll, but here the victory is clear-cut and very decisive, not clouded over with misapprehensions as before.

It should be noted here just how emphatically evil does dominate this idyll. Although Merlin has premonitions of danger and repeatedly tells Vivien he will not accede to her wishes, he seems powerless when she turns all her charms on him. At one point he even irritates her to such an extent that she completely loses control of herself and bitterly reviles everything that the Round Table stands for: she calls Arthur a fool and states that his knights do only foul deeds; she swears that if she is lying, let heaven strike her dead, and a lightning-bolt immediately hits a tree close by. But in spite of all this the man of Wisdom cannot avail against Evil, and Merlin is imprisoned in a hollow oak.

Three other points in this idyll are noteworthy with regard to the spread of evil throughout Arthur's realm. The court of Mark, the Cornish king, is described by Vivien in terms somewhat reminiscent of descriptions of the Round Table, but here everything is aimed at hate and evil instead of doing right. The court of Sir Pellam, in the previous idyll, was also against King Arthur. Secondly, Vivien's noxious influence has now gotten inside the castle itself, for she had attached herself to the Queen's retinue and spread foul rumours there. The last point is extremely important: Vivien had met the King himself at a time when Arthur was vexed concerning a rumour she had spread about corruption among his knights. Yet he said nothing to her, nor did he subsequently do anything about it. This is one of the two occasions in the *Idylls* when Arthur suspects that all is not well in the Round Table. Yet he never asserts himself to find out if anything really is wrong. His ineffectiveness in this matter shows in a rather startling manner just how powerful the influence of evil has become in his realm.

The love Elaine has for Lancelot is only a minor point in the following idyll; what is important is that, for the first time in the poem, the general laxity and corruption spreading from the Queen down through the entire court are openly discussed by everyone concerned. Hence the Complication is brought right up to the Climax, to occur in the following section.

Lies, deceit, jealousy, cowardliness—all now have their part in this court which was founded to do right and redress wrongs. Lancelot lies to the King so that he will not have to participate in the tournament; when he does participate he is disguised so that, according to Guinevere's explanation, he will not win due simply to his great reputation. But Arthur is saddened by Lancelot's "idly dallying with the truth" (377, a); he should at least have had confidence in the King. Guinevere openly avows her feelings for Arthur, calling him "that passionate perfection" (369, b); "swearing men to vows impossible,/ To make them like himself." "A moral child without the craft to rule." (370, a) And she states that she is Lancelot's except by marriage. But the actual instability of their illicit love is later sharply pointed out when Arthur tells his wife that Lancelot, while tilting, had for the first time worn some maiden's gift on his helmet. When she is alone Guinevere ragingly calls him a traitor. Then when Lancelot brings the diamonds to her, she says:

> I for you
> This many a year have done despite and wrong
> To one whom ever in my heart of hearts
> I did acknowledge nobler. (386, a)

But she later apologizes for her fit of jealousy. Lancelot seriously ponders all that has lately happened to him, and he realizes that Elaine had loved him with a love purer than the Queen's. He resolves to try to break away from Guinevere, as he says to himself: "Alas for Arthur's greatest knight, a man/ Not after Arthur's heart." (389, a)

It is quite clear at this point that the affair between Lancelot and Guinevere is beginning to break up; they both appear surfeited with their sin and tired of each other. It is also evident that the general laxity of knightly feeling, the loss of knightly tenor, has become widespread in the Round Table as the net of Evil continues to draw its occupants towards the Climax. It is said by Guinevere at the beginning of the idyll that, if Lancelot stays away from the tilts, this will be noticed and whispered about by the knights, half of whom are their enemies. This point—that half of the Round Table are enemies of its greatest knight—is quite important because it gives us an indication of the poor condition of Arthur's court. One specific example of this is the following: Arthur had given Gawain the task of finding the mysterious knight who had won the jousts and giving him the diamond. Gawain sets out, irritated because he will miss all the banquets. He courteously accepts an invitation to stay at Astolat, but "courtesy with a touch of traitor in it." (377, b) He sets his eye on Elaine, but when he cannot get her, he gives her the diamond to give to Lancelot, "and all wearied of the quest/ Leapt on his horse, and carolling as he went/ A true-love ballad, lightly rode away." (378, b) It is not surprising that Arthur is quite irritated with him, for this is most unchivalric conduct.

At the end of this idyll the Round Table is obviously not what it was meant to be. The war of the spirit against the flesh has been relegated to a secondary position; the knights have become lazy and addicted to gossiping about Guinevere and Lancelot; and half of them have even become the enemies of the greatest of Arthur's knights.

"The Holy Grail" marks the almost complete dissolution of the Round Table, and it is an ironic fact that that which should cause this breaking-up is the quest for a holy object. But for nearly all the knights the quest is not a good in itself but an evil. As Arthur bitterly points out to the assembled knights, Lancelot had been able to overthrow five knights at once; and then all the younger knights had thought themselves Lancelots until they had found out otherwise. Now Galahad has seen the Grail because he is the only one able to sit in "The Siege Perilous"; all the other knights, thinking themselves Galahads, have sworn to quest for the cup a year and a day. Arthur does not state explicitly that they have all fallen victims to pride, but the implication is certainly there. And so now for a whole year Arthur will be left alone in the castle with the women, children, and a few of the knights. It is not surprising that Arthur is grief-stricken and prophesies that most of them will not return. He also states that they will not be doing their duty according to the vows they had sworn to him:

> Your place being vacant at my side,
> This chance of noble deeds will come and go
> Unchallenged, while ye follow wandering fires
> Lost in the quagmire! (394, a)

As all the knights leave on the quest, Guinevere bewails to Lancelot that " 'this madness has come on us for our sins.' "

The truth of Arthur's prophecy is borne out when the knights return. Of all the knights who had gone on the quest only four—Galahad, Bors, Lancelot, and Percivale—had seen the Grail; of these four only Galahad had seen the sacred vessel clearly and closely, and he is now dead. Only one-tenth of the knights have come back to the court.

Arthur's court is not completely wiped out; in the "Pelleas and Ettarre" idyll he will knight more young, virtuous men to take the place of those lost on the quest, and there will be more strivings for the good. But the true spirit of the Round Table is now gone; Arthur has lost the most virtuous of his knights and the others have lost most of their virtuous qualities. The Climax of the *Idylls* occurs here not only because of the great physical transformation in Arthur's court, but also because Sin has entrapped nearly all the knights into the same sin at the same time. The events-structure and the influence of Sin have followed parallel paths to the Climax, with the latter causing the former. From this point on there will be a quick decline to the eventual complete annihilation of the court because of the complete ascendancy of Sin.

"Pelleas and Ettarre" is the last idyll to present the brave young knight jousting for his lady, but Pelleas, one of Arthur's newly-created knights, had chosen the wrong lady. All attempts to win Ettarre being in vain, he agrees to Gawain's idea of changing clothes and having Gawain plead his case. His disillusionment comes when he finds the two sleeping together. He wants to kill them, but remembers the vows he had sworn to Arthur and does not. Then he learns indirectly from Percivale that the only true knight of the Round Table is Arthur himself. Pelleas turns against the court completely:

he calls the castle a "black nest of rats," confronts the Queen with a most bitter attitude, and even fights Lancelot. It is the awakening of Innocence to the facts of evil life.

The theme of lost innocence is repeated in the following idyll, "The Last Tournament." Lancelot has grudgingly accepted to referee the Tournament of the Dead Innocence—a title some of the knights mock in obvious reference to Lancelot and Guinevere. The degeneration of Arthur's court is now shown to be complete: at the tournament itself Lancelot referees badly, a knight swears at the King, Tristram talks insultingly to Lancelot about the Queen without being punished, and then Tristram insults the ladies present. Truly, as both Lancelot and the ladies say, "The glory of our Round Table is no more." (415, a) On the field of battle Arthur faces the Red Knight, one of Arthur's former knights who now has his own court much like Arthur's, but it is a Round Table of Sin. The Red Knight falls on his face, too drunk to fight; Arthur's knights kill this helpless man and then massacre the men, women, and children of the castle. While this is going on, Tristram is having an adulterous affair with Isolt, Mark's wife, and doing so he is killed by Mark.

At the conclusion of this idyll, as the poem approaches the end, there is nothing left of the Round Table but some of its external appearance. Sin has complete dominion over everyone but Arthur himself, and there are only a few knights left who will fight for their King.

In the "Guinevere" section the affair between the Queen and Lancelot finally comes to an end as they are denounced by Modred, who has been spying on them. A slight uplifting note here is that the Queen has now begun to repent her sins, and she firmly refuses Lancelot's offer to go with him to his own land. But the most important point is Arthur's tragic realization that, in the battle between Sense and Soul, he is the only one left to fight for the Soul. With Guinevere grovelling at his feet he recalls the founding and purpose of the Round Table. But then everything had gone wrong, and it is all because of her: the sin she had committed with Lancelot had started everything. In one way Arthur as Soul had actually been fighting his own wife, initiator of eventually all-dominant Sense. Guinevere now sincerely repents her sins, and her last words are "Now I see thee what thou art,/ Thou art the highest and most human too." (433, a)

The last idyll, "The Passing of Arthur," is like a summary of the entire poem, for in it are again contrasted Good and Evil. On the one hand Arthur spends all the life he has left in a tremendous battle against some of his former knights from which he, the Good, is the only survivor. On the other hand, Bedivere, the one knight who has been with him throughout his entire career, brings Sin to Arthur's last few moments by disobeying him twice before throwing Excalibur into the lake. But the poem ends on a certain note of hope, as Bedivere now quickly does Arthur's bidding, the King disappears over the horizon and seems to be greeted by the cries of a great city cheering its returning King, and "the new sun rose bringing the new year." (441, b)

The progression of the *Idylls of the King* from Introduction through Climax to Conclusion leaves no doubt that we have here more than just a touch of the dramatic. There is a definite building-up of suspense intimately linked with the ever-more preponderant role of Sin. Immediately before and during the Climax we can even say that the court is generally so lax about its vows as to typify Sin itself, waging war against Arthur, the last proponent of Good. In a sense the Round Table is a microcosm of the world itself and its daily battle against sin and injustice. As Bedivere says in the last few lines of the poem: "But now the whole Round Table is dissolved / Which was an image of the mighty world." (440, a)

NOTES

1. Hallam Tennyson, *Alfred, Lord Tennyson: A Memoir* (New York, 1897), II, 126–27.
2. *Memoir*, II, 127.
3. Page and column references are to *Alfred Tennyson: Poetical Works* (London: Oxford University Press, 1954).

GERALD MORGAN

Narcissus Afloat

The sea, as a subject, has a way of vanishing behind the conventions of art or chronicle which spring to our minds. Trying to conceive, to represent this reality of ceaseless change of light and shape, we have recourse to fictions, to dubious notions of time and space: to pictures explaining—pictures. As with the sea, so with the universe; and so with ourselves. Reality is guessed and hinted at by analogy and symbol, within the limitations of language by which reality itself is unaffected. There are more things in heaven and earth than we can name, with worn-out coinage.

Conrad was explicitly aware of this by the time he wrote his third completed novel, *The Nigger of the Narcissus*. Nonetheless he declared in the Preface to this novel his intention of doing justice, not only to the visible aspects of the universe, but also to the truth underlying these. The visible aspects he had observed for twenty years as a seaman, in their most dramatic and mobile—and most obviously illusory—form. For months on end he had gazed at the sea horizon, the illusory straight line forever unattainable. He had for years charted the inconstant locus of his vessel in time and space, and known that his assumptions could be upset by the "eloquent facts" of the sea which "can speak for themselves with overwhelming precision."[1]

As with the sea, so with the self; for Conrad wavered constantly between an epic of the sea and an epic of the soul, and in the end wrote both by reflecting the one in the other. He averred that personality is an illusion, "an aimless mask of something hopelessly unknown."[2] His method was to descend within the unknown self and

HAB vol. xv, no. 2, autumn 1964. From an address to the annual meeting of the Association of Canadian University Teachers of English, 1964.

there find some truth of the universe; the result was symbolism, with a difference. Things become symbolic in Conrad's work by reason of the clarity, rather than the obscurity, of their perceptible aspect, which Conrad describes with as much precision as non-technical language allows.

He uses similes very often, and metaphors very seldom. More often than not his literal representation takes the propositional form: A (like x) = A (like y). When he shifts into the stronger analogy of metaphor, where A = B, the metaphor takes increased strength from its rarity. Thus a sudden metaphor of Karain, performing an Odyssey among illusions;[3] illusions elsewhere referred to as visions of remote unattainable truth dimly seen.[4] An example of Conrad's literal precision is the description, in *Typhoon,* of a vessel in the eye of a cyclone.[5] As the club-hauling manoeuvre in Marryat's *Peter Simple* became a standard recitation-piece for Royal Navy examinations in sail, so Conrad's *Typhoon* passage could serve for candidates in marine meteorology. Likewise the opening chapter of *Nostromo* could be equally a copy of, or a model for, a chapter of Admiralty Sailing Directions describing the seaward approach to Sulaco. But the whole chapter is part of an epic metaphor. The novel begins with pilotage and ends with a lighthouse; it is the converse of the metaphor in "Youth": a voyage as "a symbol of existence."[6] Within the symbolic frame, Conrad's descriptions mean exactly what they say. Thus, a storm-sunset seen from the capsized Narcissus:

> On the edge of the horizon, black seas leaped up towards the glowing sun. It sank slowly, round and blazing, and the crest of waves splashed on the edge of the luminous circle. . . . The big seas began to roll across the crimson disc; and over miles of turbulent waters the shadows of high waves swept with the running darkness the faces of men. A crested roller broke with a loud hissing roar, and the sun, as if put out, disappeared. The chattering voice faltered, went out together with the light.[7]

This passage alone would suffice to demonstrate, not only the descriptive exactitude, but also the symbolical and mythic saturation of Conrad's art. There is the Narcissus-shell, overturned; there is a capsized planet of men; a voyage of existence abruptly checked; the inept voice chattering and silenced; the sun of life swallowed up by the devouring sea, as if it had been itself a sun-myth like Balder or Osiris, doomed to be submerged in a final darkness.

Conrad begins with visible fact, vividly described, assumed to be illusion; he descends to the inner selfhood of persons affected by their pictures of visible fact and of themselves; he emerges with a vision of man in the universe voyaging through the visible toward the inscrutable, while peering within his unknown depths through the barely expressible toward the unspeakable.

Thus *The Nigger of the Narcissus.* The name of the ship is highly symbolic in Conrad, but is not invented by him. A shipowner chose to name his vessel Narcissus, and Conrad chose to sail in her. From this fact springs a novel more famous than the ship, and a symbol for the whole of Conrad's imaginative achievement; a symbol for our century. The description of visible aspects is impressive, and at first sight seems exhaustive. An early critic perceived, on reading it, that the pasteboard ocean was gone forever.[8] But Conrad himself, master mariner, made no claim to have shown the sea as reality. What the critic did not remark was that the pasteboard had been replaced by a mirror, and the saucy Arethusa by the dreaming Narcissus.

The symbolism in Conrad's art has been sketched out by Conrad himself, in the choice of titles and epigraphs for his works. Reading these, we can discard chronology as readily as Conrad did; as readily as Captain Brierley discarded his timepiece before leaping down from Ossa into the destructive element, as readily as Verloc prepared to blow up time, as casually as Marlow floated on the Thames to the Roman Empire and the Belgian Congo in the same turn of the tide. We can rearrange Conrad's titles as logicians and mathematicians reshuffle propositions, changing the sequence of these without altering their significance, the better to perceive some truth in what Ayer calls "Complex tautologies."[9] Conrad's works are complex tautologies, expressing always the same truth or illusion, variations on a constant theme. We can read his titles in the following order, the better to perceive their symbolism: "An Outpost of Progress," "The End of the Tether," "The Heart of Darkness," *The Nigger of the Narcissus, The Mirror of the Sea,* "The Secret Sharer," "The Secret Agent," *The Shadow-Line, Victory.*

The titles signify a progression of the soul, an explorer's journey into the interior, into something like the dark night of the soul known to the Spanish mystic or "the devil's poncho" known to our man—Nostromo—in Sulaco; into the reflective self-awareness of Narcissus afloat on an immense mirror in the darkness, discovering in the mirror, and sometimes overcoming, the secret agent that shares his selfhood and universe.

The title of *Victory* invited some confusion in 1915, when public interest was centred upon a struggle between anonymous masses. Some might have found in the title a heartening echo of the name of the flagship of Lord Nelson, who was in Conrad's view the "seaman of seamen," a genius of "exalted soul" who enlarged "the very conception of victory itself."[10] So said Conrad in *The Mirror of the Sea,* of the parson's sailor son; he provided a clerical origin to Leggatt in "The Secret Sharer," to Kurtz's Russian friend in "Heart of Darkness," and to Lord Jim, all of them sailors concerned with a special conception of victory or defeat. The title of *Victory* surely derives from the speech of the Polish hero in Calderon's drama *Life is a Dream* who says: "It is a question now of achieving the highest victory: the victory over the self."[11]

Conrad had already quoted the Spanish drama twenty years earlier, in the epigraph to his second novel *An Outcast of the Islands*: "The worst fault of a man is his having been born."[12] The words are spoken by Calderon's drugged hero in a moment of anguish, when he finds truth and illusion inextricably confused, before he goes on to a victory over the self. Calderon is a Baroque master of the equivocal tradition developed in the Renaissance and bequeathed to the Romantics, eventually to Conrad by his father: the convention of mirrors, dreams, dubious madness, self-portraits, optical illusions; the notion of the world as a stage, and the obverse notion of art as a mirror of nature; the taste for mingling all of these in a marriage of contraries, an equivocation between reflection and object, subject and painter, world and soul, illusion and truth, wit and madness, dream and fact. The tradition rests on the ancient principle of the *coincidentia oppositorum,* which was revived in the fifteenth century by Nicholas of Cusa with his doctrine of *Learned Unknowing.*[13] The doctrine is paralleled, with the *noche oscura* of the Spanish mystic St. John of the Cross, by Conrad's credo in the Preface to *The Nigger of the Narcissus.* The principle is best symbolized by the mirror, wherein an object reflected appears in reverse, its spatial form altered but not its significance.

The dream and the mirror are important components of Conrad's work. Both of them are equivocal. Both, it may be said, aid in the projection of a man's ideal conception of himself, which is the opening move in most of Conrad's tales. When a Conrad hero loses his ideal conception of himself, embodied in himself or in another character conceived as his "double," he is like Erasmus in Hoffmann's tale,[14] who lost his reflection and went about in secrecy and dismay. In this event Conrad's characters often commit suicide, or a moral harakiri. Thus Willems, Kurtz, Jim, Brierley, Falk, Nostromo, Decoud, Razumov, and many others, exceptions being the young anonymous captain of the nameless barque in "Secret Sharer" and *The Shadow-Line*. A rare recovery occurs in the case of Lord Jim, figuratively buried alive and reborn, after the famous "Stein" chapter which positively gleams with mirrors, doubles, and dreams, and which poses the main question of the self-questing Narcissus: "how to be?"[15] Jim is Everyman, or Everyman's double. He is "one of us," he is "an enigma," to be fathomed only by an austere naval officer (in the aspect of a priest) and by a romantic entomologist, collector of things "perishable and defying destruction." Thus Marlow in *Lord Jim*:

> [Stein] lit a two-branched candlestick and led the way. We passed through empty dark rooms, escorted by gleams . . . [which] glided along . . . sweeping here and there . . . leaped upon a fragmentary curve . . . or flashed perpendicularly in and out of distant mirrors, while the forms of two men and the flicker of two flames could be seen for a moment stealing silently across the depths of a crystalline void. . . .
>
> [Jim's] imperishable reality came to me . . . with an irresistible force! I saw it vividly, as though in our progress through the lofty silent rooms amongst fleeting gleams of light and the sudden revelations of human figures stealing with flickering flames within unfathomable and pellucid depths, we had approached nearer to absolute Truth, which, like Beauty itself, floats elusive, obscure, half-submerged, in the silent still waters of mystery.[16]

Conrad had introduced the crystalline void in his second novel, which borrowed its epigraph from Calderon. Here we find the sea extending, for the first of a hundred glimpses, as "the restless mirror of the infinite."[17]

The sea is represented as a mirror both physically and metaphysically. Its surface, when calm, is represented as polished stone or metal, "an adamantine surface,"[18] "the silvered plate-glass of a mirror,"[19] or strewn with islets "like a handful of emeralds on a buckler of steel."[20] Various similes of metal and gems are employed, on one occasion extending the sea, as an image of light, over the whole world.

> The sea was polished, was blue, was pellucid, was sparkling like a precious stone, extending on all sides, all round to the horizon—as if the whole terrestrial globe had been one jewel, one colossal sapphire, a single gem fashioned into a planet.[21]

In "The Secret Sharer" the narrator's ship is first seen near islets "set in a blue sea that itself looked solid;"[22] at the crisis the ship is immobilized on "the glassy smoothness of the sleeping surface,"[23] as befits the vessel of a dreamer on the mirror. In *The Shadow-Line* the same ship, bewitched at the same place, is like "a model ship set on the gleams and shadows of polished marble."[24] The same condition affects Lingard's brig as *The Rescue* opens:

> On the unruffled surface of the straits the brig floated tranquil and upright as if bolted solidly, keel to keel, with its own image reflected in the unframed and immense mirror of the sea. To the south and east the double islands watched silently the double ship. . . .[25]

But this imagery leads us to its own opposite, where the mirror itself becomes invisible and the sea, from being solid, becomes pure space. The same brig is later seen floating at night "between an invisible sky and an invisible sea, like a miraculous craft suspended in the air."[26] This optical phenomenon is described several times between Conrad's first work and his last. In "Karain" the light-image, which elsewhere has given the sea a universal extension as a global sapphire, is fused with the mirror-image so as to confound dimensions: "The bay was a bottomless pit of intense light. The circular sheet of water reflected a luminous sky, and the shores enclosing it made an opaque ring of earth floating in an emptiness of transparent blue."[27]

This mirror-imagery, in which the reflected and the reflection cancel out each other, producing "emptiness," is usually associated with light, but not always with the brilliance of gem-light. We can see the different hours of the day and night casting different hues about the emptiness. Renouard's schooner, for instance, "lay white, and as if suspended, in the crepuscular atmosphere of sunset mingling with the ashy gleam" of the sea.[28] At night we see Captain Whalley's Sofala: "Under the clouded sky, through the still air that seemed to cling warm, with a seaweed smell, to her slim hull . . . the ship moved on an even keel, as if floating detached in empty space."[29] The ship detached in empty transparent space is naturally comparable to a planet, and Conrad underlines the symbolic connection. "My command might have been a planet flying vertiginously on its appointed path in a space of infinite silence. I clung to the rail as if my sense of balance were leaving me for good."[30] The Narcissus in fair weather, sails "lonely and swift like a small planet. . . . Round her the abysses of sea and sky met in an unattainable frontier."[31] And again: "Our little world went on its curved and unswerving path carrying a discontented and aspiring population."[32] Eventually we see a compounding of the images of light, mirror and flaming astral body, when the Narcissus is caught in lightning: "the becalmed craft stood out with its masts and rigging, with every sail and every rope distinct and black in the centre of a fiery outburst, like a charred ship enclosed in a globe of fire."[33]

Thus it is to be observed that the mirror of the calm sea dissolves two elements, sky and water, into each other, and removes altogether two dimensions out of three, leaving only a sensation of suspension in altitude or depth. This sensation is perfectly familiar to any seaman who has floated above the stars reflected in tropic seas. The length and breadth of the sea, already compounded as the diameter of a circular horizon, disappear together with the horizon, leaving the ship at the centre of an illimitable globe as if bound to voyage forever. Space, as a measurable quantity, has vanished; and time has vanished too.

Conrad has perfectly described the phenomenon, and furnished it with appropriate imagery. This spacelessness is to be remembered when Conrad transposes the mirror of the sea as a metaphor of human life, which he often does. In this manner Conrad approaches the late-Renaissance poet Johannes Scheffler, who wrote:

> A heart that time and place suffice to satisfy
> Knows nothing of its own immeasurability.[34]

It remains only for Conrad to remove time, which he does in his storm scenes. The sea, he suggests, is not merely a light-filled mirror of space, but is also a mirror of a condition older than light; it is a revelation of Chaos, ancient and ageless. It is a vat of time; in storms it looks "as if the immemorial ages had been stirred up from the undisturbed bottom of ooze."[35]

If you would know the age of the earth look upon the sea in a storm. The greyness of the whole immense surface, the wind furrows on the faces of the waves, the great masses of foam, tossed about and waving, like matted white locks, give to the sea in a gale an appearance of hoary age, lustreless, dull, without gleams, as though it had been created before light itself.[36]

The sea, embodiment of Chaos, is shown as being prior to light, and able to extinguish "the last rays of sinister light between the hills of steep rolling waves."[37] The end is as the beginning, time is turned backwards and extinguished. The moon is seen "rushing backwards with frightful speed over the sky,"[38] just as the sun is seen swallowed up by the sea which antedates it: "Black seas leaped up towards the glowing sun. . . . A crested roller broke with a loud hissing roar, and the sun, as if put out, disappeared."[39] The ship becomes again a lonely planet through mirror-effect. In the black sky the stars gleam at a black sea that flashes back at them "the evanescent and pale light of a dazzling whiteness born from the black turmoil of the waves."[40] But at moments, on this wild mirror, even the stars and the foaming tumult are swallowed by darkness:

Nothing seems left of the whole universe but darkness, clamour, fury—and the ship. And like the last vestiges of a shattered creation she drifts, bearing an anguished remnant of sinful mankind, through the distress, tumult and pain of an avenging terror.[41]

When darkness pervades a calm, so that "your ship floats unseen under your feet, her sails flutter invisible above your head,"[42] it defeats both the eye of God Himself and the malice of the devil;[43] a ship, or a soul, is perfectly isolated, "lost in a vast universe of night and silence."[44] This is a kind of passive annihilation, which merely disorients the soul: "He had the strangest sensation of his soul having just returned into his body from the circumambient darkness in which land, sea, sky . . . were as if they had not been."[45]

But in a storm, the seaman faces annihilation by the active embodiment of chaos, where his ship becomes the last vestige of a shattered creation, itself about to be shattered by a maniac victor over space and time:

A big, foaming sea . . . made for the ship, roaring wildly, . . . as mischievous and discomposing as a madman with an axe.[46]

It wasn't a heavy sea—it was a sea gone mad! I suppose the end of the world will be something like that.[47]

Thus the storm shows the beginning of time, "before light itself," and the ending of time, "the end of the world" and "shattered creation";

the "restless mirror of the Infinite" exerts its power before and after time, its roar sounding "like an indistinct noise from another world."[48]

The mirror of the sea abolishes the meaning of up and down, of before and after, which it makes the same by reflecting, so to speak, one against the other until time and space are fused into a single dimension, an un-named condition of existence. In this condition, human experience is limited to that of elementary sight and sound; the eye perceives light delusively reflected, or else nothingness in the dark, while the ear is strained either by the silence of infinity or by the roaring of an other-worldly chaos. The condition is one of almost perfect isolation of the spirit from the senses. It is analogous to a moral isolation of a man from his fellows, and, like this latter condition, is best appreciated in solitude. "Solitude from mere outward condition of existence becomes very swiftly a state of soul . . . (which) takes possession of the mind, and drives forth the thought into the exile of utter unbelief."[49] The epigraph of *The Shadow-Line* is from Baudelaire's poem "La Musique": ". . . D'autres fois, calme plat, grand miroir / De mon désespoir."[50]

Another poem by Baudelaire, "L'Homme et la mer,"[51] prefigures in sixteen lines the whole Conradian symbolism, elaborated in twenty-nine volumes, of the seafaring Narcissus and the double in the infinite mirror. It is never quoted by Conrad. Nor is the reference to Narcissus in Milton's *Comus,* which, thirty lines earlier, provides the epigraph to Conrad's *Victory.*[52]

In a word, one might say that the Conrad *œuvre* is simply the development, or tautological transformation, of symbolic formulas worked out by Calderon and Baudelaire. To the extent that Conrad is concerned with "the truth, manifold and one,"[53] underlying every aspect of the visible universe, one might say that Conrad, inspired by these two masters, has dreamed his way to a Swedenborgian Narcissism particularly apt for our time. This would explain his present wide appeal.

Selfhood is the modern Sant-Graal, leading men to choose a flag, vote a new constitution, change their psychiatrist, by uncertain acts of a will to "be themselves." But selfhood is not readily identified. No common measure of identity is to be found in modern Western literature, except as provided in the Pythagorean utopias which Huxley, Zamiatin and Orwell described with the aim of prevention rather than promotion, though with a prospect of failure steadily before them. Selfhood in modern culture is something of an unknown soldier, giving and receiving multiple death, and symbolized by machine-cut granite blocks of sizes proportional to the density of population living or dead. Asserting selfhood nonetheless, the artist tends to waver between bravado and flight; between satire of a kind soon to be written by computers to amuse each other, and a headlong flight into irrationality—to the dark knowledge acquired in the gamekeeper's shed.

"All art is narcissistic," says a critic.[54] But how an artist may succeed as Narcissus cannot be told, in the absence of a definition of selfhood. "Man must invent himself," says Sartre.[55] But this means to cultivate the absurd, to apply Orwell's doublethink, not merely to a regimented cypher but to an individual believing himself intensely self-aware. "To thine own self be true," said Shakespeare, setting the stage for generations of walking shadows, full of sound and fury; for characters of diminishing import retreating from the throne-room to the parlour, to the bedroom, to the ashcan.

When mythology filled the place vacated by drama, as a ritual of collective identity, suffering became the measure of selfhood. Prometheus suffers with immense self-satisfaction, having invented a bird to devour him. Though in truth it would seem that it is the fire, not the bird, which punishes Prometheus; he is a "noble savage," like Caliban, who stole language in order to abuse it. Thus the Promethean and Byronic heroes, bloody but unbowed, secure in their rebellious suffering. Yet the Satanic *non serviam* does not sufficiently define selfhood. The poètes maudits were obliged to go further, to spend a season in Hell without Vergil or Dante, to cultivate flowers of evil, and induce illuminations far removed from the madness of Hamlet or Don Quixote; alienation becomes the gauge of selfhood.

Here the creative genius in Conrad shows itself in the mythmaker. He is the first author to set Narcissus on the open sea, as a double of Aphrodite in Neptune's domain. Venus arises, he says, "not from the foam of the sea, but from a distant, still more formless, mysterious and potent immensity of mankind."[56] Which reminds us of the Gnostic doctrine, that all gods and all men have their genesis in the ocean.[57] Conrad is the first modern author to identify Aphrodite's mirror with the sea itself, as a universal analogue resolving the dichotomy between world and soul, between reality and illusion. He is the first to double Narcissus with Odysseus as a wanderer upon the mirror. (Kazantzakis appears to be the second.) He is the first to bring a *doppelgänger* naked from the mirror of the sea, the first to launch an Ancient Mariner on long prose tales of communal introspection, the first to set a Flying Dutchman in the China Sea. He is the first to transcribe the voyages of archaic myth as ventures in self-discovery: the voyage out of time (*The Nigger of the Narcissus*, "Heart of Darkness"); the voyage to the isle of death or transfiguration (*Outcast, Narcissus, Lord Jim, Nostromo*, "Secret Sharer," *Shadow-Line*, "Smile of Fortune," "Planter of Malata," "Freya," *Victory, The Rescue*); the voyage to the underworld (*Narcissus*, "Heart of Darkness," "Falk"); the voyage of atonement (*Narcissus, Shadow-Line*, "Alaska" [*Last Essays*, p. 52]). All of these refashioned mythic voyages were refined by Conrad's imagination from the crude events of the maritime history of his day, with a brilliant nautical exactitude. It is illustrative of Conrad that, unlike Hardy and E. J. Pratt, he expressed only contempt for the whole episode of the Titanic.

The century of Prometheus the Titan ended symbolically with the Titanic rushing upon a mindless lump of ice, an "eloquent fact," a truth floating submerged, like that which Lord Jim's pilgrim-ship met on her course. The fire-stealer of our time is Andrew Undershaft, Shaw's precursor to Orwell's Big Brother. In our century, therefore, it is assumed that mythic selfhood must be sought in other damned heroes: in Oedipus, relic of the State founded on Kinship, for the Freudian mythology of lust; in Sisyphus, relic of Newtonian physics, for the Existentialist mythology of the absurd.

But it would seem that the proper mythical emblem for our time is Narcissus. The variety of emblems now used from mythology, in what is actually a quest for selfhood, suggests a Protean Narcissus, seeking the Procrustean couch for relief of his multiform aches and pains in murmured confessions of a fifty-minute hour, and seeing in a fluid sheet of time the shifting symbols of his mysterious identity: the Swedenborgian Narcissus. The "forest of symbols" of Baudelaire shelters a pool where Narcissus may, in constant danger of drowning, contemplate the riddle of selfhood and otherness, in what may be his own image or may be the Lady of the Lake. (There is scant need at this point to enter into the erotic connotations of narcissism and its mirror-obverse, which are visible everywhere about us, thanks to the professional voyeur. Lewd or learned, Kinsey and the camera have caught us all.)

It is to be noted that Conrad's heroes are no good at loving. Lord Jim, Heyst, Gould, Nostromo, Kurtz, M. Georges, Captain Anthony, and others are far too concerned, each with his ideal conception of himself, to inspire anything but despairing self-sacrifice in women. In some cases the weakness is shared by women. One critic has written at some length on Conrad's failure in treating sexual themes.[58] The book may be termed an erotic fallacy. The failure seems to be less in Conrad than in his characters, since Conrad portrays faithfully the vagaries of Narcissus, in plots which are adequate comment on the failure of communication which is today the agonizing concern of authors and dramatists. The whole problem is very clearly stated in Conrad's short story "The Return," a domestic tale in which a mirror figures very prominently. In the ship Narcissus, where the "Heart of Darkness" theme is rehearsed on an immense mirror, there is no woman at all. Conrad's women, as a rule, don't take seriously the complicated masculine game of self-conception.

It can be shown, however, that the vessel Narcissus, traversing the crystalline void with a "crew of shades"[59] to "the centre of the fatal circle,"[60] the "very gate of Erebus,"[61] means something more than self-absorption. The Narcissus-figures who flicker in and out of the Conradian mirror have also another quest, of solidarity and "fellowship with all creation."[62] A mirror, like a Renaissance painting or a photograph, is optically extra-dimensional; in two dimensions it represents three. The Conradian mirror is polydimensional, absorbing time and space in shifting series of spatio-temporal points of $(n + 1)$ dimensions, like the post-Einsteinian universe. On such a mirror the wandering Narcissus leaves Swedenborg behind; he is the nuclear Narcissus, a Ulysses of the interstices.

In *The Secret Agent*, a scheming diplomat meditates on the joy of dropping a bomb into pure mathematics. The event has come to pass. We are now deprived of universals, not only of selfhood, but also of a cosmos with a recognizable meaning. Our knowledge of the visible aspects of the universe has outrun our speech, as happened to Dante in Paradise. A new language is sought by mathematicians and philosophers, to represent conceptions of a cosmos in which the interstices are greater than the entities, and the entities are no more than systems of space-time points.[63] A statement of units of existential mystery conceived as having a certain order, is itself formulated as units of linguistic mystery accepted in a certain order.

What this means to literature has been demonstrated by three polyglot authors: by Hopkins, whose naming delves into the unique individuality of every thing for which he utters the inscape; by Joyce, whose Ulysses functions as a polyglot Narcissus, and by Conrad, whose Narcissus doubles Ulysses wandering among physical and psychic dimensions.

Conrad's celebrated time-shifts mean simply this: that time can be treated as a dimension. As a navigator can estimate his momentary position from points in space (and time) which he has already passed or not yet reached, so Conrad's narrator verifies the position, if not the entity, of his subject, by referring to events in time past or time to come. These events can be superimposed on the present, as points in space can be joined in a double image by the mariner's azimuth-mirror or by his sextant-mirror, and the relative angles verified. Thus in *Lord Jim* the narrator can take a hundred and seventy-five pages to discuss facts "visible, tangible, open to the senses, occupying their place in space and time, requiring for their existence a fourteen-hundred-ton steamer and twenty-seven minutes by the watch."[64]

The multiple point of view of Conrad's narrations, a device carried further in Durrell's *Alexandria Quartet* with explicit reference to the Einsteinian world,[65] is another way of taking bearings, to be drawn on a chart such as the Tudor seamen called a Mariner's Mirror.[66] This ranging on moving entities or personalities, like the juggling of antecedents and consequents, lends emphasis to Conrad's dictum that "the meaning of an event lies outside the event."[67]

It can be said that Conrad's is a navigator's art, a science of relativity, open to all the implications of a cosmology without absolutes; a literature as well devised to represent our world as Narcissus is fit to symbolize it.

What the nuclear Narcissus may hereafter communicate, concerning the enigmas of selfhood or universe, depends on the language he is able to devise. A Conrad narrator says of one event:

It had the power to drive me out of my conception of existence. . . . I seemed to have lost all my words in the chaos of dark thoughts I had contemplated for a second or two beyond the pale. These came back . . . very soon, for words belong also to the sheltering conception of light and order which is our refuge.[68]

Narcissus is cut off from his refuge, and launched on what Conrad calls the "alien sea";[69] the otherness of which has lately been stressed in French literature by the *roman de l'objet,* including *Le Voyeur.*[70] But it is still, after all, none other than Dante's ocean of being.[71]

Conrad's conception of Narcissus as a vessel recalls that of the twelfth-century mystic Hugh of St. Victor, who compared the human soul to the Ark of Noah on the universal flood.[72] It was Hugh who said "To be oneself, one should enter into oneself, and transcend oneself, moving toward God."[73] Conrad will not go so far. An author is not a monk, he says, though literary activity is a religious rite.[74] What he does seem to suggest is that if, like the chastened crew of the Narcissus, one enters unselfconsciously into one's voyage upon "the immortal sea," the "mirror of the infinite," one may possess at least the universe. Which brings him fairly close to what the existentialist Gabriel Marcel has said, in a book entitled *Reflection and Mystery.*[75]

NOTES

1. "Typhoon," in *Typhoon and Other Stories,* Dent Collected Edition, pp. 15 and 9. Except as otherwise indicated, this edition is the source of Conrad quotations.
2. Letter of 29/3/96, in J. G. Aubry, *Joseph Conrad, Life and Letters* (London, 1927), I, 186.
3. "Karain—A Memory," in *Tales of Unrest,* p. 40.
4. *Lord Jim,* p. 323.
5. *Typhoon and Other Stories,* p. 82.
6. "Youth," in *Youth etc.,* p. 4; cf. *Notes on Life and Letters,* 185–89.
7. *The Nigger of the Narcissus,* p. 75.
8. E. V. Lucas, cited by John D. Gordon, *Joseph Conrad: The Making of a Novelist* (Cambridge, Mass., 1940), p. 291.
9. A. J. Ayer, *Language, Truth and Logic* (London, 1955), p. 86.
10. *The Mirror of the Sea,* p. 187.
11. "Hoy ha de ser la mas alta / vencerme a mé." *La Vida es sueño,* Jornada Tercera, Escena XIV; ed. Angel del Río, *Antología General de la Litteratura Española* (New York, 1954), I.

12. "El mayor delito del hombre es haber nacito." *Ibid.*, Jornada Primera, Escena II.
13. E. Gilson, *History of Christian Philosophy in the Middle Ages* (New York, 1955), pp. 534–540.
14. E. T. A. Hoffmann, "The Lost Reflection," in *Eight Tales of Hoffmann*, ed. and transl. J. M. Cohen (London, 1952).
15. *Lord Jim*, p. 214.
16. *Ibid.*, p. 216.
17. *An Outcast of the Islands*, p. 12.
18. "The End of the Tether," *Youth etc.*, p. 165.
19. *Ibid.*, p. 245.
20. "Karain," *Tales of Unrest*, p. 2.
21. "Youth," *Youth etc.*, p. 20.
22. "The Secret Sharer," *Twixt Land and Sea*, p. 91.
23. *Ibid.*, p. 142.
24. *The Shadow-Line*, p. 76.
25. *The Rescue*, p. 5.
26. *Ibid.*, p. 203.
27. "Karain," *Tales of Unrest*, p. 5.
28. "The Planter of Malata," *Within the Tides*, p. 31.
29. "The End of the Tether," *Youth etc.*, p. 318.
30. *The Shadow-Line*, p. 74.
31. *The Nigger of the Narcissus*, p. 29.
32. *Ibid.*, p. 103.
33. *Ibid.*, p. 104.
34. Angelus Silesius, *The Cherubinic Wanderer*, transl. W. R. Trask (New York, 1953), p. 50.
35. *The Mirror of the Sea*, p. 71.
36. *Ibid.*, p. 71.
37. *Narcissus*, p. 53.
38. *Ibid.*, p. 55.
39. *Ibid.*, p. 75.
40. *Ibid.*, p. 77.
41. *Ibid.*, p. 54.
42. *Nostromo*, p. 7.
43. *Ibid.*, p. 7.
44. *Narcissus*, p. 104.
45. *Nostromo*, p. 262.
46. *Narcissus*, p. 57.
47. "The Secret Sharer," *Twixt Land and Sea*, p. 124.
48. *Narcissus*, p. 92.
49. *Nostromo*, p. 497.
50. Baudelaire, *Oeuvres*, ed. Y-G. Le Dantec (Paris, 1954), p. 141.
51. *Ibid.*, p. 94. See also Gide's symbolist *Traité du Narcisse* (1892) and *Voyage d'Urien* (1893); in *Oeuvres Complètes*, ed. L. Martin-Chauffier (Paris, n.d.), I, 207–20, 281–365.
52. *Comus*, lines 235–36; lines 206–8. H. F. Fletcher, ed., *The Complete Poetical Works of Milton* (Cambridge, Mass., 1941). Cf. letter cited in note 2, above.
53. Preface, *The Nigger of the Narcissus*, p. vii.
54. J. G. Weightman, "High, Low, and Modern," *Encounter*, xv, 3 (1960), 69.
55. J. P. Sartre, "Existentialism is a Humanism," in W. Kaufmann, ed., *Existentialism from Dostoevsky to Sartre* (New York, 1957), pp. 287–311.
56. "The Planter of Malata," *Within the Tides*, p. 36.

57. V. Magnien, *Les Mystères d'Eleusis* (Paris, 1950), p. 297.
58. T. Moser, *Joseph Conrad: Achievement and Decline* (Cambridge, Mass., 1959).
59. *Narcissus*, p. 173.
60. *Shadow-Line*, p. 84.
61. "Secret Sharer," p. 140.
62. Preface, *Narcissus*, p. viii.
63. See, e.g., R. Carnap, *Meaning and Necessity* (Chicago, 1956), pp. 205–221.
64. *Lord Jim*, p. 30.
65. L. Durrell, *Justine* (London, 1957), p. 248; *Balthazar* (London, 1958), p. 7; *Clea* (London, 1960), p. 5.
66. L. Brown, *The Story of Maps* (Boston, 1950), p. 145.
67. "Heart of Darkness," *Youth etc.*, p. 48.
68. *Lord Jim*, p. 313.
69. *Mirror of the Sea*, p. 101.
70. J. G. Weightman, "The Obsessive Object," *Encounter*, XIX, 1 (1962), 67–71.
71. "onde si muovono a diversi porti
per lo gran mar dell' essere"
—Paradiso I, 112–13; ed. L. Magugliani (Milano, 1949).
72. E. Gilson, *La Philosophie du Moyen Age* (Paris, 1947), p. 305.
73. Cited as epigraph to Gabriel Marcel's dissertation on Coleridge and Schelling; P. Colin, *Existentialisme chrétien* (Paris, 1947), p. 15.
74. *A Personal Record*, pp. 99–109; cf. Letter of 6/10/08; in Aubry, *Joseph Conrad*, II, 89.
75. G. Marcel, *The Mystery of Being*, I: *Reflection and Mystery* (London, 1950).

Notes on Contributors

CLAUDE T. BISSELL, FRSC, President of the University of Toronto since 1958, was President of Carleton College, and Chairman of both the Canada Council and the Canadian Universities Foundation. He has edited and contributed to four volumes, and has published a number of articles. His book *The Strength of the University* has recently appeared. Recipient of numerous honorary degrees, he spent the academic year 1967–68 as Visiting Professor of Canadian Studies at Harvard.

MICHEL BRUNET, Professor of History at the University of Montreal, received his Ph.D. from Clark University as a Rockefeller Fellow. Formerly Assistant Dean of the Faculty of Letters and Head of the Department of History at Montreal, he has published nine volumes and a large number of scholarly and popular articles in both French and English.

A. P. CAMPBELL, Professor of English at the University of Ottawa, is presently in France on a Canada Council Senior Fellowship, preparing editions of the *Tiberius Psalter* and of Guido Faba's *Rota Nova*. He has told his own children's stories on radio and television, and has published numerous articles, poems, and short stories.

REVEREND FATHER CAMILLE DOZOIS received his doctorate in theology from the University of Ottawa. Now Dean of Studies and Professor of Moral Theology at St. Joseph's Seminary, Edmonton, Alberta, he has published a series of articles on patristic sources as used in Aquinas.

A. R. C. DUNCAN is Head of the Department of Philosophy at Queen's University, Kingston. He is a graduate of Edinburgh, and taught there and at the University of London. Past President of the Canadian Philosophical Association, he has published *Practical Reason and Morality*, has translated *The Development of Kantian Thought*, and has contributed chapters to books and published articles on Wittgenstein, moral philosophy, and the philosophy of education.

MAURICE LEBEL, MSRC, est professeur de langue et de littérature grecques et directeur du Département d'études anciennes à l'Université Laval. Ancien président du Conseil canadien de recherche sur les humanités, il a publié nombreux livres sur la littérature des Grecs et sur l'éducation contemporaine.

MAURICE LEGRIS, who teaches English at the University of Oregon, was the Associate Editor of the *Humanities Association Bulletin* for four years. He has published articles on the English Renaissance and the history of the French in Western Canada, and has taught at a number of American and Canadian universities.

LE RÉVÉREND FRÈRE CLÉMENT LOCKQUELL, É.C., est professeur et directeur du Département d'études françaises à l'Université Laval. Membre de la Société royale du Canada, il est l'auteur de nombreux articles et de livres; l'excellence de son œuvre lui a valu un doctorat honorifique et deux prix littéraires.

GERALD MCCAUGHEY, currently Visiting Professor of English at San Fernando Valley State College, California, was the Editor of the *Humanities Association Bulletin* from 1963 to 1967. A graduate of McGill and Washington, he saw extensive service as a pilot with the Royal Navy and the RCAF. He has given a number of talks on the CBC radio network, and has published articles on a variety of subjects from Shakespeare to modern fiction.

MARSHALL MCLUHAN, Professor of English and Director of the Centre for Culture and Technology at the University of Toronto, is at present Visiting Professor at Fordham. He has published numerous articles on English literature and the humanities; his three books—*The Mechanical Bride, The Gutenberg Galaxy,* and especially *Understanding Media*—have achieved international repute.

ELI MANDEL, Professor of English at York University, Toronto, has received several awards, among which are the University of Western Ontario President's Medal in Poetry and a Canada Council Arts Fellowship. He has published numerous articles as well as five books, including three volumes of his own poetry: *Fuseli Poems, Black and Secret Man,* and most recently *An Idiot Joy.*

GILLES MARCOTTE est assistant-professeur au Département de français de l'Université de Montréal. Il a publié deux romans; une anthologie de textes critiques sur la littérature canadienne-française contemporaine; et *Une Littérature qui se fait,* un volume d'essais critiques sur la littérature canadienne-française qui a gagné le Prix du Gouverneur général en 1962.

GERALD MORGAN is Professor and Head of the Department of English at Royal Roads Military College, Victoria, B.C. He holds a Master Mariner's licence from the University of Southampton, and a Ph.D. from the University of Montreal. He has published a large number of poems and articles, particularly on Conrad.

F. E. L. PRIESTLEY, FRSC, is Professor of English at the University of Toronto. A former President of the Humanities Association of Canada, he has been a Nuffield Fellow and is a Fellow of the Royal Society of Literature. He is the co-author of *Science and the Creative Spirit,* a Special Editor of *The Canadian Dictionary,* and General Editor of *The Collected Works of John Stuart Mill,* now being published by the University of Toronto Press in some twenty-two volumes.

JOHN M. ROBSON, Professor of English at the University of Toronto, is Editor of the *Mill News Letter* and Advisory Editor of the *Wellesley Index to Victorian Periodicals.* He is also Associate Editor of the *Collected Works of John Stuart Mill,* of which four volumes are published and four more are in preparation. He has published three other books and numerous articles on Victorian literature and the editing of Victorian texts.

DONALD E. SOULE, who received a Ph.D. from Stanford, is now Professor in the Department of Theatre, University of British Columbia. A Fulbright Fellow at the University of London, he has produced a number of plays, including Molière's *School for Wives* and an adaptation of Aristophanes' *Lysistrata.*

G. M. STORY, Professor of English at Memorial University of Newfoundland, received a D.Phil. from Oxford. He has edited five books, including *The Sonnets of William Alabaster* (with Helen Gardner) and *Lancelot Andrewes: Sermons,* as well as numerous papers in the fields of textual criticism, dialectology, and Tudor literature and Renaissance humanism.

GUY SYLVESTRE, MSRC, est Bibliothécaire associé du Parlement, Ottawa. Il a occupé des postes importants au gouvernement, dont secrétaire particulier du Premier ministre Saint-Laurent. Il est l'auteur de plusieurs livres sur les littératures françaises et canadiennes, et d'un grand nombre d'articles et de revues.

PIERRE VAN RUTTEN, assistant-professeur à l'Université d'Ottawa, est diplômé de la Sorbonne. Il détient plusieurs médailles et distinctions honorifiques pour son service avec la Résistance belge durant la guerre. Il a publié nombreux articles au Canada et en Belgique, où il était collaborateur de la revue *Synthèses*.

WILFRED WATSON, Professor of English at the University of Alberta, won the Governor-General's Prize for his book of poems, *Friday's Child*. He has published several articles, and six of his plays have been produced.

PAUL WEST, Visiting Professor of English at Pennsylvania State University, was educated at Oxford and Columbia, and was both a Guggenheim Fellow and a Senior Fellow of the Canada Council. He has published three volumes of literary criticism, two volumes of poetry, a memoir, and numerous essays in periodicals on both sides of the Atlantic.

The late A. S. P. WOODHOUSE, for many years Head of the Graduate Department of English at the University of Toronto, exercised considerable influence on the teaching of English literature in Canadian universities. He published a large number of articles and several books, was a Guggenheim Fellow and a Fellow of the Royal Society of Canada, and held several important posts in professional organizations. He was a Visiting Professor at London, Harvard, Johns Hopkins, and Chicago, and the recipient of numerous honorary degrees from Canadian and American universities.

www.ingramcontent.com/pod-product-compliance
Lightning Source LLC
Chambersburg PA
CBHW050232110726
47898CB00007B/2123
9781487587345